"Picciano is one of our long-standing contributors t[illegible] education. In this book, he takes us on an entire journ[illegible] the online learning landscape. He navigates the landscape of the past and present foundations, frameworks, definitions, research, planning models, design of instruction, and support structures. The journey extends into the future, exploring how technological change is ever-changing the nature and conduct of teaching and learning and communication in online environments. The book builds on purposeful history, compelling research, and informative practice to provide deep understanding of where online education has been and where it is going. This book is a fine resource for the field, one that stakeholders in online education and in higher education will find useful for a long time to come."

—**Laurie P. Dringus**, *Professor, College of Engineering and Computing, Nova Southeastern University, USA*

"If I were trying to understand the past, present, and future landscape of online learning, this book would be the overwhelming choice. The range of topics, contexts, and precise language make this a tour de force for locating the epicenters of educational transformation. Tony Picciano was there from the beginning and has nurtured our understanding of online learning for decades so this work never deviates from its purpose or avoids complex issues. This book is a bold and comprehensive portrait that frames and resets how we understand then, now, and what lies ahead. A must-read for experts as well as novices."

—**Charles D. Dziuban**, *Director of the Research Initiative for Teaching Effectiveness, University of Central Florida, USA*

"Dr. Picciano is a legend in the online learning community and a colleague who I have held in the highest regard for more than two decades. He provides a critically important book that captures a thoughtful reflection on where we have been and then attends to important questions related to approaches that are appropriate in our field. This foundation enables this pioneer to offer his insight and valuable predictions about the future. Recognizing that online learning can impact virtually all instruction, this is an essential resource for any educator."

—**Eric E. Fredericksen**, *Associate Vice President for Online Learning & Associate Professor in Educational Leadership, University of Rochester, USA*

"Few individuals have a historical perspective of online/blended learning like Tony Picciano. His career in education has spanned over four decades, during which time he has served in school level positions and high level university positions. His research and leadership with the Online Learning Consortium (formally the Sloan Consortium) have given him insights related to the emergence and expansion of online learning available to few others. This book includes stories from his personal journey as well as insights about the past, present, and future of education in a digital world."

—**Charles R. Graham**, *Professor of Instructional Psychology and Technology, Brigham Young University, USA*

"Although online education has taken root at the vast majority of U.S. institutions, adoption is still a work in progress. Institutional leaders must grapple with questions about mission (why?), students to be served (who, where?), maintaining quality (how?), and the appropriate level of engagement. In *Online Education: Foundations, Planning, and Pedagogy*, Tony Picciano lays out the foundational elements of today's online education practice and forecasts the future. Institutional leaders and online education practitioners alike will find this book a very useful roadmap as they establish and scale their own online initiatives."

—**Joel L. Hartman**, *Vice President for Information Technologies & Resources and CIO, University of Central Florida, USA*

"Tony Picciano has been a leader in instructional technology for over forty years, serving as a teacher, practitioner, researcher and administrator. Perspectives from those roles are what will make this book a classic. By reflecting on the historical evolution of technology and its impact on education, Tony thoughtfully discusses its potential for the future. I can think of no author better suited to reflect on online learning."

—**Patsy D. Moskal**, *Associate Director for the Research Initiative for Teaching Effectiveness, University of Central Florida, USA*

"Anthony G. Picciano brings his unique qualifications to this history and evolution of online learning. He had an active role in much of its development, providing him with considerable perspective on the factors that have impacted its evolution. More importantly, however, his keen observation and analytic skills allow him to clearly organize the information and provide a nuanced presentation that well serves both newcomers and seasoned veterans of the online learning field."

—**Jeff Seaman**, *Director, Babson Survey Research Group, Babson College, USA*

"Tony Picciano's new book on online education considers both the foundations of online teaching and learning and its practice from multiple higher-level perspectives. Dr. Picciano is a skilled writer who makes his thoughtful overview of the foundations of online learning, including its history, theories, and research findings, eminently readable. His treatment of the practice of online learning in terms of planning, designing, and administering online courses and programs is similarly grounded in theory and research. It provides excellent general advice to guide implementation that is likewise a good read. I highly recommend this book to anyone interested in online education."

—**Karen Swan**, *Stukel Distinguished Professor of Educational Leadership, University of Illinois Springfield, USA*

Online Education

Online Education is a comprehensive exploration of blended and fully online teaching platforms, addressing history, theory, research, planning, and practice. As colleges, universities, and schools around the world adopt large-scale technologies and traditional class models shift into seamless, digitally interactive environments, critical insights are needed into the implications for administration and pedagogy. Written by a major contributor to the field, this book contextualizes online education in the past and present before analyzing its fundamental changes to instruction, program integration, social interaction, content construction, networked media, policy, and more. A provocative concluding chapter speculates on the future of education as the sector becomes increasingly dependent on learning technologies.

Anthony G. Picciano is Professor of Education Leadership at Hunter College and Professor in the PhD program in Urban Education at the City University of New York Graduate Center, USA.

Online Education

Foundations, Planning, and Pedagogy

Anthony G. Picciano

Routledge
Taylor & Francis Group
NEW YORK AND LONDON

First published 2019
by Routledge
711 Third Avenue, New York, NY 10017

and by Routledge
2 Park Square, Milton Park, Abingdon, Oxon, OX14 4RN

Routledge is an imprint of the Taylor & Francis Group, an informa business

Library of Congress Cataloging-in-Publication Data
A catalog record for this book has been requested

ISBN: 978-0-415-78411-5 (hbk)
ISBN: 978-0-415-78413-9 (pbk)
ISBN: 978-1-315-22675-0 (ebk)

Typeset in Bembo
by Apex CoVantage, LLC

I dedicate this book to colleagues around the world who see online technology as a critical means of access to education that, when done right, can result in high-quality teaching and learning.

Contents

Figures

Plates

The plate section appears after page 81.

Boxes

About the Author

Anthony G. Picciano is a professor of education leadership at Hunter College of the City University of New York (CUNY) and in the PhD Program in Urban Education at the CUNY Graduate Center of the City University of New York. He has also held faculty appointments in the masters program in Quantitative Methods in the Social Sciences and the doctoral certificate program in Interactive Pedagogy and Technology at the CUNY Graduate Center, and the CUNY Online BA Program in the CUNY School of Professional Studies. He has held several senior administrative appointments at the City University and State University of New York.

Dr. Picciano started his career working with computer systems in the late 1960s. He taught his first college-level course in computer programming and systems analysis in 1971. In the 1970s and 1980s, he was involved with developing computer facilities, computer-assisted instruction (CAI) laboratories, and data networks at the City University of New York. He started teaching online in 1996.

In 1998, Picciano co-founded CUNY Online, a multimillion dollar initiative funded by the Alfred P. Sloan Foundation that provided support to faculty using the Internet for course development. He was a founding member and continues to serve on the Board of Directors of the Online Learning Consortium (formerly the Alfred P. Sloan Consortium).

Picciano's research interests are education leadership, education policy, Internet-based teaching and learning, and multimedia instructional models. He has led major research projects funded by the United States Department of Education, IBM, and the Alfred P. Sloan Foundation. With Jeff Seaman, he has conducted major national studies on the extent and nature of online and blended learning in American K–12 school districts. He is currently working with Abt Associates on a grant-funded project to conduct a meta-analysis on *Using Instructional Technology to Support Postsecondary Classroom Instruction* for the U.S. DOE's Institute of Education Sciences for its *What Works Clearinghouse* Series. He has authored numerous articles and frequently speaks and presents at conferences on education and technology. He has edited nine journal special editions and has authored 14 books including:

CUNY's First Fifty Years: Triumphs and Ordeals of a People's University. (2018, Routledge/Taylor & Francis). Co-author: Chet Jordan.

Online Education Policy and Practice: The Past, Present and Future of the Digital University. (2017, Routledge/Taylor & Francis).

Conducting Research in Online and Blended Learning Environments: New Pedagogical Frontiers (2016, Routledge/Taylor & Francis). Co-Authors: Charles Dziuban, Charles Graham and Patsy Moskal.

Blended Learning: Research Perspectives, Volume 2 (2014, Routledge/Taylor & Francis). Co-authors: Charles Dziuban and Charles Graham.

The Great Education-Industrial Complex: Ideology, Technology, and Profit (2013, Routledge/Taylor & Francis). Co-author: Joel Spring.

Educational Leadership and Planning for Technology, 5th Edition (2010, Pearson).
Blended Learning: Research Perspectives, Volume 1 (2007, The Sloan Consortium). Co-author: Charles Dziuban.
Data-Driven Decision Making for Effective School Leadership (2006, Pearson).
Distance Learning: Making Connections across Virtual Space and Time (2001, Merrill/Prentice Hall).
Educational Research Primer (2004, Continuum).

Picciano was elected to the inaugural class of the Sloan Consortium's Fellows in recognition of "outstanding publications that have advanced the field of online learning." He was the 2010 recipient of the Sloan Consortium's National Award for Outstanding Achievement in Online Education by an Individual.

Visit Dr. Picciano's website at: http://anthonypicciano.com

Preface

In the 1950s, I attended elementary school in the South Bronx, New York City. The technology I used in kindergarten through second grade was a pencil as I learned to print the letters of the alphabet. In third grade I was taught cursive and midway through the year I was required to use a fountain pen. We were not allowed to use a ballpoint pen. My teachers also insisted that we use Waterman's washable blue ink in case we spilled any on our clothes. The only other technologies I used in elementary school were a twelve-inch ruler and a box of Crayola crayons that cost ten cents, had eight colors, and came in a familiar yellow and green box. I never had a science class in my nine years (K–8) of elementary school. The only *science* I ever experienced in my young years occurred during visits to the Museum of Natural History, the Hayden Planetarium, the Bronx Zoo, and through science fiction movies in the local theaters. Among my favorite movies were the *Flash Gordon* serials that were rerun on Saturday mornings, generally in the winter months.

In 1980, I bought my eleven-year-old son, Michael, a Radio Shack Color Computer. This was one of the very early and successful personal computers. It did not come with a screen (we had to hook it up to an old television) and there was practically no software for it except a BASIC (Beginners All-purpose Symbolic Instruction Code) interpreter. I taught Michael BASIC and after a while he was able to write rudimentary programs, mostly involving simple computations. A year later, Michael and one of his friends, Tommy, wrote a fairly sophisticated program (for the time) for a science fair. The program simulated the solar system with photos and facts about each planet. It was the only computer-based project in the fair. I was proud of what Michael and Tommy had achieved and the project won an award.

In 2017, I visited my daughter Dawn Marie and her family in Poulsbo, Washington. She has two children, twelve-year-old Michael Anthony and ten-year-old Ali. They showed me the Chromebooks that all students receive free of charge from their Klahowya School in the Central Kitsap School District 401. Their Chromebooks are connected to the cloud-based platform PowerSchool that provides them with a variety of instructional services including all of their textbooks as well as supplementary curricula material that teachers and students can use in class, at home, or on the school bus. In addition to basic software such as Google Docs and ClassLink, the Chromebook provides access to a host of instructional packages such as Imagine Learning for language arts, Renaissance for reading, and the Destiny Library Catalog. The Chromebook also allows parents and the children access to all grades and assessments. Another major benefit is that students can collaborate easily with one another on group projects. The Chromebook also comes with screening software so that the children can only use it for instructional activities. If you think the Klahowya School is unique, my two granddaughters, Isabella and Gracie, who attend school in Mahopac, New York, also use Chromebooks. In fact, it is estimated that more than half the nation's primary- and secondary-school students—more than 30 million children—use Google education applications (Singer, 2017). I mention these three vignettes to demonstrate how our schools have advanced incredibly in their use of technology in teaching and learning. From no technology in my generation, to a novelty in my son's generation, to becoming an essential part of the learning experience in my grandchildren's generation. Just imagine what my great grandchildren will be doing in the not too distant future.

I hope that you will find this book helpful as you consider the issues involving online education. I have tried to provide the reader with a foundation for online education focusing on history, theory, research, planning, and practice including instructional design, pedagogical models, and current advances. Quality instruction must be at the top of our priorities in the online environment as well as in the face-to-face classroom, and student success must be maintained as the foremost goal regardless of modality. I enjoyed working on this book because one learns so much when trying to share knowledge with others using the written word. I sincerely hope that this book lives up to your expectations and wish you much success in your endeavors.

Reference

Singer, N. (2017, May 13). How Google took over the classroom. *New York Times*. Retrieved December 21, 2017 from www.nytimes.com/2017/05/13/technology/google-education-chromebooks-schools.html

Acknowledgments

This is the sixth book that I have published with Routledge/Taylor & Francis. I am very pleased with my association with this fine company. The editors and support staff there have become colleagues with whom it is a pleasure to work. First and foremost, I thank my editors, Alex Masulis and Dan Schwartz, who have assisted this project from the very beginning. Second, the support staff at Routledge/Taylor & Francis including Jamie Magyar, Jonathan Pennell, Helen Strain and Kerry Boettcher are a talented and able group of individuals whose contributions made this book better as it came to fruition. Third, I have been blessed to be a part of the Online Learning Consortium, formerly the Sloan Consortium, where the seeds of online learning in this country were planted in the 1990s. I have had the pleasure of working with a number of amazing colleagues through this Consortium including Chuck Dziuban, Patsy Moskal, Karen Swan, Peter Shea, Eric Fredericksen, Frank Mayadas, Joel Hartman, Mary Niemiec, Tanya Joostens, Meg Benke, Charles Graham, Burks Oakley, Gary Miller, Steven Laster, Bob Ubell, Jacquie Moloney, Kathleen Ives, Jill Buban, and others. Their friendships and collaborations have helped form many of my ideas about online education. Fourth, I have had the good fortune to spend more than a half of a century at the City University of New York as a student, an administrator, and a faculty member. I have enjoyed this journey immensely because of the people who work, study, and teach at CUNY. My faculty colleagues, especially at Hunter College and the Graduate Center, have helped me become a productive scholar and researcher. My students over the years have been an inspiration to me and continue to help me to become a better teacher and adviser. Lastly, God has blessed me with a loving family. My grandmother, parents, brothers, children, and grandchildren were and are the air that I breathe. My wife, Elaine, has been the 35-year partner who has been there to help in good times and not so good times. She has assisted me in everything I do and I am who I am because of her.

My humble thanks to all of you!

Tony

Acknowledgements

Chapter 1

Introduction to *Foundations, Planning, and Pedagogy*

In 1971, I taught my first college course on computer systems and programming. The student computer laboratory housed a remote job entry (RJE) station with a card reader and printer. Students keypunched decks of cards that contained their COBOL program instructions and datasets and then submitted them on the RJE station for processing on a mainframe computer that was housed miles away. Turnaround time was usually 10 to 15 minutes assuming there were no technical communications problems between the RJE station and the mainframe. When problems did occur, students might have to wait hours or until the next day to receive the results of their programming efforts.

In 1981, BITNET ("Because It's There Network" which eventually came to mean "Because It's Time Network") was launched by the City University of New York, Yale University, and IBM. It provided basic data file transfer and email services using point-to-point or store and forward transmission where entire files and messages were sent from one node in the network to another node. At its height, BITNET included more than 500 organizations and 3,000 nodes. Connections to BITNET from home computers generally operated at speeds between 320 and 9600 bits per second.

In 1992, the Alfred P. Sloan Foundation established the Learning Outside the Classroom Program later renamed the Anytime, Anyplace Learning Program. This was quite a significant development given that the Internet and World Wide Web as we came to know it did not exist until 1992 and didn't become a major resource until the mid-1990s. Over the 20-year life cycle of this grant program, the Foundation made awards in excess of $72 million to colleges and universities developing online education programs.

In 2004, the University of Illinois at Chicago sponsored an invitation-only workshop to explore blended learning, a relatively new phenomenon which sought to integrate online technology into mainstream higher education courses. Thirty experienced online education course developers debated definitions, pedagogical techniques, and the possibilities of blending online learning into all aspects of college teaching.

In 2014, I gave the keynote address titled *The Online Learning Landscape* at a conference in New York City. The purpose of this talk was to provide an overview of the current state of online education and to offer possible scenarios regarding its future. After the address, an associate professor from a local community college came up to me and asked if I thought that she would be out of a job in ten years. I told her that I didn't think she would be out of a job, but it was very likely that the way she teaches and the way her students learn would change. As instructional software evolves, making greater use of artificial intelligence and adaptive learning techniques, it is possible that teaching and learning will look very different in the not too distant future.

These ten-year scenarios of occurrences in my personal background provide examples and illustrate where I am coming from in presenting the material for this book. Online technology, as manifested by the ubiquitous Internet, has impacted all aspects of human endeavor including education. As a result, understanding this technology has become fundamental in the 21st century to understanding humankind's existence including how we teach and learn from one another. The purpose of this book is to examine the foundations of online education focusing on its historical, theoretical, and pedagogical bases as well as its practical applications in our schools and colleges. These bases and applications are critical to understanding online education's present proliferation as well as speculating on its future.

Foundations, Planning, and Pedagogy!

Foundations are the bedrock of a society, its organizations, and its functions. Foundations of education focus on the history, theory, research, pedagogy, and societal influences of what we do in schools. In the first part of this book, each of these will be explored as related to online education. It is important to understand them if we are to understand how online education has achieved its prominent position in what we are doing in education in general.

During the past several decades, there have been debates about the relationship between online education and distance education and whether the former is an outgrowth of the latter. Keegan (1993) conducted a review of the literature in the 1990s just as the Internet was evolving. He concluded that online technology had the potential to change the concept of distance education and make existing distance education theories and practices less applicable. He recommended research "theoretical or otherwise, to determine if virtual systems were a subset of distance learning or a new field of study in their own right" (Keegan, 1996, pp. 214–215). More recently, there have been several fine texts that begin with a distance education perspective that examine the foundations of online education such as Terry Anderson's *Theory and Practice of Online Learning* (Au Press, 2009) and Michael Moore and Greg Kearsley's *Distance Education: A Systems View of Online Learning* (Wadsworth Publishing, 2011). Building on Keegan's work, they examine how online education has developed as the next technological step in the evolution of distance education following earlier radio, television, and videocassette-based course packs. But with the convergence (Tait & Mills, 1999) of distance and online education models and especially the development of blended learning models, the case can be made that online education has evolved as a distinct movement resulting in its own modes, applications, and dynamics. A case can also be made that online education evolved from earlier digitally-based instructional software as developed by B.F. Skinner, Patrick Suppes, Donald Bitzer, and others who focused on traditional education applications and not just on distance education. An important consideration of this book is that online instructional technology had much of its genesis in digital technologies developed for traditional learning applications and not solely or directly for distance education.

In the second part of this book, planning and pedagogy, or the application of technology for learning, will be examined. In the last 20 years, "how to" books and articles have proliferated offering recommendations and guidance on how to develop online programs and courses. While some of the "how to" is covered in this book, foundational contexts provide insights as to "why" certain approaches are appropriate and useful. Practices based on theories and concepts such as learning styles, teaching styles, community of inquiry, and blending with pedagogical purpose shape parts of this book. Critical aspects of developing online education applications including institutional planning, policy issues, instructional design, and library and student services are also considered.

Foundations, planning, and pedagogy help us to speculate on and plan for the future. The third part of this book suggests that online education as made popular by the Internet and World Wide Web, has a future that is both bright and threatening. The future is explored in depth in the concluding chapter of this work.

Definitions

This book focuses on online education as provided by the Internet and World Wide Web starting in the early 1990s. Online education applications using local and wide area networks existed before the Internet; however, the primary model that has evolved over the past 20 years relies on data and communications equipment that are owned and operated routinely by students in their homes, places of business, and increasingly on mobile devices. Large percentages of people living in countries all over the world are now using laptops, tablets, and cell phones to stay connected with family, friends, and their studies.

The term *online education* is defined as all forms of teaching and learning using the Internet. It refers to the plethora of names and acronyms that have evolved over the past two decades including: online learning, e-learning, blended learning, web-enhanced learning, hybrid learning, flipped classrooms, MOOCs (massive open online courses), and adaptive learning. Notice that the terms *distance education* or *distance learning* are not included in the previous sentence. While it can be argued that online education is the latest evolution of distance education, it is the position of this author, as mentioned earlier in this chapter, that online education is not just an evolution of distance education; it is a distinct entity that has provided new instructional models for all education and not just for students who study at a distance. Blended models, possibly the most popular use of online education technology today, have blossomed and represent instructional applications across a wide spectrum of education. However, a definition of blended learning is elusive at best and perhaps impossible because there are so many different varieties of it in operation at all levels of education. It will receive a more thorough treatment later in this book.

Allen and Seaman (2016) and Picciano and Seaman (2009) have conducted a number of studies on the development of online education. Their work, going back to the early 2000s, represents the most comprehensive treatment of the evolution of online education that presently exists. For the purpose of their national surveys, they defined an online or fully online course as one where 80% or more of the seat time is replaced by online activity. The word *blended* was used to designate courses where some percentage of seat time (less than 80%) was conducted online. Web-enhanced courses were defined as courses that do not necessarily replace seat time but have substantial Internet-based activity. The point is quickly being reached in education where the majority of all courses will have some Internet components ranging from the fully online to blended to Web enhancements. In a mere 20 years, online education has become integral to the delivery of instruction in our schools and colleges. No longer a novelty, it is becoming integrated into all teaching and learning. As Larry Ellison, the founder and CEO of Oracle Corp., has often been quoted as saying "The Internet changes everything, I really mean everything" (Schlender, 1999).

Forces Shaping Education

While technology is considered as a driving force in bringing about change in our schools and colleges, it must be recognized that other developments both outside and inside of education are just as important. Social, political, and economic concerns focusing on global competition, income inequality, and social justice dominate and influence much of what is being done in education. Policymakers in countries around the globe see a desperate need to advance and improve education opportunities for their citizens. Primary, secondary, and postsecondary schools are seen as critical for their future and their stability. Investments are being made, but the resources frequently are not sufficient to address the needs of growing populations or years of neglect. In looking for economies of scale, online education increasingly is being considered as one of the vehicles for bringing education access to students at reasonable costs in countries desperate to catch up to those more economically advanced.

Even in the economically-developed countries, there is a concern that education systems are not doing as much as they can. In the United States, for instance, the call for more accountability and assessment has increased over the past 20 years as policymakers question whether the schools and colleges are as effective as they should be. Calls for school choice, common core curricula, and teacher accountability all relate to a desire on the part of policymakers to improve K–12 education while controlling costs. At the postsecondary level, there have also been calls for greater accountability and cost efficiency. The non-profit public higher education sector where the majority of American college students are enrolled has seen a significant shift in funding away from government subsidy to student tuition. Contingent faculty, especially lower-paid adjuncts, now teach the majority of all postsecondary courses. It is not by accident that public higher education systems have emerged (along with for-profit institutions) as among the most prolific in developing online education programs. They were forced to do so to meet student demand for their academic programs. Increasing enrollments and stagnant state government subsidies moved many public systems to adopt online instructional technology in hopes of stabilizing costs especially for capital and campus-building projects. As we approach the 2020s, practically all segments (non-profit, private, public, and for-profit) of higher education have embraced online technology as critical for their academic programs. The same is true for the K–12 sector where online technology has become integrated for many of the same reasons as it has in higher education.

Cost-efficiencies were not the only drivers for expanding online education programs. A good number of teachers and faculty saw the pedagogical benefits to integrating technology into their courses and programs. Many of the blended learning models, for instance, were not developed for cost efficiency as much as for pedagogical benefits. These models were seen as helping to prepare young people for 21st century skills. Finally, fully online models were seen as important vehicles for expanding education access to more students who, because of geographical distance or time commitments, found it difficult to receive an education in traditional brick and mortar institutions.

Technological Change

Much of this book will deal with technological change. Over the years, and especially as applied to education, digital technology has been both canonized and demonized as a vehicle for change, transformation, and disruption. This book will consider technological change in terms of evolution rather than revolution. The word *technology* derives from the ancient Greek "*techne*" that translates to art or craft-knowledge. It specifically refers to the knowledge and practice of making things. Technological change has been a fundamental aspect of human existence since homo-sapiens started to walk on two legs and possibly before. Stone tools, metals, and the wheel have each had a profound impact on how the members of our species have interacted with the environment and with each other. Aristotle wrote about and examined the dichotomy between things that occurred naturally and those that were made by humans. Francis Bacon in *New Atlantis*, written in 1623, presented a vision of society in which natural philosophy and technology coexisted in the centrality of human endeavor. Hegel's dialectics—thesis, antithesis, and synthesis—served as a foundation for Marx and Engels in terms of the effect of technology on societies and the interplay of capital and workers. In the modern era, Neil Postman (1993) refers to the dialectic of technological change and warns of its light and dark sides. Clayton Christensen (1997) sounded the alarm throughout corporate America to be aware of "disruptive technology" that can cause great firms to fail. Christensen and Eyring (2011) have since sounded a similar alarm to public service organizations including schools and colleges. A major focus of this book will be to examine technology's influence on education and specifically how online technology is changing the fundamental way instruction is delivered. However, this influence cannot be separated from the larger societal influence that technology has had and will continue to have on all aspects of human endeavor.

Since the industrial revolution of the late 19th century to the present, American society and culture have embraced new technology. Automobiles, air travel, television, and mobile devices have found producers and consumers interested and willing to invest their resources. Over the past 50 years, this has been particularly true of digital technology. The computer age of the 1960s–70s gave way to the information/knowledge age of the 1980s which, in turn, gave way to the age of the Internet in the 1990s to the present. Public and private organizations and companies have changed in most aspects of their operations including the production and delivery of goods and services. Companies such as Apple, Google, Facebook, and Microsoft, which did not exist 50 years ago, now lead the list of stocks on the major national stock exchanges. Amazon re-conceptualized the book retailing business. Books can now be proposed, written, edited, published, and sold without a single printed page. In education, the Florida Virtual High School, which conducts all of its teaching online, enrolls more than 100,000 students each year. The for-profit University of Phoenix enrolled more than 400,000 online students at its peak. Change brought on by digital technologies, and specifically, the Internet, to the broad spectrum of education will serve as a recurring theme in this book.

A Word About Networks!

Any treatment of online education requires a discussion about the power of networks and especially the mother of all networks, the Internet. Networks are not just simply the latest technological advancement designed to move data more efficiently from one location to another. They can have profound effects on how people interact with one another. Watts (2003) and Barabasi (2002) have studied the effects of networks on various people-intensive processes including education. They found that networks enable individual behavior to aggregate into collective behavior. Crowdsourcing, for instance, has evolved into a highly sophisticated approach to bringing the expertise of thousands of people to problem solving. Something special happens when individual entities (nodes, components, people) are able to interact to form larger wholes (networks, systems, communities). Furthermore, the "interaction effect" or collective behavior may result in a far more productive environment than individuals acting by themselves: one individual working with another individual does not simply comprise two individuals but a third, more powerful *collaborating entity* that can extend the benefits beyond two. The Internet now makes it possible for many individuals to share and work with one another, and their collective behavior can be most effective in supporting complex processes including education. The ability of teachers and students to interact with one another across space and time is proving to have many effects on teaching and learning, much of which is in need of careful study and research. While there has already been a great deal of research on online networked education, the dynamics and ever-changing nature of the Internet and data communications warrant further investigation and inquiry.

Organization of This Book

Chapter 1—Introduction to Foundations, Planning, and Pedagogy

The present chapter provides an overall introduction to the main topics in this book emphasizing both foundations and applied practices in the development of online education.

SECTION I—FOUNDATIONS

Chapter 2—The History and Evolution of Online Education

This chapter focuses on the evolution of online education from three perspectives. First, it starts with an overview of the history of distance education in all its technological forms (mail, radio, television, and the Internet). Secondly, it examines online education's evolution from digital forms of instructional technology that can be traced to individuals such as B.F. Skinner, Pat Suppes, and Donald Bitzer who were developing generic models for all segments of education. Lastly, it examines online education from the 1990s with the advent of the Internet and World Wide Web to the present. It traces the development of online education as a series of waves that continues to the present time and that will continue to evolve in the future.

Chapter 3—Theoretical Frameworks for Online Education: Seeking an Integrated Model

Perhaps one of the most challenging chapters of this book, Chapter 3 examines whether a comprehensive theoretical framework for online education can be developed. It will examine whether the frameworks that do exist are incomplete as a result of narrow perspectives that may limit their overall appropriateness. The chapter also will specifically separate the distance education theories and models from those for traditional mainstream education. An important question is whether a convergence of the two is occurring. It concludes with the author's suggestion for a new integrated model that encompasses both distance education and traditional education perspectives.

Chapter 4—Research on Online Education

This chapter takes a critical look at the research in online education. It will start with a review of research paradigms used for studying online education and then move to exemplar studies in the field. It will also trace the nature of the research on online education over the past 20 years to demonstrate how it has evolved and changed. The chapter will conclude with recommendations for continuation of this research, suggesting areas in need of more study and investigation.

SECTION II—PLANNING AND PEDAGOGY

Chapter 5—Planning for Online Education: A Systems Model

Chapter 5 presents a social systems planning model that can serve as a guide to the development and implementation of online education. The model will focus on goals and objectives (defined as applications) appropriate for moving online education initiatives in a college or school. Online education initiatives might consist of developing new courses, programs, or entire schools. The operational components of the model include hardware, software, staffing/professional development, facilities/student/tech infrastructure, finances, and policies. The chapter concludes with an emphasis on the importance of evaluation.

Chapter 6—Designing Instruction for Online Environments

Chapter 6 focuses entirely on the design of instruction for online education and provides a good follow up to Chapter 5. It briefly reviews the extensive literature on this topic and moves into critical aspects of good design. A holistic approach dominates the discussion on this topic, emphasizing that good instructional design depends extensively on good support services especially when designing entire programs. Chapter 6 concludes with examples of scripts for three online education models.

Chapter 7—Academic, Administrative, and Student Support Structures

Chapter 7 focuses on the non-instructional side of online education. Successful online education initiatives require leadership and support from all parts of a school organization. Dependable technology infrastructure and support services frequently can "make or break" academic programs especially those that are serving fully online distance students. Administrative leadership that can work with various constituents, especially faculty governing bodies, can go a long way to bring an institution together in many aspects of the education enterprise but especially in moving forward with online initiatives that might be viewed with skepticism. This chapter will also review a number of policy issues that have arisen as colleges and schools move to more online instruction.

Chapter 8—Navigating the Current Landscape—Blending It All Together!

Chapter 8 examines the current landscape of online education that is incorporating a variety of pedagogical approaches using multiple formats and instructional tools. Social- and multimedia use has expanded significantly throughout society as well as in education. Mobile devices (laptops, tablets, PDAs) for accessing and participating in course activities are forcing even experienced online education providers to upgrade their course and program delivery. In addition, a number of new facilities and approaches that were in their nascent stages in previous years are now expanding significantly. These include:

1. learning analytics
2. adaptive or differentiated learning
3. expansion of competency-based instruction
4. open resources including material meant to replace traditional textbooks
5. gaming and multiuser virtual environments (MUVE).

All of the listed approaches, as well as traditional lectures, class discussions, laboratory work, internships, etc. that are typical in face-to-face classes, are at the disposal of faculty and instructional designers. How to harness all of these facilities is the challenge facing many education administrators.

Chapter 9—The 2020s, 2030s, and Beyond!

This final chapter speculates on the future and examines possible scenarios that may evolve as new technologies are introduced, spurring greater development of online education. Society in general and education at all levels are moving to much greater reliance on online technologies. Students will come to expect that every course will have online components. The future portends even greater reliance as massive cloud computing services and mobile technologies advance and expand. It is also likely that in the not too distant future, new technological breakthroughs in man–machine interfaces related to artificial intelligence and bio-sensing will likely mean major new approaches to many societal activities including education. It will be a different world.

Appendices

The appendices provide resources that readers might find helpful. Appendix A provides case studies of colleges and schools that developed online education programs and have provided important insights into our understanding of the field. The institutions selected for this chapter are not intended to represent a national selection of "the best" online education programs but are examples of colleges and schools that have added some distinct aspects to the study of online education. Readers who may be considering using this book as a text for a course may find these case studies to be excellent supplements for class discussions and other activities. These case studies represent various types of institutions in both K–12 and higher education including public and private colleges, non- and for-profit schools, virtual high schools, community colleges, and schools with special purposes.

Appendices B, C, and D provide evaluation criteria for three aspects of online education development including:

1. The Administration of Online Education Programs;
2. Blended Learning Programs;
3. Quality Course Teaching and Instructional Practice.

These criteria were developed by the Online Learning Consortium and derived from its Five Pillars of quality online education.

Appendix E is an overview of the European Union's General Data Protection Regulation (GDPR).

References

Allen, E., & Seaman, J. (2016). *Online report card: Tracking online education in the United States.* Needham, MA: Babson College Survey Research Group.

Barabasi, A. L. (2002). *Linked: The new science of networks.* Cambridge, MA: Perseus Publishing.

Christensen, C. (1997). *The innovator's dilemma: When new technologies cause great firms to fail.* Boston, MA: Harvard Business Review Press.

Christensen, C., & Eyring, H. J. (2011). *The innovative university: Changing the DNA of higher education from the inside out.* San Francisco, CA: Jossey-Bass, Inc.

Keegan, D. (1993). *Theoretical principles of distance education.* London: Routledge.

Keegan, D. (1996). *Foundations of distance education* (3rd ed.). London: Routledge.

Picciano, A. G., & Seaman, J. (2009). *K–12 online learning: A 2008 follow up of the Survey of U.S. School District Administrators.* Needham, MA: The Sloan Consortium.

Schlender, B. (1999, May 24). Larry Ellison Oracle at Web Speed: 'The Internet changes everything,' and the CEO of Oracle is living proof. *Fortune Magazine.* Retrieved January 31, 2017 from http://archive.fortune.com/magazines/fortune/fortune_archive/1999/05/24/260276/index.htm

Tait, A., & Mills, R. (Eds.). (1999). *The convergence of distance and conventional education: Patterns of flexibility for the individual learner.* London: Routledge.

Watts, D. (2003). *Six degrees: The science of a connected age.* New York, NY: Norton.

Section I

Foundations

Chapter 2

The History and Evolution of Online Education

This chapter focuses on the history and evolution of online education from differing perspectives. The work of Desmond Keegan, Terry Anderson, Michael Moore, and Greg Kearsley provide an historical overview from the perspective of individuals who have devoted extensive time to studying distance education. Seen from another perspective, online education evolved essentially from digital forms of instructional technology that can be traced to individuals such as B.F. Skinner, Pat Suppes, and Donald Bitzer. In the following paragraphs, histories from both the distance education and digital instructional technology perspectives will be presented. These will be followed by an examination of online education as it evolved starting in the 1990s with the advent of the Internet and World Wide Web.

The Distance Education Perspective

Distance education has an extensive history that focuses to an extent on the available communications technology of a given time. Exactly when distance education began is hard to say but it likely existed in many cultures going back hundreds of years or more. Tifflin and Rajasingham (1995) describe the epistles of the apostles as a form of religious correspondence education. The epistles or letters were written on papyrus by scribes and delivered by messengers to early Christian communities to promulgate and explain religious dogma. In colonial America in the 1700s, public lectures in Lyceum halls were frequently supplemented by mail and correspondence courses (Willis, 1993).

In Europe, more formal distance education programs appeared in the mid-19th century as postal systems were developed and more people learned to read and write. Holmberg (1986) traces the development of correspondence courses as far back as the 1830s in Sweden and Germany. Isaac Pitman established a most successful correspondence program in Great Britain in 1940 using the *Penny Post* for teaching shorthand. Other successful correspondence courses appeared at Skerry College in Edinburg in 1878 and at the University Correspondence College in London in 1887. Charles Toussaint and Gustav Langensheidt began offering foreign language correspondence instruction in Germany in 1873. One of the most successful of the early correspondence schools was started by H.S. Hermod and began in Sweden in 1873. By 1998, Hermods was one of the largest distance education organizations in the world.

In the United States, William Rainey Harper, who would go on to become president of the University of Chicago, developed one of the first degree-granting distance education programs at Chautauqua College of Liberal Arts in New York. In 1883, Harper developed the University Extension Center at the University of Chicago that offered a variety of correspondence courses and programs. Other early correspondence-based distance education programs of note were developed at Illinois Wesleyan (1877), the University of Wisconsin (1885), and Pennsylvania State University (1892).

During the early part of the 20th century, correspondence and home-study programs began to be established for primary and secondary education. The Calvert School, a correspondence-based primary school in Baltimore, enrolled its first students in 1906. Calvert continues today and is an important provider of home-schooling options for primary, middle, and secondary school students.

While many of the early correspondence schools struggled financially, several such as Hermods and Calvert have become quite successful. In the 1920s, a number of correspondence schools converted or supplemented their academic programs with radio transmission. Buckland and Dye (1991) estimated that at least 176 radio stations were established at education institutions for the purpose of delivering distance education. However, many of these were subsequently replaced a few years later by television.

The State University of Iowa, Purdue University, and Kansas State University were among the first schools to use television in distance education. Most transmissions were of material from selected courses within state and local communities. The televised materials were supplemented with course-packs. In the 1950s, more extensive televised academic programs such as *Sunrise Semester* (New York University) and *Continental College* (Johns Hopkins University) were developed with the assistance of major television networks such as CBS and NBC. Public Broadcasting (PBS) in the 1970s made a major thrust into national education television and became involved with a number of distance education projects. In the late 1970s and 1980s, cable (CATV) became a primary partner with a number of distance education providers in Alaska, Texas, Hawaii, and Iowa. Oklahoma State University initiated a consortium, the National University Teleconference Network (NUTN) in 1982. Sixty-six colleges agreed to work with each other via NUTN. Today almost 100 colleges are active members of NUTN. Consortia arrangements among colleges and school districts particularly at the state level have also emerged which provide a full range of educational, library, and other services including distance education to students and faculty. In 1989, the Iowa Communications Network (ICN) was established that provided a fiber-optic based system to support a full range of digital connectivity, interactive video communications, and voice services for school districts, colleges, hospitals, and government agencies. In 2013, ICN completed a $24 million infrastructure upgrade providing service capacity of up to 100 gigabytes. Many other states have followed the ICN model to provide a wide range of education services to their citizens.

During much of the 20th century, most of the distance education programs were affiliated with or extensions of traditional colleges and schools. This was not necessarily true in other countries such as Australia, France, and Canada where greater national control of education led to the creation of institutions whose missions were primarily distance education. The Open University of the United Kingdom, established in 1969, for example, has enjoyed a fine reputation for providing distance education services throughout the world. In fact, The Open University is one of most successful distance education providers in the world with a current enrollment of 173,000 students, having enrolled almost 2 million students over its lifetime (The Open University, 2017). In the past several decades many countries in Asia, Africa, and South America have also established substantial distance education programs as the demand for education increased throughout the world.

Many of the students who enrolled in distance education programs, particularly in the colleges, were adults looking to advance careers. Most of them were geographically distant from traditional brick and mortar schools and colleges. Distance education also tended to provide entire degree and certificate programs rather than individual courses. The faculty, with the assistance of instructional designers, took great pains to develop high-quality, self-paced materials to help these students succeed. By the late 1990s, and surely by the beginning of the 2000s, most of these schools started to make use of the Internet as a primary vehicle for making curriculum material available to students.

The Digital Instructional Software Perspective

The history of online education can also be viewed through the development of digital or computer-based instructional software that was occurring in many schools, colleges, and private companies for the purpose of improving instructional technique or delivery. Like the distance learning perspective discussed earlier, this development was dependent upon available hardware and software technologies. Furthermore, because digital data communications were rudimentary during most of the 20th century, the models developed were originally adapted for traditional schools and colleges using stand-alone computers or proprietary local and later, wide area networks. There is a very extensive literature on this development and below are several of the more important contributors. This surely is not an all-inclusive treatment.

B.F. Skinner, Sidney L. Pressey, and Edward L. Thorndike

> "There are more people in the world than ever before, and a far greater part of them want an education. The demand cannot be met simply by building more schools and training more teachers. Education must become more efficient. To this end curricula must be realized and simplified, and textbooks and classroom techniques improved. In any other field a demand for increased production would have led at once to the invention of labor-saving capital equipment. Education has reached this stage very late, possibly through a misconception of its task. Thanks to the advent of [various technologies] . . . These tools are finding their way into American schools and colleges."

This commentary is the kind of narrative heard regularly today from those who promote the use of technology as a way to reach the masses around the world. Policymakers, MOOC providers, and corporate America have used this narrative as a rationale for infusing more online technology into teaching and learning. They see technology as a cost-benefit that can greatly expand educational opportunity. The opening quote, however, was taken from an article written by B.F. Skinner in 1958, and the various technologies to which he referred in the brackets were film projectors, television sets, phonographs, and tape recorders (Skinner, 1958, p. 969).

Skinner is perhaps the best-known behavioral psychologist of the 20th century. He was a prolific writer who taught at the University of Minnesota and Indiana University but spent most of his career at Harvard University. Skinner was a great believer in technology as a teaching aid and developed a teaching machine based on a number of sound instructional design principles. In the quoted *Science* article, he summarized the benefits of a teaching machine as:

> "allowing each student to proceed at his own pace"
> ". . . immediate feedback"
> ". . . permitted the student to play an active role"
> ". . . constant interchange between program and student"
> "In addition to charts, maps, graphs, models, students would have access to auditory material"
>
> (Skinner, 1958, pp. 969–972)

All of the quotes from Skinner's article referred specifically to the work of Sidney I. Pressey who designed his own teaching machine in the 1920s (Pressey, 1926). Pressey was a professor of psychology at Ohio State University from 1921 to 1959. His machine incorporated the basic programmed instruction principles of self-paced learning using multiple-choice questions. Interestingly, Pressey credits Edward I. Thorndike, for providing him with the insights needed to build his machine. Thorndike was a professor of psychology at Teachers College of Columbia University. He designed multiple-choice tests, teaching aids, and wrote extensively about adult education. He was also a critic of textbooks. A common fault in textbooks, Thorndike wrote, is that "habits to be formed are stated but the reader does not have the chance to practice." In addition, textbooks do not give the reader a chance to think out conclusions for her or himself:

> "If, by a miracle of mechanical ingenuity, a book could be so arranged that only to him who had done what was directed on page one would page two become visible, and so on, much that now requires personal instruction could be managed by print."
>
> (Thorndike, 1912, pp. 164–165)

Skinner, Pressey, and Thorndike made important contributions to our understanding of instructional technology. Their principles reflected sound pedagogical practices that are still respected today by faculty, instructional designers, and commercial developers. In 2011, a new adaptive learning platform debuted at Arizona State University. The announcement in *The Chronicle of Higher Education* commented:

> Knewton is a new computerized-learning program that features immediate feedback and adaptation to students' learning curves. The concept can be traced back a half-century or so to a "teaching machine" invented by the psychologist B.F. Skinner, then a professor at Harvard University. Based on principles of learning he developed working with pigeons, Skinner came up with a boxlike mechanical device that fed questions to students, rewarding correct answers with fresh academic material; wrong answers simply got them a repeat of the old question. "The student quickly learns to be right," Skinner said.
>
> Fifty years later, that basic idea has evolved into a hot concept in education: adaptive learning. Programs like Knewton can pace an entire math course using sophisticated tracking of skill development, instant feedback, and help levels based on mastery of concepts, as well as something the Harvard students did not get: the enjoyment of a video-game-like interface.
>
> (Fischman, 2011)

Skinner and Pressey were recognized for their ideas and models, but the technologies of their eras were not robust enough to provide stimulating learning environments in the teaching machines that they envisioned. By the early 1960s, teaching machines were still considered "boring" and impersonal ways to learn and had not caught on in a major way at any level of education (Seattler, 2004, p. 303).

Patrick Suppes and Richard Atkinson

With the advent of computer technology in the mid-1960s, a number of projects at the University of Texas, Florida State University, the University of Pittsburgh, and the University of California at Santa Barbara converted the programmed instruction ideas of Skinner and Pressey to digital platforms. Perhaps the most extensive work in this area was carried out at The Institute for Mathematical Studies in the Social Sciences at Stanford University under the direction of Patrick Suppes and Richard Atkinson.

Suppes and Atkinson first partnered in developing what became known as computer-assisted instruction (CAI) for teaching basic mathematics. The digital technology of the latter 1960s and the 1970s afforded them more capability than the teaching machines of earlier times. Suppes and Atkinson were able to attract a good deal of funding support from IBM, the National Science Foundation, the Carnegie Foundation, and the U.S. Department of Education. IBM in particular invested significant resources and developed the IBM 1500 instructional system in 1966 primarily for implementing CAI. Using either an IBM 1130 or IBM 1800 computer, the IBM 1500 system supported 32 terminals in a local area network and integrated what were at the time interesting audiovisual capabilities. Course materials were developed by Science Research Associates, Inc., an IBM subsidiary, and the programming was done in a specialized language called *Coursewriter.*

Just after the debut of the IBM 1500 instructional system, Suppes and Atkinson formed the Computer Curriculum Corporation (CCC) to develop drill and practice materials in mathematics, reading, and the language arts. CCC evolved into one of the most successful CAI companies of all time. It was bought by Simon & Schuster Publishing in 1990 which in turn was bought by Pearson Education. It continues to develop and market CAI software and professional development programs for teachers under the Pearson umbrella. The work of Suppes and Atkinson had profound impact on CAI at the K–12 level and for remedial education at the college level. After Patrick Suppes died in 2014, his *New York Times* obituary noted:

> Patrick Suppes . . . sketched a vision of the democratic future of computerized education.
>
> "In a few more years," he predicted in 1966, "millions of schoolchildren will have access to what Philip of Macedon's son Alexander enjoyed as a royal prerogative: the personal services of a tutor as well informed and as responsive as Aristotle."
>
> (Markoff, 2014)

Donald Bitzer: Loomis Laboratory/CERL, University of Illinois

Donald L. Bitzer is generally considered to be the "father" of the PLATO (Programmed Logic for Automatic Teaching Operations) software system developed at the University of Illinois at Urbana Champaign (UIUC). While Bitzer gets most of the credit for the development of PLATO, he was assisted by a number of colleagues at the Loomis Laboratory at UIUC including Daniel Alpert, Chalmers Sherwin, and Paul Tenczar. PLATO was conceived in 1959 and by 1960 a working model (PLATO I) was running on an ILLIAC I computer. It was designed to run on a network and can be considered the prototype for Internet-based online learning. Several versions of PLATO (II, III, IV) were developed in the 1960s and early 1970s, all of which expanded its functionality. A most important feature of PLATO II allowed a teacher or faculty member to design her/his own lesson modules using the TUTOR programming language developed in 1967 by Paul Tenczar. Another unique feature was added in 1972 (PLATO IV): a plasma display terminal that provided far more interesting graphics than any other display at the time. Bitzer developed the plasma display and received a number of awards for his invention. Music synthesizer and limited speech recognition features were also added in the 1970s. PLATO attracted a good deal of attention and in turn funding from both the federal government and private industry. The National Science Foundation, for instance, provided funding in 1967 for Bitzer to set up the *Computer-Based Education Research Laboratory (CERL)* dedicated essentially to developing and enhancing the PLATO system. PLATO no doubt set the standard for computer-assisted hardware and software in the early days of networked-based learning and had several hundred customers operating on 1,000 or more terminals throughout the country at all levels of education by the mid-1970s. It should also be mentioned that much of the curriculum development on PLATO was for course modules designed to be used with traditional face-to-face instruction.

A most generous funder of PLATO was Control Data Corporation (CDC) which in the 1960s was one of the major manufacturers of large mainframe computers. William Norris, the CEO of CDC, donated several large mainframe computers to CERL to continue PLATO development and to provide the computer hub for the PLATO network. Norris' equipment donation helped to keep the costs reasonable. This was critical because a single PLATO terminal cost $12,000. In addition, users paid for log-in hours. A PLATO lab of 25 terminals minimally cost $300,000 in start-up funds plus the on-going costs for connectivity infrastructure, personnel, and training. Nevertheless, Norris was convinced of the future of PLATO and purchased its commercial rights in 1976. Over the next ten years CDC would invest hundreds of millions of dollars into PLATO services, but CDC's timing was not good as the industry moved away from mainframe computing toward inexpensive microcomputers. In fact, by the 1980s, the entire large mainframe computer business collapsed as companies moved to distributed desktop computing devices. CDC did try to market a mini version of PLATO to operate on microcomputer platforms but it was too late. When asked about CDC's failure to make PLATO profitable, Donald Bitzer commented that the product was too expensive and the need to keep itself profitable resulted in higher user fees. In his opinion, CDC "produced an inferior program at a very high cost" (Van Meer, 2003). By the end of the 1980s, CDC had sold off many of its assets including its PLATO business. The PLATO name is now associated with one of the online services sold by the company, Edmentum (www.edmentum.com/about/mission-values). The University of Illinois continued development of PLATO at CERL and eventually set up a commercial on-line service called NovaNET in partnership with University Communications, Inc. (UCI). CERL was closed in 1994, with the maintenance of the PLATO code passing to UCI. UCI was later renamed NovaNET Learning, which was bought by National Computer Systems (NCS). Shortly after that, NCS was bought by Pearson in 2000. A free, open access version of PLATO is still available online.

The software development as just described is but a quick snapshot of decades of experiment and development in instructional computer software during the 20th century. Much of this development, while starting in schools and colleges, moved quickly to commercial vendors. In the end, cost and lack of widespread connectivity made it difficult to have a broad-based impact on education. This would all change with the advent of the Internet in the 1990s.

Internet-Based Online Education (1990s to the Present)

The advent of Internet-based online education in the 1990s was a major leap forward in terms of how teachers teach and students learn. Internet technology provided far more facility for interaction among and between students and faculty than had previous technologies. As a result, online education evolved in a mere 20-plus years into an integral part of instructional delivery at all levels of education

Online education applications using local and wide area networks existed before the Internet and the World Wide Web, but the model that evolved over the past 20 or so years relies on ubiquitous data communications that are owned and operated routinely by all segments of the population. People now have access to vast digital depositories and applications using their laptops, cellphones, and other portable devices. Looking at how online education developed during this period, a series of waves or stages becomes discernible.

The First Wave (the Beginning)—1990s

The major data communications technology available to the general populace during the First Wave of online education was based on accessing the Internet via slow-speed, dial-up modem lines. As a result, many of the earliest online courses were text-based and relied heavily on asynchronous learning. Digital multimedia with no generally agreed upon standards was difficult and time-consuming to develop and was very slow in downloading to student computers. While a college or a business might have access to high-speed data communications lines, it made little sense to develop instructional approaches which would frustrate students who had slower speed access to the Internet in their homes. The main pedagogical model of the time was a highly interactive, asynchronous learning network (ALN) made popular by the Alfred P. Sloan Foundation's grant program titled Learning Outside the Classroom/Anytime, Anyplace Learning. The underlying concept of the ALN was that faculty and students need not log on at the same time for instruction. Students could participate at the times most convenient for them (i.e., after work, after the children were put to bed, etc.).

The schools, colleges, and universities most interested in online learning during the 1990s were those that had established distance education programs using other modalities such as television, radio, and course packs. Public institutions such as the Penn State World Campus and the University of Maryland University College were early leaders in the development of online education programs. For-profit colleges such as the University of Phoenix also invested heavily in developing online education programs. The Virtual High School in Massachusetts and the Florida Virtual High School were also founded during this period. The students enrolled in most of these institutions lived and/or worked a good distance from their schools and colleges and were typically enrolling in fully online programs and courses. These institutions naturally gravitated to providing instruction and most support services via online technology.

One of the significant catalysts for online education during this period came from the Alfred P. Sloan Foundation. In the early 1990s, Ralph Gomory, its president, envisioned the Learning Outside the Classroom/Anytime, Anyplace Learning Program, based on the idea that students could learn in their homes, places of business, or just about anywhere or anytime they could connect to a digital network. Joel Hartman, Vice Provost for Information Technologies and Resources at the University of Central Florida, commented that "Dr. Ralph Gomory and the Foundation were way ahead of their time in promoting digital teaching and learning especially considering that the Internet as we know it did not exist" (Interview, Picciano, 2013, p. 2). At that time, the vast majority of households in the United States did not have connections to digital networks and no one was predicting that within a decade the populace would be willing to pay for high-speed communications lines in order to use the vast information resources of the Internet including access to online courses and degrees. Nevertheless, in 1992, the Alfred P. Sloan Foundation formally funded the Learning Outside the Classroom Program and began accepting grant proposals. The purpose of the program was to explore educational alternatives for people who wanted to pursue higher education but who could not easily attend regularly scheduled college classes. The name was changed in 1993 to the Anytime, Anyplace Learning Program. As previously described, this grant program promulgated a major development in pedagogical practice referred to as the asynchronous learning network (ALN) and favored proposals for online education projects that were faculty led and offered in this mode.

Over the 20-year life-span of the successful Anytime, Anyplace Learning Program, 346 grants totaling $72,197,965 were awarded. Of these grants, $40 million were awarded to just 22 institutions (Picciano, 2013). Major distance and adult learning providers such as the University of Maryland University College, the Penn State World Campus, Rio Salado Community College, and Northern Virginia Community College were early grantees. Following on the heels of these institutions, large mainstream public university systems such as the University of Illinois, the State University of New York, the University of Massachusetts, and the University of Central Florida also received funding. In the early 2000s, large urban universities in New York, Chicago, and Milwaukee were funded to develop and expand blended learning environments. The awarding of grants to public university systems and community colleges was not accidental, but by design, as confirmed by Frank Mayadas, the Sloan Foundation program officer for the Anytime, Anyplace Learning Program:

> In discussing the focus on large public universities with Frank Mayadas, it becomes clear that the Foundation's early attempts to work with elite institutions such as M.I.T., Cornell, and Brown did not yield tangible results with the exception of Stanford University . . . So early on, we gained the conviction that if the ALN program was to succeed, it needed to direct grant resources to academic programs at the large public university systems. These institutions were an excellent fit for the ALN program, and most (e.g., SUNY Learning Network, Penn State World Campus, UMASS Online) formalized their grant programs into major university operations involving traditional departments.
>
> (Interview, Picciano, 2013, p. 29)

At the turn of the 21st century, public institutions represented approximately 76% of all student enrollments in American higher education and many of them, especially the community colleges, focused on the importance of access to higher education. The strategy of the Foundation to support the public sector made sense and enabled it to penetrate the largest segment of American higher education.

The Foundation also developed a strategy wherein individual faculty or administrators initially received small or modest grants to demonstrate their capability before establishing larger ALN projects at their institutions. If successful, they were encouraged to apply for larger grants. Examples of this approach were evident at the University of Illinois, SUNY Learning Network, and the University of Massachusetts. Eric Fredericksen of the State University of New York described the concept as follows:

> a three-phase progression from small proof of concept projects, to larger university-wide proof of scale projects, and finally to full expansion and proof of sustainability projects. The smaller initial projects brought in "early-adopter" faculty and administrators who then formed a "grassroots" base of individuals willing to support the larger, system-wide effort. The larger system-wide efforts brought ALN to scale; and the grassroots base that supported these efforts gave credence to the overall scaling-up of ALN . . .
>
> Dr. Fredericksen also emphasized that the proposals submitted to the Sloan Foundation focused on "doing or accomplishing something with tangible results."
>
> (Interview, Picciano, 2013, p. 22)

The Anytime, Anyplace Learning Program lasted 20 years but its importance really stems from the early years of online education in the 1990s. At the time, there was widespread belief that online education represented low quality instruction. The investment of the Foundation gave online education credibility and built a community of educators and scholars known as the Sloan Consortium (later renamed the Online Learning Consortium) devoted to promoting quality education practice based on careful pedagogical design.

Online learning during this First Wave was not without its critics. Social commentators such as Neil Postman (1992) and David Noble (1998) cautioned against the new online technology and its incursion into teaching and learning. Neil Postman (1992) saw virtual learning as a poor substitute for face-to-face instruction and said so in *The End of Education*. David Noble (1998) went further in his criticism and warned that online learning would usher in the era of "digital diploma mills." Regardless, online education development pushed on. By the end of the 1990s, hundreds of thousands of college students were enrolling in online courses every year. Allen and Seaman (2014) estimated that 1.6 million college students were enrolling yearly in fully online courses by 2002.

The Second Wave (Into the Mainstream)—Early 2000s

By the early 2000s, Internet technology had advanced to a place where most of the general population was able to afford high-speed cable modems or DSL. This enhanced connectivity opened up the possibility of incorporating multimedia (pictures, sound, video) into online learning development. Social media such as blogs, wikis, podcasting, and YouTube also came on the scene, allowing for greater interaction. Faculty from around the country began sharing learning tools and objects in digital depositories such as Merlot. The most important development of this Second Wave was that online education was no longer seen solely as a vehicle for distance education but could be used in mainstream education in almost any course and any subject matter. The dominant pedagogical model that evolved during this wave was blended learning, as faculty and teachers from most sectors of education began to use online facilities to enhance their courses and to replace some portion of seat time in face-to-face courses.

In 2004, the Alfred P. Sloan Foundation funded an invitation-only workshop focusing on blended learning hosted by the University of Illinois—Chicago (Picciano, 2009). One of the major purposes of this workshop was to develop a definition of blended learning. The workshop participants were unable to agree until almost a year later, and even then the definition was imperfect. The issue of a definition or lack thereof continues to dominate any discussion of blended learning today, as educators continue to define blended learning to suit their own institutions and academic departments. This issue will be discussed in greater depth later in this book.

Also during the Second Wave, many schools and colleges scaled up their online and blended learning activities. Learning/course management systems such as Blackboard, Desire2Learn, and Moodle were acquired throughout education. For-profit colleges expanded their programs significantly as venture capital flooded into the sector. The fully online model continued to be the mainstay of the for-profit colleges mainly because it was very cost effective for those institutions that did not have brick and mortar campuses.

Perhaps the most serious concerns of the Second Wave were in response to the remarkable growth of the for-profit sector which came under scrutiny for questionable recruitment and financial aid practices. The Education Trust estimated that the for-profit higher education sector grew 236% from 1998 to 2008 while the public and non-profit sectors grew 21% and 17% respectively (Lynch, Engle, & Cruz, 2010). The University of Phoenix, one of the top recipients of federal student financial aid, was the focus of highly-publicized federal government investigations into their recruitment practices in 2003 and 2004. The University subsequently settled these investigations by making significant payments to the federal government without admitting wrongdoing.

It is estimated that by 2008, 4.6 million college students enrolled yearly in fully online courses in public and non-profit colleges and universities (Allen & Seaman, 2014). Data for the for-profit colleges and universities are sketchy, but it is likely that over 1 million additional students were enrolled in fully online courses in this sector. In K–12 education, current data on the number of students enrolled was difficult to come by. One study published in 2008 estimated the enrollment to have been 1,030,000 students (Picciano & Seaman, 2009). A more recent estimate was 2.7 million students for the 2014–15 academic year. The fact is that no one really knew the extent of online education in K–12 schools. No agency at the federal or state levels was collecting these data at the time of this writing (Herold, 2017).

The Third Wave (The MOOC Phenomenon)—2008 to 2013

The term "MOOC" (Massive Open Online Course) was coined in 2008 by Dave Cormier and Bryan Alexander to describe an online course led by George Siemens of Athabasca University and Stephen Downes of the National Research Council. The course enrolled more than 2,000 students. With this course the Third Wave of online learning development began. In 2011, Stanford University offered several MOOCs—one of which, led by Sebastian Thrun and Peter Norvig,—enrolled more than 160,000 students. Thrun shortly thereafter started a MOOC company, Udacity. A few months later, Andrew Ng and Daphne Koller, both from Stanford University, launched Coursera, another MOOC provider. The MOOC model was grounded in improving student access to higher education and cost effectiveness. The emphasis was surely on "massive" enrollments. Venture capital from private investors and philanthropies flowed into MOOC development, especially as for-profit colleges lost some of their appeal because of the ongoing federal investigations of recruitment and financial irregularities.

The major interest in MOOC technology was not its pedagogical benefits but the possibility of access to an education. Courses that were enrolling hundreds of thousands of students attracted deserved attention. In addition, faculty from big name institutions such as Stanford University, Harvard, and the Massachusetts Institute of Technology became associated with the MOOC phenomenon. MOOCs were glamorized by their founders at companies such as Udacity, Coursera, and edX as the technological revolution that would indeed change higher education. As a result, the media went into a frenzy. The *New York Times* declared 2012 as "The Year of the MOOC" (Pappano, 2012). Education policymakers and university trustees took notice and thought they had found a solution to their education funding woes. Some such as in the California State University System and the University of Virginia pushed for major new MOOC initiatives.

As the MOOC phenomenon took off, a closer examination of the pedagogical basis of their design was made by faculty and instructional designers, many of whom were experienced online learning developers. The mechanistic style of many early MOOCs, based on "read, watch, listen, and repeat" course materials, was questioned by experienced online learning developers who preferred more socially constructed pedagogical approaches that emphasized extensive interaction among students and faculty. In addition, the high student dropout rates of 90% in some MOOC courses could not be easily explained away. Lastly, but perhaps most significant, was the failure by educational leaders and faculty to jump at the chance to use MOOC course materials developed by the faculty at Ivy League and other highly selective universities. To the contrary, faculty and administrators saw this as elitism and arrogance on the part of the MOOC providers.

At the end of 2013, the media's infatuation with MOOCs receded. The story of new technologies overhyped by the media only to be followed by a backlash has been a recurring theme in American culture. Products such as the Apple Liza, Windows Vista Operating System, Microsoft Zune, and Linden Labs Second Life are examples of technologies that never lived up to their promotion. To a degree, MOOCs followed the same pattern. One major incident that occurred in 2013 spurred the backlash. California's San Jose State University was the focus of a well-publicized experiment in which several basic courses in mathematics and statistics were developed by Udacity and offered in spring 2013. In comparing completion rates and grades, students taking the MOOC courses did not fare as well as students in previous years' face-to-face courses (Collins, 2013). In December 2013, Sebastian Thrun, the founder of Udacity, opened the flood gates for criticism when in an interview with *Fast Company*, he was quoted as saying that he was throwing in the towel and that "we [Udacity] have a lousy product" (Chafkin, 2013).

Actually Thrun may have been too harsh on his company, but the quote was out there and doubts about the efficacy of MOOCs grew. Daphne Koller, founder of Coursera, was more moderate in her comments about her own company's MOOC products. In November 2013, she commented at the Sloan Consortium International Conference on Online Learning that students who have remediation and other learning needs and who lack the basic skills of reading, writing, and arithmetic would probably better be served by face-to-face instruction (Koller, 2013). Koller went on to say that MOOC companies should consider the development of more pedagogically sound course materials that can be used in blended online formats rather than fully online formats. In a sense, Coursera and other MOOC providers might rebrand themselves as producers of high-quality content that gives faculty to use the materials to their best advantage.

It also needs to be mentioned that as MOOCs developed, a number of different definitions and models evolved. There has not been general agreement on the types of MOOCs. For example, Clark (2013) identified eight different MOOC models as follows:

> transferMOOCs—take existing courses and transfer them into a MOOC;
> madeMOOCs—take innovative approaches to the creation of course material;
> synchMOOCs—have fixed start and end dates and deadlines for assignments;
> asynchMOOCs—do not have fixed start and end dates and deadlines for assignments;
> adaptiveMOOCs—use adaptive algorithms to present personalized learning experiences;
> groupMOOCs—emphasize group work among students;
> connectivistMOOCS—rely on connectivity as afforded by digital networks that focus on knowledge creation and generation rather than content delivery;
> miniMOOCSs—course and module activity that lasts for short periods of time (days, weeks) rather than entire semesters.
>
> (Clark, 2013)

There can be a good deal of overlap within these models. For instance, a MOOC could easily include transfer, synch, adaptive, and group characteristics.

Perhaps the most common difference between MOOCs is based on the terms cMOOC and xMOOC (Bates, 2014). cMOOCs are based on connectivist theory as promoted by George Siemens and focus on the development and creation of knowledge by the interactions of students in a network environment such as an online course (Kop, 2011). Individuals are responsible for their own learning and for establishing their own learner structures. The cMOOC provides the environment but students are responsible for making the connections that are most important to their learning and the construction of their knowledge. cMOOCs use pedagogical approaches that are highly interactive; students develop their own subgroups of individuals with common goals and interests. While interesting and even provocative, it will take a while for connectivism to be accepted by the majority of faculty and students. Many students, for instance, are not necessarily interested in developing their own learning groups and would rather have a structured environment with a teacher and content-driven course.

An xMOOC allows for a variety of learning theories but focuses on providing quality content in the form of media, promoting student interaction, and assessing student progress. An xMOOC typically takes existing course material, converts it to a new medium (i.e., video, simulations) and integrates it with the interactive facilities that the online environment provides. In comparing the cMOOC and xMOOC models, the xMOOC is by far the more commonly used mainly because most faculty are interested initially in converting their existing course materials or relating their content to other content developed by a MOOC provider (Bates, 2014). As of this writing, terms and definitions of MOOCs were very fluid and in some cases even moving away from the root term "MOOC."

The Fourth Wave (Reconciliation of the Blended and MOOC Models)—2014→

In 2014, the (current) Fourth Wave of online education arrived wherein blended learning technologies that allowed for more extensive and personal faculty interaction were integrated with well-financed course content as developed by MOOC providers and others that instructors can use as they see fit. The Fourth Wave model extends and combines the development of the Second Wave (blended learning) and the Third Wave (MOOC content) and incorporates a variety of pedagogical approaches using multiple content forms and instructional tools. Social and multimedia use is expanding and students are relying extensively on portable devices (laptops, tablets, iPhones, PDAs) for accessing and participating in course activities. In addition, a number of new facilities and approaches that were in their nascent stages in previous waves are expanding. These include:

1. learning analytics;
2. adaptive or differentiated learning;
3. competency-based instruction;
4. open resources, including material meant to replace traditional textbooks;
5. gaming and multiuser virtual environments (MUVE);
6. mobile technology.

All of these approaches, as well as traditional lectures, class discussions, laboratory work, and internships, etc. that are typical in face-to-face classes, are at the disposal of faculty. Pedagogy does will continue to drive technology in a comprehensive and sophisticated blended learning environment. The evolution of the Fourth Wave blended/MOOC model will require careful nurturing while avoiding sudden or disruptive changes.

Who Directs the Design and Development of Online Education?

The potential for friction over whether content and course material for online education are developed within or outside of individual schools, colleges, and universities is great. What used to be the purview of teachers and faculty—that is, the design and choice of their own curriculum materials—is giving way to several possibilities inside and outside schools and colleges. For-profit instructional software providers that have well-designed materials are proliferating and cannot be ignored. Many non-profit content providers are making their material available as free, open-source content. The result is that educators increasingly have access to a good deal more content and other course material than ever before thanks to the facilities of the Internet. In a survey of college presidents conducted by *The Chronicle of Higher Education* on change and innovation, important insights were provided as to where campus leaders think online education is going. The following is an excerpt from the Executive Summary:

> *Direction*: Two-thirds of presidents of public institutions think that higher education is headed in the right direction, as do well over half of their private campus peers.
>
> *Modality*: An overwhelming majority of presidents—three quarters at private institutions and even more at public campuses—think that blended courses that contain both face-to-face and online components will have a positive impact on higher education.
>
> *Focus*: Presidents say that when it comes to innovation in higher education, reformers pay too much attention to cutting costs and not enough to changing the model of teaching and learning.
>
> *Change Drivers*: Two-thirds of public-institution presidents think that politicians are the most influential drivers of change in higher education and half of private-campus presidents agree with that assessment. The presidents on both types of campuses believe strongly that faculty should be the number one drivers of change.
>
> (Selingo, 2014)

The last item of the summary, *Change Drivers*, is most telling. Faculty indeed should be the number one drivers of change and to some degree many have been on the frontlines during the 20-year period of the evolution of online and blended learning. Faculty must be vigilant and increase their presence at the forefront, understanding full well that forces inside and outside of education will be moving to extend the integration of online technology into all aspects of teaching and learning. The same is true for teachers in K–12 schools. How gracefully this integration occurs is rooted in important theoretical issues that will be explored in the next chapter.

Summary

This chapter focused on the evolution of online education from two perspectives. It began with an overview of the history of distance education in all its technological forms (mail, radio, television). The work of Desmond Keegan, Terry Anderson, Michael Moore, and Greg Kearsley was referenced. It then examined online education's evolution from digital forms of instructional technology that can be traced to individuals such as B.F. Skinner, Pat Suppes, and Donald Bitzer, who were developing generic models for all segments of education. Finally, the chapter traced online education since the advent of the ubiquitous Internet and World Wide Web in the 1990s as it developed as a series of waves or stages that will continue into the foreseeable future.

Further Reading/Case Studies

Readers may wish to refer to Appendix A—Case Studies in Online Education specifically to:

Penn State World Campus
Embry-Riddle Aeronautical University
Florida Virtual High School
Northern Virginia Community College
University of Maryland University College
University of Phoenix

References

Allen, E., & Seaman, J. (2014). *Grade change: Tracking online education in the United States.* Needham, MA: Babson College Survey Research Group.

Bates, T. (2014). Comparing xMOOCs and cMOOCs: Philosophy and practice. *Blog posting.* Online and distance education resources. Retrieved May 6, 2017 from www.tonybates.ca/2014/10/13/comparing-xmoocs-and-cmoocs-philosophy-and-practice/

Buckland, M., & Dye, C. (1991). *The development of electronic distance education delivery systems in the United States: Recurring and emerging themes in the history and philosophy of education.* Unpublished manuscript (ERIC Document No. ED345713).

Chafkin, M. (2013, December). Udacity's Sebastian Thrun, godfather of free online education, changes course. *Fast Company.* Retrieved February 22, 2017 from www.fastcompany.com/3021473/udacity-sebastian-thrun-uphill-climb

Clark, D. (2013). MOOCs: Taxonomy of 8 types of MOOCs. *Blog posting plan B.* Retrieved May 6, 2017 from http://donaldclarkplanb.blogspot.co.uk/2013/04/moocs-taxonomy-of-8-types-of-mooc.html

Collins, E. D. (2013, September). *Preliminary summary: SJSU and Augmented Online Learning Environment Pilot Project.* The Research and Planning Group for California Community Colleges (RP Group). Retrieved February 22, 2017 from www.sjsu.edu/chemistry/People/Faculty/Collins_Research_Page/AOLE%20Report%20Final%20Version_Jan%201_2014.pdf

Fischman, J. (2011, May 8). The rise of teaching machines. *The Chronicle of Higher Education.* Retrieved April 5, 2017 from http://chronicle.com/article/The-Rise-of-Teaching-Machines/127389/

Herold, B. (2017, June 12). Online classes for K–12 schools: What you need to know. *Education Week*. Retrieved October 14, 2017 from www.edweek.org/ew/articles/2017/06/14/online-classes-for-k-12-schools-what-you.html

Homberg, B. (1986). *The growth and structure of distance education*. London: Croom Helm.

Koller, D. (2013, November). *Online learning: Learning without limits*. Keynote presentation at the 19th Annual Sloan Consortium Conference on Online Learning, Orlando, FL.

Kop, R. (2011). The challenges to connectivist learning on open online networks: Learning experiences during a massive open online course. *International Review of Research in Open and Distance Learning, 12*(3). Retrieved on May 6, 2017 from http://nparc.cisti-icist.nrc-cnrc.gc.ca/eng/view/accepted/?id=2d83ddb7-b3cd-45cd-8371-92a94e5dd349

Lynch, M., Engle, J., & Cruz, J. L. (2010). *Subprime opportunity: The unfulfilled promise of for-profit colleges and universities*. Washington, DC: Education Trust.

Markoff, J. (2014, December 2). Patrick Suppes, pioneer in computerized learning, dies at 92. *New York Times*. Retrieved April 6, 2017 from www.nytimes.com/2014/12/03/us/patrick-suppes-pioneer-in-computerized-learning-dies-at 92.html?emc=edit_th_20141203&nl=todaysheadlines&nlid=1596194&_r=1

Noble, D. (1998). *Digital diploma mills: The automation of higher education*. New York, NY: Monthly Review Press.

The Open University. (2017). *Fact and figures*. Retrieved February 20, 2017 from www.open.ac.uk/about/main/strategy/facts-and-figures

Pappano, L. (2012, November 2). The year of the MOOC. *New York Times*. Retrieved February 22, 2017 from www.nytimes.com/2012/11/04/education/edlife/massive-open-online-courses-are-multiplying-at-a-rapid-pace.html?pagewanted=all&_r=0

Picciano, A. G. (2009). Blending with purpose: The multimodal model. *Journal of the Research Center for Educational Technology, 5*(1), 4–14.

Picciano, A. G. (2013). Pioneering higher education's digital future: An evaluation of the Alfred P. Sloan Foundation's *Anytime, Anyplace Learning Program* (1992–2012). *Monograph*. Retrieved October 14, 2017 from https://aalp-sloan-report.gc.cuny.edu

Picciano, A. G., & Seaman, J. (2009). *K–12 online learning: A 2008 follow-up of the Survey of U.S. School District Administrators*. Needham, MA: The Sloan Consortium.

Postman, N. (1992). *The end of education: Redefining the value of school*. New York, NY: Random House Digital, Inc.

Pressey, S. L. (1926). A simple apparatus which gives tests and scores and teaches. *School and Society, 23*, 373–376.

Seattler, P. (2004). *The evolution of American educational technology*. Charlotte, NC: Information Age Publishing.

Selingo, J. J. (Ed.). (2014). The innovative university: What college presidents think about change in American higher education. *The Chronicle of Higher Education*. Retrieved February 24, 2017 from http://app.results.chronicle.com/e/es.aspx?s=2423&e=89593&elq=cd9973526e504845837bbada16e5b345

Skinner, B. F. (1958). Teaching machines. *Science, 128*(3330), 969–977.

Thorndike, E. L. (1912, published 1923). *Education: A first book*. New York: Macmillan.

Tifflin, J., & Rajasingham, L. (1995). *In search of the virtual class: Education in an information society*. London: Routledge.

Van Meer, E. (2003, November 3). PLATO: From computer-based education to corporate social responsibility. *Iterations: An Interdisciplinary Journal of Software History*. Retrieved April 7, 2017 from www.cbi.umn.edu/iterations/vanmeer.html

Willis, B. (1993). *Distance education: A practical guide*. Englewood Cliffs, NJ: Educational Technology Publications.

Chapter 3

Theoretical Frameworks for Online Education

Seeking an Integrated Model

In a provocative chapter of *The Theory and Practice of Online Learning*, Terry Anderson (2011) examined whether a common theory for online education can be developed. While recognizing it is a difficult and perhaps fruitless task, he nonetheless examines possibilities and proposes his own theory which he admits is not complete. The purpose of this chapter is to examine theoretical frameworks relevant to the pedagogical aspects of online education. It starts with a consideration of learning theories and funnels down to their specific application to online education. The chapter concludes with a proposal for an integrated model for online education based on pedagogical purpose.

Big Picture

As mentioned in Chapter 1, a number of major Western theorists such as Aristotle, Bacon, Hegel, Marx, and Engels have all made important observations on the influence of technology on society and humankind. Of these, the dialectics as defined by Hegel are most appropriate in terms of the broad perspective of technological and society. The dialectics' framework of thesis, antithesis, and synthesis is an elegant yet simple view of the effects of technological change on cultures and societies. In the modern world, we are in a constant state of flux and readjustments to never-ending developments of technology, especially related to digitization and communication. Mobile devices, self-driving cars, drones, the Internet of things, etc. are changing society in more ways than we fully understand. Hegelian dialectics posit that a society evaluates, adjusts, and realigns itself to accommodate new technologies. Some technologies such as mobile devices are widely accepted and the society provides mechanisms to produce and make available phones, tablets, and PDAs to the populace. Other technologies such as self-driving cars are slower to be accepted. A society may accept and then reject a technology. Nuclear energy for example has been seen as enormously cost beneficial energy technology but the danger of a nuclear disaster may not be worth the benefits.

Neil Postman (1992) applied Hegelian dialectics to media such as television, computers, and communications networks. These technologies did not destroy societies and its institutions but changed them and continues to do so. He also proposed that new technologies have the potential to change societies in ways not readily apparent. He used an ecological example as follows:

> One significant change can generate total change. If you remove caterpillars from a given environment, you are not left with the same environment minus the caterpillars: you have a new environment, and you have reconstituted the conditions for survival; the same is true if you add caterpillars to an environment that had had none. This is how the ecology of media works as well. A new technology does not add or subtract something. It changes it.
>
> (Postman, 1992, p. 18)

Postman's comments echo Marshall McLuhan's (1964) thesis that "the medium is the message," that a major new medium has the potential to shape and control human associations and actions. It is fair to say that the Internet and World Wide Web have in fact brought major changes to our societies and institutions. They are not just add-ons but are society-altering technologies. They provide all of the audiovisual stimulation of television plus levels of global and personal communications and interactivity never before witnessed by humankind.

Manuel Castells (2014) comments that the Internet has, in fact, led humankind to become a "networked society." He sees the Internet as the decisive technology of the Information Age, and with the explosion of wireless communication in the early 21st century, we can say that humankind is now almost entirely connected albeit with varying levels of inequality in bandwidth, efficiency, and price.

> People, companies, and institutions feel the depth of this technological change, but the speed and scope of the transformation has triggered all manner of utopian and dystopian perceptions . . . Our current "network society" is a product of the digital revolution and major sociocultural changes. . . . social relationships are being reconstructed on the basis of individual interests, values, and projects. Community is formed through individuals' quests for like-minded people in a process that combines online interaction with offline interaction, cyberspace, and the local space. . . . The virtual life is becoming more social than the physical life, but it is less a virtual reality than a real virtuality, facilitating real-life work and urban living.
>
> (Castells, 2014)

Castells goes on to suggest that without the Internet we would not have seen the large-scale development of networking as the fundamental mechanism of social structuring and social change in every domain of social life. In sum, the Internet, the World Wide Web, and a variety of data networks increasingly based on wireless platforms constitute the technological infrastructure of the network society.

As applied to education, the Internet is not simply a technological tool that is being used but is fundamentally changing instruction in ways not anticipated. Fully online courses and blended learning models are being integrated in all manners of instruction at all levels of education to the point that teachers and students alike would have difficulty participating in many class activities without access to the Internet.

Learning Theory

Learning theory is meant to explain and help us understand how people learn; however, the literature is complex and extensive enough to fill entire sections of a library. It involves multiple disciplines including psychology, sociology, computer science, and of course, education. Three of the more popular learning theories—behaviorism, cognitivism, and social constructivism—will be highlighted to form the foundation for further discussion. Mention will also be made of several other learning theories that are relevant to online education. Before reviewing these theories, it will be worthwhile to have a brief discussion of definitions of the term *theory* itself.

Theory is defined as a set of statements, principles or ideas that relate to a particular subject. A theory usually describes, explains, and/or predicts phenomena. The definition of theory also varies depending upon disciplines, especially when related to the term *model*. As noted by Graham, Henrie, and Gibbons (2013), the two terms are used interchangeably and generally refer to the same concept. However, a model is more frequently a visual representation of reality or a concept. In this discussion, the terms theory and model will be used interchangeably.

The purpose of a theory or model is to propose the answers to basic questions associated with a phenomenon. Graham et al. (2013) reviewed this issue as related to instructional technology and recommended a three-part taxonomy first proposed by Gibbons and Bunderson (2005) that includes theories that:

1. *Explore*—answer "What exists?" and attempt to define [describe] and categorize;
2. *Explain*—answer "Why does this happen?" and look for causality and correlation and work with variables and relationships;
3. *Design*—Answer "How do I achieve this outcome?" and describe interventions for reaching targeted outcomes and operational principles.

(Graham et al., 2013, p. 13)

This taxonomy will serve as an overall guiding principle for the discussion of learning theories and models in this chapter.

Behaviorism

Cognitivism has been considered a reaction to the "rigid" emphasis by behaviorists on predictive stimulus and response (Harasim, 2012, p. 58). Cognitive theorists promoted the concept that the mind has an important role in learning and sought to focus on what happens in between the occurrence of the environment stimulus and the student response. They saw the cognitive processes of the mind such as motivation and imagination as critical elements of learning that bridge environmental stimuli and student responses. For example, Noam Chomsky (1959) wrote a critical review of Skinner's behaviorist work in which he raised the importance of creative mental processes that are not observable in the physical world. Although written mainly from the perspective of a linguist, Chomsky's view gained popularity in other fields including psychology. Interdisciplinary in nature, cognitive science draws from psychology, biology, neuroscience, computer science, and philosophy to try to understand the workings of the brain as well as levels of cognitive development that form the foundation of learning and knowledge acquisition. As a result, cognitivism has evolved into one of the dominant learning theories. The future for cognitivism is particularly interesting as more advanced online software evolves into adaptive and personalized learning applications that seek to integrate artificial intelligence and learning analytics into instruction with cognitive processes.

Behaviorism led to the development of taxonomies of learning because it emphasized the study and evaluation of multiple steps in the learning process. Behaviorists would study a learning activity repeatedly to deconstruct and define the elements of learning. Benjamin Bloom (1956) was among the early psychologists to establish a taxonomy of learning that related to the development of intellectual skills and stressed the importance of problem solving as a higher order skill. Bloom's (1956) *Taxonomy of educational objectives handbook: Cognitive domains*, remains a foundational text and essential reading within the educational community. Bloom's taxonomy is based on six key elements (see Figure 3.1) as follows:

- **Creating**: Putting elements together to form a coherent or functional whole; reorganizing elements into a new pattern or structure through generating, planning, or producing;
- **Evaluating**: Making judgments based on criteria and standards through checking and critiquing;
- **Analyzing**: Breaking material into constituent parts, determining how the parts relate to one another and to an overall structure or purpose through differentiating, organizing, and attributing;

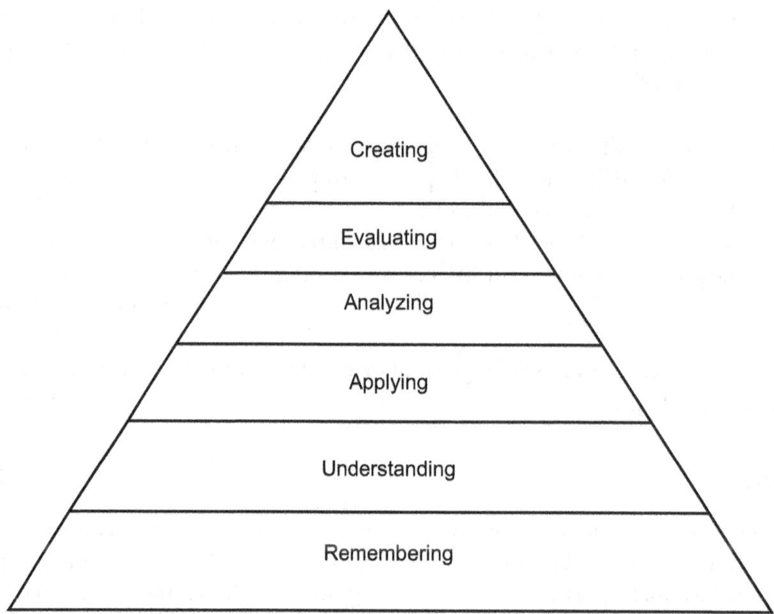

Figure 3.1 Bloom's Taxonomy

- **Applying**: Carrying out or using a procedure through executing or implementing;
- **Understanding**: Constructing meaning from oral, written, and graphic messages through interpreting, exemplifying, classifying, summarizing, inferring, comparing, and explaining;
- **Remembering**: Retrieving, recognizing, and recalling relevant knowledge from long-term memory.

Bloom in developing his taxonomy essentially helped move learning theory toward issues of cognition and developmental psychology. Twenty years later, Robert Gagne (1977), an educational psychologist, developed another taxonomy (events of instruction) building on Bloom, which became the basis for cognitivist instructional design (Harasim, 2012). Gagne emphasizes nine events in instruction that drive the definitions of objectives and strategies for the design of instructional material (see Box 3.1).

Box 3.1 Gagne's Nine Events of Instruction

1. **Gain attention**: Use media relevant to the topic;
2. **Describe the goal**: Provide clear objectives to the overall course goals;
3. **Stimulate prior knowledge**: Review previously presented material and concepts and connect them to the material to be addressed in the current module;
4. **Present the material to be learned**: Readings, presentations, demonstrations, multimedia, graphics, audio files, animations, etc.;
5. **Provide guidance for learning**: Discussions to enable learners to actively reflect on new information in order to check their knowledge and understanding of content;

6. **Elicit performance**: Activity-based learning such as group research projects, discussion, homework, etc.;
7. **Provide feedback**: Immediate, specific, and constructive feedback is provided to students;
8. **Assess performance**: Assessment activity such as a test, research project, essay, or presentation;
9. **Enhance retention and transfer**: Provide opportunities for additional guided practice or projects that might relate learning to other real-life activities.

Social Constructivism

A number of major education theorists have been associated with social constructivism including Lev Vygotsky, John Dewey, and Jean Piaget. The focus for social constructionism was to describe and explain teaching and learning as complex social phenomena where teachers and students interact with one another. Vygotsky posited that learning is problem-solving and that the social construction of solutions to problems is the basis of the learning process. Vygotsky described the learning process as the establishment of a "zone of proximal development" in which the teacher, the learner, and a problem to be solved exist. The teacher provides a social environment in which the learner can assemble or construct with others the knowledge necessary to solve the problem. John Dewey likewise saw learning as a series of practical social experiences in which learners learn by doing, collaborating, and reflecting with others. While developed in the early part of the 20th century, Dewey's work is very much in evidence in a good deal of present-day social constructivist instructional design. The use of reflective practice by both learner and teacher is a pedagogical cornerstone for interactive discussions that replaces straight lecturing whether in a face-to-face or online class. Jean Piaget, whose background was in psychology and biology, based his learning theory on four stages of cognitive development that begin at birth and continue through one's teen years and beyond. Seymour Papert, in designing the Logo programming language, drew from Jean Piaget the concept of creating social, interactive, microworlds or communities where children, under the guidance of a teacher, solve problems while examining social issues, mathematical, and science equations, or case studies. Papert's approach of integrating computer technology into problem-solving is easily applied to many facets of instructional design.

Derivatives of the Major Learning Theories

There have been a number of theories and models with roots in one or more of the previously described concepts. In the latter part of the 20th century, the major learning theories, especially cognitive theory and social constructionism, began to overlap one another. For example, Wenger and Lave (1991) and Wenger (1998) promoted concepts such as "communities of practice" and situated learning. Their position was that learning involves a deepening process situated in and derived from participation in a learning community of practice. Their work is very much in evidence in many studies including those related to online education.

Information processing learning theory is a variation of cognitivism that views the human mind as a system that processes information according to a set of logical rules. In it, the mind is frequently compared to a computer that follows a set of rules or a program. Research using this perspective attempts to describe and explain changes in the mental processes and strategies that lead to greater cognitive competence as children develop. Richard Atkinson and Richard

Shiffrin (1968) are generally credited with proposing the first information processing model that deals with how students acquire, encode, store (in short-term or long-term memory), and retrieve information.

One of the more popular, and at times controversial, theories relates to learning styles and posits that individuals learn differently depending upon their propensities and personalities. Carl Jung (1921) posited that individual personality types influence various elements of human behavior including learning. Jung's theory focuses on four basic psychological dimensions:

1. Extroversion vs. Introversion;
2. Sensation vs. Intuition;
3. Thinking vs. Feeling;
4. Judging vs. Perceiving.

While each unique dimension can influence an individual learning style, it is likely that learning styles are based on a combination of these dimensions. For example, a learning style might include elements of extroverted, sensing, feeling, and perceiving personality dimensions. Readers may be familiar with the Myers-Briggs Type Inventory (MBTI) which has been used for decades to assist in determining personality types, including how they relate to student learning. The MBTI is based extensively on Jung's theories and has been used to predict and develop different teaching methods and environments and to predict individual patterns of mental functioning, such as information processing, idea development, and judgment formation. It can also be used to foretell patterns of attitudes and interests that influence an individual's preferred learning environment and to predict a person's disposition to pursue certain learning circumstances and avoid others. Lin, Cranton, and Bridglall (2005) remind us that much of the work of Carl Jung and the MBTI is applicable to learning environments, whether face-to-face or online. For example, the extrovert may prefer active, highly collaborative environments whereas the introvert would prefer less interaction and less collaboration. This suggests that instruction should be designed to allow both types of individuals—the outgoing social organizer as well as the introspective reflective observer—to thrive.

Howard Gardner (1983) has developed a theory of "multiple intelligences" that proposes that intelligence is not just a singular entity but consists of multiple entities used by individuals in different proportions to understand and to learn about the world. Gardner has identified nine basic intelligences: linguistic, logical/mathematical, spatial, musical, bodily kinesthetic, interpersonal, intrapersonal, naturalistic, and existential (see Box 3.2). Gardner's theory has come under criticism from both psychologists and educators. Critics posit that his nine different "intelligences" simply represent talents, personality traits, and abilities. His work has also been questioned by those who propose that there is in fact a root or base intelligence that drives the other "intelligences." Gardner does not necessarily disagree with this latter position but maintains that other intelligences can be viewed as main branches off the base root intelligence. This theory has important pedagogical implications and suggests the design of multiple learning modalities, allowing learners to engage in ways they prefer by way of their interest or ability, while also challenging them to learn in other ways that are not as well-related to their preferences, interests, or abilities. Gardner's work also addresses the common concern that too much teaching and learning is linguistically-based (reading, writing, speaking) and that the other intelligences are underutilized.

Modern-day neuroscience research also suggests that students learn in different ways depending upon a number of factors including age, learning stimuli, and the pace of instruction. Willingham (2008) suggests that learning is a dynamic process that may evolve and change

Box 3.2 Gardner's Multiple Intelligences

1. **Verbal-linguistic intelligence** (well-developed verbal skills and sensitivity to the sounds, meanings, and rhythms of words);
2. **Logical-mathematical intelligence** (ability to think conceptually and abstractly, and capacity to discern logical and numerical patterns);
3. **Spatial-visual intelligence** (capacity to think in images and pictures, to visualize accurately and abstractly);
4. **Bodily-kinesthetic intelligence** (ability to control one's body movements and to handle objects skillfully);
5. **Musical intelligences** (ability to produce and appreciate rhythm, pitch, and timber);
6. **Interpersonal intelligence** (capacity to detect and respond appropriately to the moods, motivations, and desires of others);
7. **Intrapersonal intelligence** (capacity to be self-aware and in tune with inner feelings, values, beliefs, and thinking processes);
8. **Naturalist intelligence** (ability to recognize and categorize plants, animals, and other objects in nature);
9. **Existential intelligence** (sensitivity and capacity to tackle deep questions about human existence such as: What is the meaning of life? Why do we die? How did we get here?).

from one classroom to another, from one subject to another, and from one day to another. This research also supports the concept that multiple intelligences and mental abilities do not exist as yes-no entities but within continua which the mind blends into the manner in which it responds to and learns from the external environment and instructional stimuli. Conceptually, this suggests a framework for a multimodal instructional design that relies on a variety of pedagogical techniques, deliveries, and media.

Lastly, Malcom Knowles (Knowles, Holton, & Swanson, 1998) needs to be mentioned as sounding a call that adult learning or andragogy is different than child learning or pedagogy. Adults, whether seeking to enhance their professional skills or to satisfy curiosity about a subject, are different from children. Courses designed for them should try to tap into their adult social contexts and their experiences. Knowles' insights are especially important for higher education where online technology is used extensively for adult students in traditional and continuing education programs, competency-based learning, and career/professional development.

In sum, a number of theories have been and will continue to be applied to instruction including online and blended learning. Several theories specifically related to online education will now be examined.

Learning Theories for Online Education

Just as no single learning theory has emerged for instruction in general, the same is true for online education. A number of theories have evolved, most of which derive from the major learning theories discussed previously. In this section, several theories will be examined in terms of their appropriateness for the online environment.

Community of Inquiry

The "community of inquiry" model for online learning environments developed by Garrison, Anderson, and Archer (2000) is based on the concept of *presence* with three essential components: cognitive, social, and teaching (see Figure 3.2). While recognizing the overlap and relationship among the three components, Anderson, Rourke, Garrison, and Archer (2001) advise further research on each of these individual components. Their model supports the design of online and blended courses as active learning environments or communities dependent on instructors and students sharing ideas, information, and opinions. What is critical here is that presence in a course is a social phenomenon and manifests itself through interactions among students and instructors. The community of inquiry has evolved as one of the more popular models for online and blended courses that are designed to be highly interactive among students and faculty using discussion boards, blogs, wikis, and videoconferencing.

Connectivism

George Siemens (2004), one of the early MOOC pioneers, has been the main proponent of connectivism, which is a learning model that acknowledges major shifts in the way knowledge and information flows, grows, and changes because of vast data communications networks. Internet technology has moved learning from internal, individualistic activities to group, community, and even crowd activities. In developing the theory, Siemens acknowledges the work of Alberto Barabasi (2002) who was mentioned in Chapter 1, and the power of networks. He also references an article written by Karen Stephenson (1998) titled "What Knowledge Tears Apart, Networks Make Whole," which accurately identified how large-scale networks become indispensable in helping people and organizations manage data and information.

Siemens describes connectivism as:

> the integration of principles explored by chaos, network, and complexity and self-organization theories [where] learning is a process that occurs within nebulous environments of shifting core elements—not entirely under the control of the individual. Learning (defined as actionable knowledge) can reside outside of ourselves (within an organization or a database), is focused on connecting specialized information sets, and the connections that enable us to learn more and are more important than our current state of knowing.
>
> (Siemens, 2004)

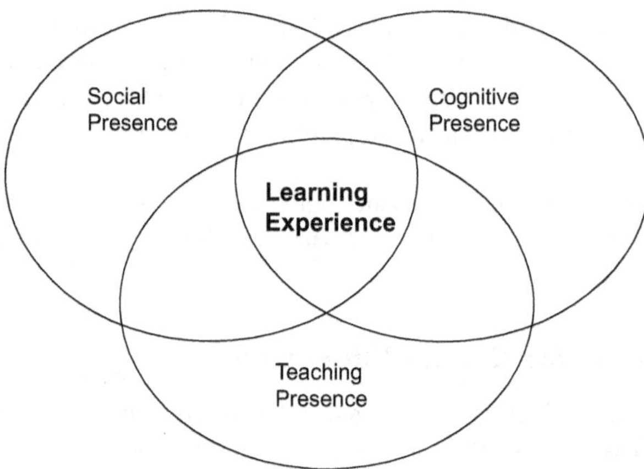

Figure 3.2 Community of Inquiry

Box 3.3 Siemens' Eight Principles of Connectivism

1. Learning and knowledge rests in diversity of opinions;
2. Learning is a process of connecting specialized nodes or information sources;
3. Learning may reside in non-human appliances;
4. Capacity to know more is more critical than what is currently known;
5. Nurturing and maintaining connections is needed to facilitate continual learning;
6. Ability to see connections between fields, ideas, and concepts is a core skill;
7. Currency (accurate, up-to-date knowledge) is the intent of all connectivist learning activities;
8. Decision-making is itself a learning process. Choosing what to learn and the meaning of incoming information is seen through the lens of a shifting reality. While there is a right answer now, it may be wrong tomorrow due to alterations in the information climate affecting the decision.

Siemens goes on to comment that connectivism as a theory is driven by the dynamic of information flow. Students need to understand and be provided with experiences in navigating and recognizing the oceans of information that are constantly shifting and evolving. Siemens has proposed eight principles of connectivism (see Box 3.3). Connectivism is particularly appropriate for courses with very high enrollments and where the learning goal or objective is to develop and create knowledge rather than to disseminate it.

Online Collaborative Learning (OCL)

Online collaborative learning or OCL is a theory proposed by Linda Harasim that focuses on the facilities of the Internet to provide learning environments that foster collaboration and knowledge building. Harasim describes OCL as:

> a new theory of learning that focuses on collaborative learning, knowledge building, and Internet use as a means to reshape formal, non-formal and informal education for the Knowledge Age.
>
> (Harasim, 2012, p. 81)

Like Siemens, Harasim sees the benefits of moving teaching and learning to the Internet and large-scale networked education. In some respects, Harasim is also channeling Alberto Barabasi's position on the power of networks. In OCL, *there exist three phases of knowledge construction through discourse in a group:*

1. **Idea generating**: the brainstorming phase, where divergent thoughts are gathered
2. **Idea organizing**: the phase where ideas are compared, analyzed and categorized through discussion and argument
3. **Intellectual convergence**: the phase where intellectual synthesis and consensus occurs, including agreeing to disagree, usually through an assignment, essay, or other joint piece of work.

(Harasim, 2012, p. 82)

OCL also derives from social constructivism where students are encouraged to collaboratively solve problems through discourse and where the teacher plays the role of facilitator while also being a member of the leaning community. This is a major aspect of OCL but also other constructivist theories where the teacher is not someone necessarily separate and apart but an active facilitator of knowledge building. Because of the importance of the role of the teacher, OCL is not easy to scale up. Unlike connectivism, which is suited for large-scale instruction, OCL is best situated in smaller instructional environments. This last issue becomes increasingly important when seeking commonality among online education theories.

There are many other theories that can be associated with online education but rather than present more theories, and in keeping with one of the major purposes of this chapter, it is appropriate to ask whether an integrated or unified theory of online education is possible.

Can We Build a Common Integrated Theory of Online Education?

As mentioned earlier, Terry Anderson (2011) examined the possibility of building a theory of online education starting with the assumption that it would be a difficult and perhaps impossible task. He approached this undertaking from a distance education perspective, having spent much of his career at Athabasca University, the major higher education distance education provider in Canada. While he acknowledged that many theorists and practitioners consider online education as "a subset of learning in general" (Anderson, 2011, pp. 46–47), he also stated:

> online learning as a subset of distance education has always been concerned with provision of access to educational experience that is, at least more flexible in time and in space as campus-based education.
>
> (Anderson, 2011, p. 53)

These two perspectives (subset of learning in general and subset of distance education) complicate any attempt at building a common theory of online education. Blended learning models, for instance, do not easily fit into the distance education schema even though they are evolving as a prevalent component of traditional face-to-face and online education environments.

Anderson considered a number of theories and models but focused on the well-respected work of Bransford, Brown, and Cocking (1999) who posited that effective learning environments are framed within the convergence of four overlapping lenses, namely community-centeredness, knowledge-centeredness, learner-centeredness, and assessment centeredness. These lenses provided the foundational framework to Anderson's approach to building an online education theory, as he examined in detail the characteristics and facilities that the Internet provides with regard to each of the four lenses. Secondly, he noted that the Internet had evolved from a text-based environment to one in which all forms of media are supported and readily available. He also accurately commented that the Internet's capacity for hyperlinking is most compatible with the way human knowledge is stored and accessed. In this regard, he referred to the work of Jonassen (1992) and Shank (1993) who associated hyperlinking with constructivism. Finally, he examined extensively the importance of interaction in all forms of learning and refers to a number of mostly distance education theorists such as Holmberg (1989), Moore (1989), Moore and Kearsley (1996), and Garrison and Shale (1990). The essence of interaction among students, teachers, and content is well understood and is referenced in many theories of education, especially constructivism. Anderson's evaluation of interaction concludes that interactions are critical components of a theory.

With these three elements in mind (the Bransford, Brown, and Cocking lenses; the affordances and facilities of the Internet; and interaction), Anderson then proceeded to construct a model (see Figure 3.3). He did add one important element by distinguishing community/

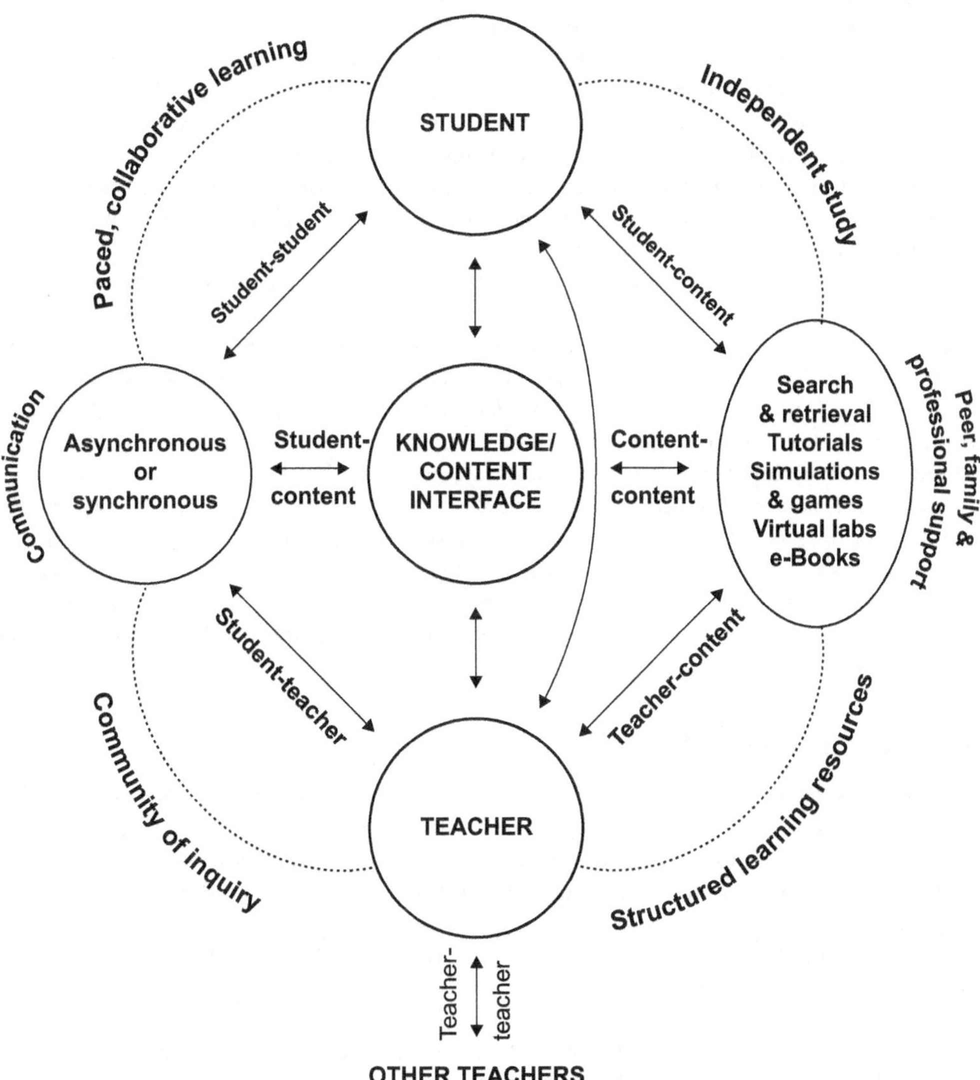

Figure 3.3 Anderson's Online Learning Model

Reprinted with permission from Anderson, T. (2011). *The theory and practice of online learning* (2nd Edition). Edmonton, AB: AU Press.

collaborative models from self-paced instructional models. He makes the comment that community/collaborative models and self-paced instructional models are inherently incompatible. The community/collaborative models do not scale up easily because of the extensive interactions among teachers and students. On the other hand, the self-paced instructional models are designed for independent learning with much less interaction among students and teachers.

Figure 3.3 illustrates:

> the two major human actors, learners and teachers, and their interactions with each other and with content. Learners can of course interact directly with content that they find in multiple formats, and especially on the Web; however, many choose to have their learning

> sequenced, directed, and evaluated with the assistance of a teacher. This interaction can take place within a community of inquiry, using a variety of Net-based synchronous and asynchronous activities . . . These environments are particularly rich, and allow for the learning of social skills, the collaborative learning of content, and the development of personal relationships among participants. However, the community binds learners in time, forcing regular sessions or at least group-paced learning . . . The second model of learning (on the right) illustrates the structured learning tools associated with independent learning. Common tools used in this mode include computer-assisted tutorials, drills, and simulations.
>
> (Anderson, 2011, pp. 61–62)

Figure 3.3 demonstrates the instructional flow within the two sides and represents the beginnings of a theory or model from the distance education perspective. Anderson concludes that his model "will help us to deepen our understanding of this complex educational context" (Anderson, 2011, p. 68), of which he notes the need to measure more fully the direction and magnitude of each input variable on relevant outcome variables.

Anderson also commented about the potential of the Internet for education delivery and that an online learning-based theory or model could subsume all other modes with the exception of the "rich face-to-face interaction in formal classrooms" (Anderson, 2011, p. 67). This becomes the quandary for Anderson in trying to develop a common theory of online education in that it does not provide for any face-to-face activity and is problematic for those who see online education as a subset of education in general.

An Integrated Model

Anderson's model assumes that none of the instruction is delivered in traditional, face-to-face mode, and so excludes blended learning models that have some face-to-face component. Is it possible, therefore, that in seeking an integrated model for online education, one might consider approaching it from the general (face-to-face) education or even the blended learning perspective?

Bosch (2016), in a review of instructional technology, identified 4 models specific to blended learning and compared them against 21 different design components. These models emphasized, to one degree or another, the integration of pedagogy and technology in the course design. Among the models was a Blending With Pedagogical Purpose Model (see Figure 3.4) developed by this author (Picciano, 2009) in which pedagogical objectives and activities drive the approaches, including the online technology that faculty use in instruction. The model also suggests that blending the objectives, activities, and approaches within multiple modalities might be most effective for and appeal to a wide range of students. The model contains six basic pedagogical goals and approaches for achieving them to form learning modules. The model is flexible and assumes that other modules can be added as needed and where appropriate. The most important feature of this model is that pedagogy drives the approaches that will work best to support student learning. The modules are also shown as intersecting but this is optional. They may or may not intersect or overlap depending upon the approaches used. For instance, some reflection can be incorporated into collaboration or not depending upon how the collaborative activity is designed. It might be beneficial to have the collaborative groups reflect specifically on their activities. Similar scenarios are possible for the other modules. What is ultimately important is that all the modules used blend together into a coherent whole. The following paragraphs briefly review each of these modules.

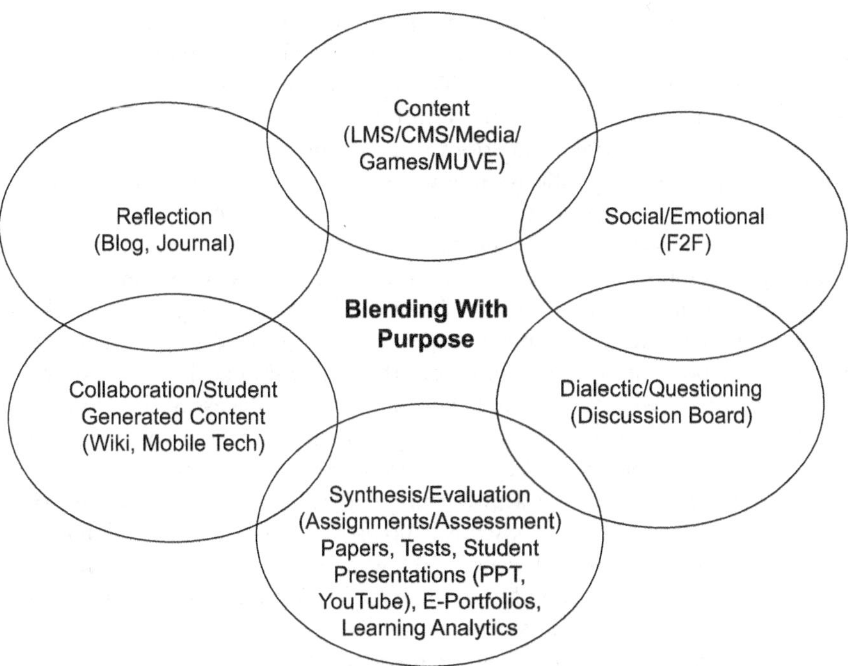

Figure 3.4 Blending With Pedagogical Purpose Model

Content is one of the primary drivers of instruction and there are many ways in which content can be delivered and presented. While much of what is taught is delivered linguistically (teacher speaks—students listen; or teacher writes—students write), this does not have to be the case either in face-to-face or online environments. Mayer (2009) has done extensive reviews of the research and has concluded that learning is greatly enhanced by visualization. Certain subject areas such as science are highly dependent upon using visual simulations to demonstrate processes and systems. The humanities, especially art, history, and literature, can be greatly enhanced by rich digital images as well. Course/learning management systems (CMS/LMS) such as Blackboard, Canvas or Moodle provide basic content delivery mechanisms for blended learning and easily handle the delivery of a variety of media including text, video, and audio. Multi-user virtual environments (MUVEs) and gaming are also evolving and playing more of a role in providing instructional content. In providing and presenting content, the Blending With Purpose model suggests that multiple technologies and media be utilized.

The Blending With Pedagogical Purpose model posits that instruction is not always just about learning content or a skill but is also about supporting students ***socially and emotionally***. A physical teacher or tutor in addition to providing instruction is a familiar and comforting presence. As mentioned earlier, constructivists see teaching and learning as inherently social activities. Perhaps more readily recognized for younger K–12 students, social and emotional development is an important part of anyone's education. Faculty who have taught graduate courses know that students, even at this advanced level, frequently need someone with whom to speak, whether to help understand a complex concept or to provide advice on career and professional opportunities. While fully online courses and programs have evolved to the point where faculty can provide some social and emotional support where possible and appropriate, in blended courses and programs this is more frequently provided in a face-to-face mode.

Dialectics or questioning is an important activity that allows faculty to probe what students know and to help refine their knowledge. The Socratic Method remains one of the major techniques used in instruction, and many successful teachers are proud of their ability to stimulate discussion by asking the "right" questions to help students think critically about a topic or issue. In many cases, these questions serve to refine and narrow a discussion to very specific "points" or aspects of the topic at hand and are not meant to be open-ended "anybody can say anything at any time" activities. For dialectic and questioning activities, a simple to use, threaded electronic discussion board or forum and its derivatives, such as VoiceThread, are as effective as most other approaches. A well-organized discussion board activity generally seeks to present a topic or issue and have students respond to questions and provide their own perspectives, while evaluating and responding to the opinions of others. The simple, direct visual of the "thread" also allows students to see how the entire discussion or lesson has evolved. In sum, for instructors wanting to focus attention and dialogue on a specific topic, the main activity for many online courses has been and continues to be the electronic discussion board.

Incorporating ***reflection*** can be a powerful pedagogical strategy under the right circumstances. There is an extensive body of scholarship on the "reflective teacher" and the "reflective learner" dating from the early 20th century (Dewey, 1916; Schon, 1983). While reflection can be a deeply personal activity, the ability to share one's reflections with others can be beneficial. Pedagogical activities that require students to reflect on what they are learning and to share their reflections with their teachers and fellow students extend and enrich reflection. Blogs and blogging, whether as group exercises or for individual journaling activities, are evolving as appropriate tools for students reflecting on their learning and other aspects of course activities.

Collaborative learning has been evolving for decades. In face-to-face classes, group work has grown in popularity and become commonplace in many course activities. Many professional programs such as business administration, education, health science, and social work rely heavily on collaborative learning as a technique for group problem solving. In the past, the logistics and time needed for effective collaboration in face-to-face classes were sometimes problematic. Now email, mobile technology, and other electronic communications alleviate some of these logistical issues. Wikis, especially, have grown in popularity and are becoming a staple in group projects and writing assignments. They are seen as important vehicles for creating knowledge and content as well as for generating peer-review and evaluation (Fredericksen, 2015). Unlike face-to-face group work that typically ends up on the instructor's desk when delivered in paper form, wikis allow students to generate content that can be shared with others during and beyond the end of a semester. Papers and projects developed through wikis can pass seamlessly from one group to another and from one class to another.

Perhaps the most important component of the model is the ***evaluation*** of learning. CMSs/LMSs and other online tools and platforms provide a number of mechanisms for assisting in this area. Papers, tests, assignments, and portfolios are among the major methods used for assessing student learning and are easily done electronically. Essays and term projects pass back and forth between teacher and student without ever being printed on paper. Oral classroom presentations are giving way to YouTube videos and podcasts. The portfolio is evolving into an electronic multimedia presentation of images, video, and audio that goes far beyond the three-inch, paper-filled binder. Weekly class discussions that take place on discussion boards or blogs provide the instructor with an electronic record that can be reviewed over and over again to examine how students have participated and progressed over time. They are also most helpful to instructors in assessing their own teaching and in reviewing what worked and what did not work in a class. As mentioned earlier in this chapter, the online environment also provides the facility for more peer review and evaluation. With all of these evaluation capabilities, learning analytics increasingly are being seen as the mechanisms for mining this trove of data to improve learning and teaching. In sum, online technology allows for a more seamless sharing of evaluation and assessment activities and provides an on-going record that can be referred to over and over again by both students and teachers.

The six components of the model described previously blend together into an integrated whole to form a community of learning in which rich interaction, whether online or face-to-face, can be provided and integrated across all modules. Furthermore, not every course must incorporate all of the activities and approaches of the model. The pedagogical objectives of a course should drive the activities and hence the approaches. For example, not every course needs to require students to do collaborative learning or to use dialectic questioning. In addition to individual courses, faculty and instructional designers might consider examining an entire academic program to determine which components of the model best fit which courses to cohesively serve overall programmatic goals and objectives. Here the concept of learning extends beyond the course to the larger academic program where activities might integrate across courses. For example, some MBA programs have a cohort of students enroll in three courses in the same semester but require one or more assignments or projects common to all three courses.

The critical question for our discussion, however, is whether this Blending With Pedagogical Purpose model can be modified or enlarged to be considered a model for online education in general. By incorporating several of the components from other theories and models discussed earlier in this chapter this is a possibility. Plate 1 (see plate section) presents a Multimodal Model for Online Education that expands on the Blending With Pedagogical Purpose approach and adds several new components from Anderson and others, namely community, interaction, and self-paced, independent instruction.

First, the concept of a learning community as promoted by Garrison et al. (2000) and Wenger and Lave (1991) is emphasized. A course is conceived of as a learning community. This community can be extended to a larger academic program. Second, it is a given that interaction is a basic characteristic of the community and permeates the model to the extent needed. Third, and perhaps the most important revision is the addition of the self-study/independent learning module that Anderson emphasized as incompatible with any of the community-based models. In this model, a self-study/independent learning can be integrated with other modules as needed or as the primary mode of instructional delivery. Adaptive learning software, an increasingly popular form of self-study, can be used stand alone or integrated into other components of the model. The latter is commonly being done at the secondary school level where adaptive software programs are used primarily in stand-alone mode with teachers available to act as tutors as needed. Adaptive software is also integrated into traditional, face-to-face classes such as in science, where it is common to see the instructor assign a lab activity that uses adaptive learning simulation software.

This Multimodal Model of Online Education attempts to address the issues that others, particularly Terry Anderson, have raised regarding elements that might be needed for an integrated or unified theory or model for online education.

Applying the Integrated Model

To provide a clearer understanding of the integrated model, several examples of its application follow. Plate 2 (see plate section) provides an example of the model as a representation of a self-paced, fully online course. The three major components [in green] for this course are content as provided on an CMS/LMS, a self-paced study module, and assessment/evaluation. Other components of the model such as a blog or discussion board to allow some interaction among students could be included but are not necessarily needed. This example is most appropriate for online programs that have rolling admissions where students can register at any time and are not limited by a semester schedule. Students can proceed at their own pace to complete the course as is typical in many distance education programs. This example is scalable and can be used for large numbers of students.

Plate 3 (see plate section) provides an example of another course that is primarily a self-paced online course similar to that described in Plate 2 but is designed to have a teacher or tutor available as needed. A discussion board is also included to allow for ongoing interaction among students and teacher. This course would follow a semester schedule and would have a standard class size; however, most of the instruction would be provided by the self-paced study module. A standard course organization would be used with a teacher or tutor assigned to guide and assist with instruction. A teacher or tutor could help students who are struggling with any of the self-paced material. This type of course is increasingly common in secondary schools such as in credit-recovery courses.

Plate 4 (see plate section) provides an example of a teacher-led, fully online course. Presentation of the course content is provided by an CMS or LMS along with other media and are used as needed by the teacher. The discussion board, blog, and wiki provide facilities for interaction among teachers and students, students and students, and students and content. In this course, the teacher could direct students to watch a 15-minute lecture that is available in the LMS database and then ask students to respond to a series of questions on the discussion board. The student responses can then be used as the basis for an interactive discussion board activity among students guided by the teacher. The model also provides for reflection and collaborative activities.

Plate 5 (see plate section) provides an example of a blended course with instruction provided primarily by a teacher. The other modules are used to extend and enrich instruction. The teacher is the major guide for instruction and would be supplemented by content as needed by an CMS/LMS. The course would meet in a face-to-face classroom; however, some instructional activity would also be conducted online either on a discussion board, a blog or a collaborative wiki. The teacher would establish beforehand portions of the course that would meet in the face-to-face and online modes.

Attributes and Limitations of the Multimodal Model

The proposed Multimodal Model for Online Education includes many of the major attributes of other learning and online education theories and models. For example, behaviorists will find elements of self-study and independent learning in adaptive software. Cognitivists might appreciate reflection and dialectic questioning as important elements of the model. Social constructivists will welcome the emphasis on community and interaction throughout the model. Connectivists might relate to the collaboration and the possibility of student-generated content. Perhaps the most significant element of the model is its flexibility and ability to expand as new learning approaches, perhaps spurred by advances in technology, evolve.

The model is not without its limitations. Learning theories can be approached through a number of perspectives and disciplines. Behavioral psychologists, cognitive psychologists, sociologists, and computer scientists might emphasize the need for deeper considerations of their perspectives in an online learning theory. The multimodal model here represents an integrated composite of several such perspectives, but is essentially a pedagogical model and therefore may have greater appeal to instructional designers, faculty, and others who focus on learning objectives.

Summary

In this chapter, a number of major theories related to technology were presented starting with a review of the major theories associated with learning. A critical question concerned whether an integrated or unified theory of online education could be developed. The work of Terry Anderson was highlighted. The chapter concluded with a proposal for an integrated model that describes the phenomenon of pedagogically-driven online education. Key to this model is the assumption that online education has evolved as a subset of learning in general rather than a subset of distance learning. Blended learning, which combines face-to-face and online instruction, is evolving as the dominant form of instruction throughout all levels of education, and is the basis for the integrated model. It is likely that in the not-too-distant future, all courses and programs will have some online learning components as suggested in this integrated model.

Further Reading/Case Studies

Readers may wish to refer to the Appendix A—Case Studies in Online Education specifically to:

Athabasca University

References

Anderson, T. (2011). *The theory and practice of online learning* (2nd ed.). Edmonton: AU Press.

Anderson, T., Rourke, L., Garrison, D. R., & Archer, W. (2001). Assessing social presence in asynchronous text-based computer conferencing. *Journal of Asynchronous Learning Networks*, *5*(2). Retrieved March 3, 2017 from http://immagic.com/eLibrary/ARCHIVES/GENERAL/ATHAB_CA/Anderson.pdf

Atkinson, R. C., & Shiffrin, R. M. (1968). Human memory: A proposed system and its control processes. In K. W. Spence & J. T. Spence (Eds.), *The psychology of learning and motivation* (Volume 2, pp. 89–195). New York, NY: Academic Press.

Barabasi, A. L. (2002). *Linked: The new science of networks*. Cambridge, MA: Perseus Publishing.

Bloom, B. S. (1956). *Taxonomy of educational objectives handbook: Cognitive domains*. New York, NY: David McKay.

Bosch, C. (2016). *Promoting self-directed learning through the implementation of cooperative learning in a higher education blended learning environment*. Doctoral dissertation at North-West University, Johannesburg, SA.

Bransford, J., Brown, A., & Cocking, R. (1999). *How people learn: Brain, mind experience and school*. Washington, DC: National Academy Press/National Research Council. Retrieved March 5, 2017 from www.colorado.edu/MCDB/LearningBiology/readings/How-people-learn.pdf

Castells, M. (2014, September 8). The impact of the Internet on society: A global perspective. *MIT Technology Review*. Retrieved February 26, 2017 from www.technologyreview.com/s/530566/the-impact-of-the-internet-on-society-a-global-perspective/

Chomsky, N. (1959). A review of B. F. Skinner's *Verbal Behavior*. *Language*, *35*(1), 26–58.

Dewey, J. (1916). *Democracy and education*. New York, NY: The Free Press.

Fredericksen, E. (2015, February 4). Is online education good or bad? And is this really the right question? *The Conversation*. Retrieved April 22, 2017 from https://theconversation.com/is-online-education-good-or-bad-and-is-this-really-the-right-question-35949

Gagné, R. M. (1977). *The conditions of learning*. New York, NY: Holt, Rinehart & Winston.

Gardner, H. (1983). *Frames of mind: The theory of multiple intelligences*. New York, NY: Basic Books.

Garrison, D. R., Anderson, T., & Archer, W. (2000). Critical inquiry in a text-based environment: Computer conferencing in higher education model. *The Internet and Higher Education*, *2*(2–3), 87–105.

Garrison, D. R., & Shale, D. (1990). *Education at a distance: From issues to practice*. Malabar, FL: Robert E. Krieger.

Gibbons, A. S., & Bunderson, C. V. (2005). Explore, explain, design. In K. K. Leondard (Ed.), *Encyclopedia of social measurement* (pp. 927–938). New York, NY: Elsevier.

Graham, C. R., Henrie, C. R., & Gibbons, A. S. (2013). Developing models and theory for blended learning research. In A. G. Picciano, C. D. Dziuban, & C. R. Graham (Eds.), *Blended learning: Research perspectives* (Volume 2). New York, NY: Routledge.

Harasim, L. (2012). *Learning theory and online technologies*. New York, NY: Routledge/Taylor & Francis.

Holmberg, B. (1989). *Theory and practice of distance education*. London: Routledge.

Jonassen, D. (1992). Designing hypertext for learning. In E. Scanlon & T. O'Shea (Eds.), *New directions in educational technology* (pp. 123–130). Berlin: Springer-Verlag.

Jung, C. (1921). *Psychological types*. Zurich: Rascher Verlag. Original in German. There are a number of English translations.

Knowles, M. S., Holton, E. F., & Swanson, R. A. (1998). *The adult learner* (5th ed.). Houston, TX: Butteworth-Heineman Publishers.

Lin, L., Cranton, P., & Bridglall, B. (2005). Psychological type and asynchronous written dialogue in adult learning. *Teachers College Record, 107*(8), 1788–1813.

Mayer, R. E. (2009). *Multimedia learning* (2nd ed.). New York, NY: Cambridge University Press.

McLuhan, M. (1964). *Understanding media*. London: Routledge.

Moore, M. (1989). Three types of interaction. *American Journal of Distance Education, 3*(2), 1–6.

Moore, M., & Kearsley, G. (1996). *Distance education: A systems view*. New York, NY: Wadsworth Publishing Company.

Picciano, A. G. (2009). Blending with purpose: The multimodal model. *Journal of Asynchronous Learning Networks, 13*(1), 7–18.

Postman, N. (1992). *Technopoly: The surrender of culture to technology*. New York, NY: Vintage Books.

Schon, D. (1983). *Reflective practitioner: How professionals think in action*. New York, NY: Basic Books.

Shank, G. (1993). Abductive multiloguing: The semiotic dynamics of navigating the Net. *The Arachnet Electronic Journal of Virtual Culture, 1*(1). Retrieved March 5, 2017 from http://serials.infomotions.com/aejvc/aejvc-v1n01-shank-abductive.txt

Siemens, G. (2004). *Connectivism: A learning theory for the digital age*. Paper Retrieved March 5, 2017 from www.elearnspace.org/Articles/connectivism.htm

Stephenson, K. (1998). *Internal communication, No. 36: What knowledge tears apart, networks make whole*. Retrieved March 5, 2017 from www.netform.com/html/icf.pdf

Wenger, E. (1998). *Communities of practice: Learning, meaning, and identity*. Cambridge: Cambridge University Press.

Wenger, E., & Lave, J. (1991). *Situated learning: Legitimate peripheral participation (Learning in doing: Social, cognitive and computational perspectives)*. Cambridge: Cambridge University Press.

Willingham, D. (2008, Summer). What is developmentally appropriate? *American Educator, 32*(2), 34–39.

Chapter 4

Research on Online Education

In October 2017, an article appeared in *The Chronicle of Higher Education* titled "Undergraduate Research Surges, Despite Uncertainties Over Best Practices" (Baskin, 2017). The article featured several research projects conducted by undergraduates and went on to indicate that undergraduate research had expanded in the last couple of decades in hundreds of colleges of all sizes and types. An important aspect of the article was the assertion that undergraduate research was also expanding into all of the disciplines, including the humanities and social sciences. As an example, a 70-page research thesis titled *What You Look At, You Make: Menstruation and Fertility in Italian Renaissance Art* by an undergraduate at the University of Vermont, was featured. The point was made that this thesis in just a few months following publication had more than 400 downloads. Just as research as an activity is exploding throughout the world, the Internet provides a ready distribution mechanism. No longer must a researcher submit manuscripts to journal editors and book publishers in order to make them available to others. And so, while the Internet greatly facilitates access to information, trying to review and synthesize the research literature becomes an ever increasingly difficult and time-consuming task.

This chapter will take a critical look at the research on online education including a review of research paradigms used for studying online education and an examination of major studies in the field. It will also trace the nature of the research on online education over the past 20 years to demonstrate how it has evolved and changed. The chapter will conclude with recommendations for continuation of this research, suggesting areas in need of more study and investigation.

Research Paradigms

Different disciplines approach research in different ways and rely more or less on particular paradigms. Since the focus of this book is online education, paradigms appropriate for research in education will be presented. A paradigm is defined as a philosophical or theoretical framework within which theories, laws, generalizations, and the research performed in support of them are formulated. Other terms are sometimes substituted for paradigm. In a textbook on research design, Creswell (2013) uses the term "worldview." Crotty (1998) uses the term "epistemology." Regardless of terminology, a paradigm influences the way research is conducted and the way knowledge is studied and interpreted. It establishes the aim, motivation, and expectations for the research. In conducting research, choices of methodologies, methods, and design should follow only after a paradigm has been established. In fact, without establishing a paradigm as the first step, there is little basis for subsequent choices regarding methodology and methods. A standardized taxonomy of research paradigms in the social sciences does not exist. Like the word paradigm itself, different terms have been used to describe similar paradigms, some of which overlap and can be the source of confusion. Among the most popular paradigms in social science research are positivism, postpositivism, constructivism, interpretivism, transformativism, emancipation, advocacy, critical research, pragmatism, and deconstructivism. In the following sections, several popular applicable paradigms will be briefly examined.

Positivism

Positivism views the universe as operating according to rational principles that can be studied empirically and quantified. Determinism is generally accepted as a guiding positivist tenet and accepts the existence of absolute truths that relate to causes and effects. Positivism can be seen in the ancient world (Aristotle) and was promoted during the Enlightenment by Francis Bacon, Rene Descartes, and John Locke. Positivistic approaches were first used widely by researchers and philosophers studying the natural world and were later adopted by social scientists. Positivism, for the most part, follows the scientific method and aims to test theories and hypotheses through observation and measurement. However, the fit of positivism with the social sciences has not always been graceful and has been the subject of much debate. As succinctly stated by Pring (2000), the language of atoms and particles is not the same as the language of intensely complex human interactions such as teaching and learning. While many scientists accept a natural world order where cause and effect variables can be controlled and quantified, the social world is a far more ambiguous one where many variables interact and intervene in ways that make it difficult if not impossible to achieve conclusive findings. As a result, a movement away from positivism evolved in the middle of the 20th century and evolved into what came to be called postpositivism.

Postpositivism

Postpositivism has been a source of confusion with regard to its relationship to positivism. Creswell (2013) sees postpositivism as a refinement that tempers the positivist working with theory, hypotheses, and measurement. The postpositivist is reluctant to assert that there are all-encompassing principles governing the social world. On the other hand, Trochim (2006) commented "I don't mean a slight adjustment to or revision of the positivist position—post-positivism is a wholesale rejection of the central tenets of positivism." In 2006, Mackensie and Knipe commented on this confusion:

> Postpositivists work from the assumption that any piece of research is influenced by a number of well-developed theories apart from, and as well as, the one which is being tested (Cook & Campbell 1979, p. 24). Also, since theories are held to be provisional and new understandings may challenge the whole theoretical framework (Kuhn, 1962). In contrast, O'Leary (2004) provides a definition of postpositivism which aligns in some sense with the constructivist paradigm claiming that postpositivists see the world as ambiguous, variable and multiple in its realities—"what might be the truth for one person or cultural group may not be the 'truth' for another" (p. 6). O'Leary (2004) suggests that postpositivism is intuitive and holistic, inductive and exploratory with findings that are qualitative in nature (pp. 6–7). This definition of postpositivism seems to be in conflict with the more widely used definition provided by Mertens (2005). Positivists and postpositivist research is most commonly aligned with quantitative methods of data collection and analysis.
>
> (Mackensie & Knipe, 2006)

In sum, postpositivists see the limitations of the world order. They may approach research deterministically and seek cause and effect, but understand that these are subject to change and are not absolute. They assume that findings may only be applicable to the situation at hand and are open to revision and reinterpretation in other environments. While tending to the quantitative, they also use qualitative methodologies.

Social Constructivism/Interpretivism

The social constructivist/interpretivist paradigm sees the world as socially constructed (Mertens, 2005). Realities are in the minds of the beholders and subject to multiple interpretations. Social constructivism/interpretivism posits that researchers' as well as subjects' views of the situation being studied are critical to the inquiry. In contrast to positivist and postpositivists, social constructivists do not always begin with a theory, rather they inductively develop a theory or pattern of meanings throughout the research process. Social constructivist/interpretivist researchers must understand their own subjectivity in conducting their inquiries. Creswell (2013) emphasizes that social constructivists understand that their own personal, cultural, and historical experiences shape their interpretations of the situations under study. Furthermore, in this paradigm, the context of the research situation plays a critical role in shaping the interpretation, and hence no attempt can be made to generalize beyond the setting under study. While mostly using qualitative methodologies, quantitative data may also be used to support or expand the analysis. Lincoln and Guba (1985) describe social constructivism as a naturalistic inquiry that is not anti-quantitative and in fact can utilize quantitative data when appropriate.

Advocacy/Critical Research

Advocacy/critical research emerged in the 1980s by researchers who believed that social constructivism did not do enough to address the issues of social justice and the causes of marginalized individuals (Creswell, 2013). Drawing from the philosophies of Marx and Engels and more recently from Freire, this paradigm advocates political action to address social issues such as poverty, domination, and inequality. Freire, especially, saw advocacy/critical research as a tool to lift colonized populations out of their suppressed conditions. In conducting advocacy/critical research, subjects of the inquiry are seen as collaborators who help design the study, assist in data collection, and participate in the analysis. Participatory action research (PAR), for example, is a common manifestation of the paradigm. Quantitative, qualitative, and mixed methodologies can be used equally well with this paradigm.

Pragmatism

Pragmatism emanates from the work of a number of individuals, although John Dewey is considered a prime mover in its development. Dewey espoused finding solutions that work in education. Pragmatism draws on other paradigms, if needed, but does not get bound by philosophical or theoretical entanglements. Pragmatists are free to design research that best meets the needs of the questions at hand. Like social constructivism, it tends to be more context-based and is not interested in finding absolute truths. It supports quantitative, qualitative, and mixed methodologies equally. Evaluation studies of instructional programs and processes frequently fall within the pragmatic paradigm.

These descriptions do not constitute an all-inclusive discussion but serve to provide an overview of the more popular paradigms of interest here. Readers should also be aware that paradigms overlap and studies can, in fact, be multi-paradigmatic. Taylor and Medina (2013) comment that rather than standing alone as individual paradigms for framing the design of a researcher's inquiry, the newer paradigms can serve as referents. In other words, research can be designed by combining methods that apply to two or more of the paradigms. For example, it is not uncommon for a research study to combine methods from the social constructivist and critical paradigms to create a "critical auto/ethnography." This multi-paradigmatic approach can prove powerful and should be considered where appropriate.

Decades of Research on Online Education

In this section, a number of major studies on online education that examine several issues related to students and faculty will be presented. Perhaps the most studied issues relate to student outcomes including grades, attrition/retention, and other performance indicators.

It is important to understand that the study of student outcomes related to the use of instructional technology predates the Internet. James Kulik and his associates at the University of Michigan were among the first researchers to conduct extensive reviews of the effects of technology on instruction. They conducted a series of meta-analyses in the 1970s and 1980s that included hundreds of studies dealing with the effects of technology at different grade levels (elementary, secondary, college, and adult). Their general conclusion was that computer-based education had a beneficial effect on academic achievement, although it was not uniformly true at all grade levels and all subject areas (Kulik, 1984; Kulik, Bangert, & Williams, 1983; Kulik, Kulik, & Bangert-Downs, 1984; Kulik, Kulik, & Cohen, 1980; Kulik, Kulik, & Schwab, 1986).

Richard E. Clark (1983, 1985, 1989) refuted these findings by questioning the research controls used in most of the studies in the Kulik meta-analyses. Clark, however, went further and proposed that technology or any medium was basically a vehicle carrying an instructional substance and that real improvement in achievement only comes with improving the substance, not the vehicle. Unlike Marshall McLuhan's thesis that the "medium is the message," Clark posited that in education the message or content is the substance that matters. Clark's position has been challenged over the years by a number of researchers such as Robert Kozma (1991, 1994a, 1994b) and Jack Koumi (1994) who see the medium as integral to the delivery of instruction. The two differing opinions on this issue remain to this day and the "great debate" continues. As an indication of the on-going nature and importance of this debate, a search of "Clark vs. Kozma" on Google provides over a million URLs, many of which refer to websites and blogs created in the past several years. Any researcher contemplating the examination of the effects of technology on learning would be well-served by reading and rereading the articles by Clark, Kozma, and Koumi cited previously. They provide valuable insight into the research issues.

The basis for the debate was ignited by the meta-analyses conducted by Kulik and his colleagues in the late 1970s and 1980s that synthesized much of the previous research on the issue. Since the Kulik work, thousands of studies have been conducted on the same issue as the nature of the technology (i.e., computer-assisted instruction, simulation software, online learning, etc.) keeps changing and evolving.

The 1990s

During the 1990s, in the early years of online education, there was a good deal of small-scale research conducted by individual faculty examining results in individual courses. This was to be expected as faculty shared what they had learned from using the new online technology in their teaching. A number of journals such as the *Journal of Asynchronous Learning Networks* (renamed the *Online Learning Journal*) dedicated to the research in online education emerged and provided vehicles for publication. Not unexpectedly, most of the early studies concluded positive student experiences and outcomes comparable to face-to-face instruction. John Hattie (2009) invested 15 years of research in examining 800 plus meta-analyses and concluded that the vast majority, as much as 90%, of the studies in education result in positive findings about the technique, strategy or policy being examined. Gladieux and Swail (1999) and Phipps and Merisotis (1999) in reviews of the available research on online education at the time concluded that there were shortcomings in much of this early research and there needed to be more systematic collection of data across programs with larger sample sizes. A group of researchers at the SUNY Learning Network addressed some of this need by conducting student and faculty satisfaction studies across programs and colleges within the State University of New York system (Fredericksen, Pickett, Shea, Pelz, & Swan, 1999a, 1999b). They reported broad satisfaction among students and faculty enrolled and teaching in online courses and programs. Among the factors that led to student and faculty satisfaction was the increase in both the quantity and quality of interaction during instruction. The issue of improved interaction became a dominant theme in much of the early research on online education.

The Early 2000s

At the turn of the millennium, the research on online education expanded, especially as the technology moved into the mainstream and was no longer seen as strictly a vehicle for distance education. Blended learning arrived and had an appeal in many sectors of K–12 and higher education. While individual cases based on course and program experiences still dominated the research literature, a substantial body of work also evolved that looked at online education across multiple institutions. In addition to student outcomes, studies considered other research topics related to faculty development and attitudes, administrative planning, funding, and implementation issues. A significant body of research evolved which examined the extent and nature of online education throughout the United States. Allen and Seaman (2013), with funding from the Alfred P. Sloan Foundation, undertook an annual study starting in 2002 of chief academic officers in colleges and universities. The American Association of Public Land-Grant Colleges conducted several studies of faculty, presidents, and chancellors across multiple institutions (McCarthy & Samors, 2009). Picciano and Seaman (2007) conducted national studies of K–12 school administrators. The United States Department of Education collected data on a three-year cycle on generic distance learning that included modalities other than online technology such as televised courses. The main conclusion of these national studies was that online technology was rapidly being deployed throughout all sectors of education. In addition, these studies identified concerns associated with implementation issues regarding student readiness, faculty development, and technology infrastructure to support large-scale online education initiatives. In a span of a little more than a decade, online education had become a hot research issue and was the focus of numerous studies and examinations. Hattie (2009) estimated that more than 5,000 studies were conducted on the use of technology in teaching and learning during the period.

Perhaps one of the most important studies was a meta-analysis funded by the United States Department of Education (U.S. ED). In 2007, the U.S. ED contracted with SRI International to conduct a meta-analysis of the effects of online learning on student achievement. Barbara Means, the lead researcher for this project, acknowledged the work done by a large team of staff members at SRI and named more than 20 individuals. The project was completed and a report prepared in 2009 and revised in 2010. As part of its work, the project team conducted a systematic search of the research literature published from 1996 through July 2008 and identified more than a thousand empirical studies of online learning. In total, 1,132 studies were screened, of which 45 were fully usable for the meta-analysis. An important aspect of this study was that it tried to separate fully online instruction from blended learning. The overall finding of the meta-analysis was that classes with online learning (whether taught completely online or blended) on average produce stronger student learning outcomes than do classes with solely face-to-face instruction. The mean effect size for all 50 contrasts was +0.20, $p < .001$ (U.S.ED, p. 18). It is important to keep in mind that an effect size of +0.20 is considered small, but is nonetheless positive. However, the researchers for the meta-analysis went a step further by separating the findings for fully online versus blended learning. To quote:

> The conceptual framework for this study, which distinguishes between purely online and blended forms of instruction, calls for creating subsets of the effect estimates to address two more nuanced research questions:
>
> 1. *How does the effectiveness of online learning compare with that of face-to-face instruction?*
>
> Looking only at the 27 Category 1 effects that compared a purely online condition with face-to-face instruction, analysts found a mean effect of +0.05, $p = .46$.
>
> This finding is similar to that of previous summaries of distance learning (generally from pre-Internet studies), in finding that instruction conducted entirely online is as effective as classroom instruction but no better.
>
> 2. *Does supplementing face-to-face instruction with online instruction enhance learning?*
>
> For the 23 Category 2 contrasts that compared blended conditions of online plus face-to-face learning with face-to-face instruction alone, the mean effect size of +0.35 was significant ($p < .0001$). Blends of online and face-to-face instruction, on average, had stronger learning outcomes than did face-to-face instruction alone.
>
> A test of the difference between Category 1 and Category 2 studies found that the mean effect size was larger for contrasts pitting blended learning against face-to-face instruction ($g+ = +0.35$) than for those of purely online versus face-to-face instruction ($g+ = +0.05$); the difference between the two subsets of studies was statistically significant ($Q = 8.37, p < .01$).
>
> (U.S.ED, p. 12)

The effect size comparing blended learning and face-to-face instruction was much stronger at +0.35 and made this finding far more significant. The researchers commented later in the study that some of the difference in the effects of blended learning might be attributed to more time on task than in fully online or face-to-face instruction. This meta-analysis was viewed as a major endorsement of online education particularly blended learning, and became one of the most cited studies from the early 2000s. It served its purpose as a well-conducted recap of the research on online education during this period.

Research on MOOCs

As noted in Chapter 2 of this book, the period between approximately 2008 and 2013 was dominated by the development of massive open online courses or MOOCS and the popular and professional literature was dominated by the MOOC phenomenon as well. One of the most important studies on MOOCs took place in California and was based on a well-funded, high-profile research initiative at San Jose State University in 2012–13. Six basic courses in mathematics and statistics were carefully planned and offered at San Jose State using materials developed by Udacity, one of the major MOOC providers in the country. Course enrollments were limited and similar in size to traditional, face-to-face courses. Personnel from Udacity were highly-involved with the faculty in the development and subsequent teaching of the courses. The results were not very positive. The average pass rate across all six courses was 33.3% and ranged from a low of 11.9% to a high of 54.3%. These pass rates were considerably lower than those in the same courses taught in traditional, face-to-face modes in previous years where average pass rates were closer to 75% and ranged from 30.4% to 80.4% (Collins, 2013). An important aspect of this study was the diverse characteristics of the student participants and the controls for matriculation status, age, gender, underrepresented minority (URM), and PELL eligibility. A criticism of many other freely-available MOOC courses was that they appealed to a certain population of mainly older male students, who already had college credentials. Of the 213 student participants in the San Jose University study, 54% were non-matriculants, 79% were under the age of 24, 51% were female, 40% were URM, and 31% were Pell eligible. As a side note, 274 students originally enrolled in the MOOC courses at San Jose State University; 249 students remained in the study sample after data cleaning. In addition, 36 students who withdrew from the course or received a final grade of Incomplete were removed, leaving a study sample of 213 students (Collins, 2013). As mentioned in Chapter 2, this study began an avalanche of adverse publicity for the MOOC movement, so much so that Sebastian Thrun was quoted during an interview that his company had "a lousy product" (Chafkin, 2013).

Another important study was conducted on 16 Coursera-developed MOOC courses taught by University of Pennsylvania faculty between June 2012 and July 2013. This study examined success as defined by a final grade of "80% or higher" and retention rates as defined by the number of students who accessed a lecture in the last module divided by the number who accessed a lecture in the first module. The authors of the study also collected data on students who progressed sequentially through a course versus those who opted to progress non-sequentially or as they wished. They defined

> sequential movement as the progression of a user through a course in the sequential order identified by the instructor. The second [non-sequential] "user-driven" approach considered the share of users who accessed a lecture in any course module, ignoring the order or sequencing of lecture access or whether the user accessed any other lecture. This second approach recognized that a user may choose whether and when to access learning materials.
>
> (Perna et al., 2014, p. 424)

The percentage of students who successfully completed a course with an "80%" or above ranged from 0% to 12%. Retention rates ranged from 11% to 39%. There were not significant differences between sequential and non-sequential or user-driven students. The authors of the study concluded:

> Additional research is needed to understand how course design characteristics and pedagogical practices influence user outcomes. Some portion of the low completion rates in this study is likely attributable to the failure of these first-generation courses to adequately engage students in the course content or utilize effective instructional practices. Future research should consider whether these outcomes reflect insufficient interaction with students, the absence of effective pedagogical approaches, and/or failure to motivate students to learn.
>
> (Perna et al., 2014, p. 429)

The pedagogical issues raised in this study were well-known to faculty and instructional designers who had experience in developing online learning courses and materials going back to the

1990s. The fundamental model promoted in the early years of online education (1990s–early 2000s) was the highly-interactive, asynchronous learning network (ALN) made popular by the Alfred P. Sloan Foundation's Anytime, Anyplace Learning Program. The results of the U Penn study gave credence to the concern that many of those involved in MOOC development at companies like Coursera did not pay enough attention to the nuances involved in developing online learning materials. In addition, the size of MOOC courses enrolling tens of thousands of students made meaningful interaction with faculty difficult at best and impossible at worst. This study, however, provided important new insights into the concept of "sporadic participation": students proceeding and progressing through course material non-sequentially at their own pace (Haggard, 2013). These students may not complete or do well in a course but they still derive meaningful learning experiences by accessing portions of the course content. It might have been their intention all along to simply study and learn from one or two modules and not the entire course. In addition, the findings in this study support the concept that self-regulated or self-determined learning may be at play (Wiebe, Thompson, & Behrend, 2015). As the authors of the U Penn study concluded, the future of MOOCs may lie in supporting other types of learning rather than providing entire courses:

> Future research should consider how user outcomes vary for MOOCs that are specifically targeted to such groups as individuals seeking personal enrichment, adult learners needing vocational or occupational training, currently enrolled college students seeking supplemental learning resources, secondary school students looking to improve academic readiness for college, and prospective college students considering whether college is right for them.
>
> (Perna et al., 2014, p. 429)

Perhaps the most comprehensive review of MOOC technology was conducted by Ho et al. (2015) as a collaboration between the HarvardX Research Committee at Harvard University and the Office of Digital Learning at MIT. The study was based on data collected over two academic years (2012–13 and 2013–14) from 68 edX courses, 1.7 million participants, 10 million participant hours, and 1.1 billion logged events. Two of the major foci of the study were student characteristics and student performance as defined by those who received/did not receive certificates of completion. Among the key student demographic data findings were the following:

> 30% of the students were female;
> 69% had bachelor's degrees;
> the median age was 28; and
> 29% resided in the United States.
>
> (Ho et al., 2015, p. 10)

This study supported earlier research that established that many MOOCs appealed to older male students who already held bachelor degrees. It also supported the fact that many MOOCs had great appeal to students in other countries where there were limited opportunities for higher education.

Certificates of completion were awarded to 7% of the students in 2012–13 and 8% in 2013–14. These findings supported other studies such as Perna et al. (2014). The study also surveyed student intentions when registering for a MOOC and the results indicated that a range of 19% to 57% intended to earn a certificate. It was concluded that large percentages of students had no intention of completing or receiving a certificate. The authors stated that the certification rate was a poor indicator of course efficacy and student performance, but that without any other agreed-upon measure, would have to do. In the study at the University of Pennsylvania cited earlier, a retention rate measure was used as an indication of course efficacy but this was not a generally agreed-upon measure either. Study of the efficacy of MOOC technology continued but many of the findings indicated weak completion rates whatever the definition. One conclusion of these studies was that the major role for MOOCs would be in providing resources such as multimedia, assessment tools, and online delivery platforms in addition to complete courses. This would give faculty the option of making best use of these materials and would also allow students to access these materials to meet their own self-directed learning needs. It was also concluded that MOOC courses may have greater appeal in other countries where access to higher education was limited.

Current Research

Online education is currently in a fourth wave or stage of development and seeks to integrate blended and MOOC models that can be used throughout all of education. Social and multimedia use is expanding and students are relying extensively on portable devices (laptops, tablets, iPhone, PDAs) for accessing and participating in course activities. In addition, a number of new software facilities and approaches associated with adaptive learning techniques are expanding. In this section, several studies that focused on at a variety of current online education issues including adaptive learning, cost-benefits, K–12 models, faculty workload, and flipped classrooms will be presented.

Adaptive Learning

Adaptive learning was introduced in Chapter 2 as the latest generation of computer-assisted instruction (CAI) capable of personalizing learning to meet individual student needs. Research has begun on the implementation of these systems including one comprehensive study conducted under the auspices of ITHAKA, a non-profit organization originally affiliated with Carnegie Mellon University, that involved 605 students ($N = 605$) enrolled at six public colleges at the State University of New York, the University of Maryland, and City University of New York (Bowen, Chingos, Lack, & Nygren, 2012). The purpose of the study was to assess the educational outcomes of students enrolled in adaptive learning courses offered in a blended format (treatment group) and students enrolled in the same courses in a traditional face-to-face format (control group). The course used in the study was an early generation of adaptive learning.

Learning outcomes were compared between the treatment and control groups in terms of the rate at which students completed and passed the course, their performance on a standardized test of statistics (the Comprehensive Assessment of Statistics—CAOS test), and their score on a set of final exam questions that were the same for both groups. The researchers found no statistically significant differences in learning outcomes between students in the traditional and blended-format sections. Blended-format students did perform slightly better than traditional-format students on the three outcomes, achieving pass rates that were about three percentage points higher, CAOS scores about one percentage point higher, and final exam scores two percentage points higher—but none of these differences passed traditional tests of statistical significance.

In addition to the findings, the authors also provided important insights into their difficulties in conducting randomized experimental studies on student populations. They provided a ten-page appendix that reviewed these difficulties, which included maintaining control of student course preferences such as the desire to withdraw or switch sections, gaining the approvals of Institutional Review Boards, recruiting and training enough instructors for the courses, and maintaining data controls over time across different data collection systems. In fact, the original research started with nine colleges (three community colleges in addition to the six senior colleges previously mentioned), but after a number of difficulties, especially with data collection, the authors decided that they had jeopardized their research protocols and could not in good conscience include the subjects from the three community colleges.

Another important study on adaptive learning was conducted at the University of Central Florida in a fully online General Psychology course (N-292) by Dziuban, Moskal, Cassisi, and Fawcett (2016). While students expressed satisfaction with the adaptive learning software, they also provided interesting feedback on the issue of interaction, which in a fully online adaptive course may be somewhat less if not minimal compared to other types of courses. The fundamental nature of these adaptive systems allows students to immerse themselves in the content and progress through the material at their own pace—in theory, as quickly or as slowly as the course structure allows. This creates the possibility of an isolated environment for students who interact primarily with the system and infrequently with each other. In examining this question, the survey results indicated that students perceived themselves as interacting less or much less (75%) with each other than in a course not using the adaptive learning platform. However, the researchers wondered how much students wanted to interact with each other in the classroom. Only 20% of them preferred some or substantial interaction with other students; 29% had no preference; and 52% of those responding indicated that they preferred little or no interaction with other students in their classes. When indicating their preferred method of interacting, the majority of students (59%) indicated discussion boards—possibly because this is the predominate method used within the online instructional environment and therefore the one with which they are most familiar. This study won the United States Distance Learning Quality Research Paper Award for 2017 mainly because it provided new insights into the issue of student interactions in online learning and specifically in adaptive learning environments.

K–12

Hoxie, Stillman, and Chesal (2014) conducted a study of 125 blended learning courses offered in New York City middle and high schools during the 2011–2012 school year. Survey data were collected from teachers (N = 126) to determine their perceptions and satisfaction with the rotation and flex models of blended learning. The rotation (N = 62) and flex (N = 64) models of blended learning were selected based on definitions established by Staker and Horn (2014), Hoxie et al. (2014) defined rotation and flex as follows:

> Rotation—students rotate between online and face-to-face learning activities;
> Flex—students learn primarily online but work individually with a teacher as needed based on data generated by the online learning software.

The critical difference between the two models was that the rotation model is basically teacher-led and integrated with vendor-developed software while the flex model is dependent primarily on vendor-developed software as the main driver of instruction. Major findings from the teacher surveys were that teachers who used a rotation approach to blended learning perceived significantly more positive effects with regard to what blended learning can do for students than the flex model:

> Rotation teachers were more likely to agree or strongly agree that blended learning makes students more engaged with content (M = 3.15, SD = .77) than Flex teachers (M = 2.79, SD = .65); $t(103) = -2.60, p < .01$. Rotation teachers also saw a greater increase in student motivation for low performing students (M = 3.01, SD = .80) compared to Flex teachers

> (M = 2.62, SD = .77); $t(104) = -2.61, p < .01$, as well as a greater increase in motivation for average performing students (M = 3.14, SD = .68) compared to Flex (M = 2.84, SD = .59); $t(102) = -2.46, p < .05$. Rotation teachers were also more likely to view blended learning as creating opportunities for students to self-regulate their learning (M = 3.42, SD = .65) compared to Flex (M = 3.00, SD = .68); $t(119) = -3.44, p < .001$, and creating a learning experience that is more personalized for each student (M = 3.39, SD = .65) compared to Flex (M = 2.98, SD = .78); $t(103) = -3.08, p < .01$.
>
> (Hoxie et al., 2014, p. 314)

In analyzing these findings, the authors concluded that the major reason for these perceptions was that rotation teachers sensed that they retained more control over content and pedagogical decisions than did the flex teachers. The rotation teachers, who were more the "creators" of instructional approaches, perceived blended learning as being more beneficial for their students than the teachers who were more "utilizers" of provided approaches. Furthermore,

> Teachers who take on the challenge of becoming blended instructors must make many decisions about how to combine online and face-to-face learning, including crucial decisions about what the online content will be, and how often to use it. These decisions, however, are clearly impacted by what is available in the blended learning marketplace, thus complicating our findings. While our research suggests that choosing to use online learning as only one element that students rotate through, and choosing to create one's own online learning content both have important positive associations with teachers' perceived effectiveness as blended instructors, these choices are undoubtedly driven, in part, by a marketplace that is constrained in two major ways. First, much of the online courseware that is available can't be easily modularized, and teachers are not free to easily pick and choose the parts of an online course that work for them in the context of their own classroom. Accordingly, they may choose not to use vendor content at all, creating their own, or they may only choose those vendors that do provide easy modularity of content. Thus, the higher satisfaction rates of teachers who used a rotation approach compared to a flex approach and of the creators compared to the utilizers could be a comparison of this: those who have found a happy modular medium compared to those who took the plunge in an all or nothing situation, and now have lingering doubts about the usefulness of their courseware.
>
> (Hoxie et al., 2014, p. 323)

The comment made by the researchers that "much of the online courseware that is available can't be easily modularized" is an important observation that has been heard in other blended learning environments and one that commercial software providers are investing significant resources to address.

Cost Benefits in Corporate Training

In addition to colleges, universities, and K–12 education, there is a respectable amount of online education occurring in corporate professional development and training. In fact, *Training* magazine estimated that corporate America expended approximately $112.5 billion in corporate training in 2015 (Staff, 2015). There have been several studies examining the benefits of blended learning in corporate training, especially in terms of cost benefits. Blended learning courses, for example, can reduce travel costs for national and international companies. By reducing travel for training, they also increase productivity by allowing employees to remain on their work sites to perform their regular responsibilities.

Intel Corporation employs thousands of manufacturing technicians around the globe who are responsible for operating, performing preventative maintenance, and troubleshooting its equipment. As a result, Intel focuses on hiring technicians with core technical competencies while also devoting resources to maintaining competencies throughout their careers. A technician's time is a precious commodity, so when developing training programs for these technicians, instructional designers at Intel have to consider their formal education, their experience, and the time required away from their responsibilities.

To reduce training costs and to minimize any disruption in factory operations, Intel developed a blended learning approach that was focused on enabling technicians to accomplish learning goals using a combination of solutions including experiential learning and self-paced learning, as well as collaborative and instructor-led models. The instructional design team implemented four different courses for Fabrication (Fab) and Sort and Assembly-test audiences in the domain of factory equipment training. The team took what had been a fully in-person, 12-day instructor-led course requiring 16 days of tool downtime and converted it to a blended learning course requiring a 5-day, instructor led course, 3 hours of Web-based work, and only 2 days of tool downtime.

The evaluators of the blended learning program carefully collected data on a number of student outcomes and cost-beneficial factors. They summarized their findings as follows:

> The program was able to show 30% reduction in travel costs. When implemented in partnership with factory resources and equipment suppliers, blended learning helped mitigate the costs associated with technician time away from the factory and tool downtime for training while enabling the reduction of Technician Time Away from Factory (TTAF) by over 50%. The Managed Preventative Maintenance (MPM) solution resulted in a 30% increase in availability of production tools through reduction of tool usage for training. This also enabled increased availability of technician time for problem solving. Creation of the Intel blended learning courses resulted in resolution to both the impacts while ensuring a quality solution resulting in significant cost-savings for Intel. The blended learning solution was able to reduce the time required to bring a manufacturing tool down for a predetermined amount of time for training through implementation of the MPM solution. The result was an additional 11 days of tool up-time each time the course was implemented . . . A detailed ROI analysis on the program revealed an ROI roughly of 157% with a benefits-cost ratio of 2.27.
>
> (Mahesh & Woll, 2007, p. 56)

The Intel evaluators who conducted this study concluded that blended learning accomplished the goals of decreasing costs while improving the quality of the learning experience.

Comparing Synchronous and Asynchronous Interactions in a Flipped Classroom

Because online education provides opportunities for using a variety of instructional approaches, there are a number of studies that compare pedagogical techniques to determine which might be more or less effective. For example, researchers at Stockton University, New Jersey, examined the interaction behaviors and metacognitive behaviors of graduate students ($N = 125$) in the online portion of a flipped classroom (Meyers & Feeney, 2016). In-person class time was used for student/faculty interaction. Instructors clarified concepts, responded to questions, and facilitated small group activities where content was applied to real world experiences. For their time outside the face-to-face classroom, students were given the choice of two online methods for their interactions—synchronous verbal discussions and asynchronous written discussions. Discussions were analyzed and interactive and metacognitive behaviors were categorized and counted. Interaction behaviors and metacognitive behaviors were reported and presented for both environments.

There were two null hypotheses:

1. Incidents of interactions are not significantly different when comparing the synchronous and asynchronous communications;
2. Incidents of metacognition are not significantly different when comparing the synchronous and asynchronous environments.

Results of the data collection indicated that synchronous verbal discussions were found to include more interaction behaviors in five of six categories. There were no significant differences in the number of metacognitive behaviors. Students demonstrated the same level of learning behaviors in both environments.

In examining these results in more detail, important pedagogical techniques for designing blended courses were being evaluated. Student interaction—whether with faculty, with other students, or with curricular material—is generally considered an indicator of student engagement with a class. Many studies have examined both the quantity and quality of student interactions. This study concluded that there were significant differences in the quantity of the student interactions. However, quantity does not indicate quality. The authors of the study took the inquiry a step further and considered meta-cognitive behaviors to provide insight into the quality of the student interactions. They used Bloom's Taxonomy, as described in Chapter 3, to present six examples of meta-cognitive behaviors. Using a prepared coding scheme and observations by an independent reviewer of student interactions in both the synchronous and asynchronous discussions, the researchers concluded that incidents of metacognition were not significantly different in the two populations. An additional important finding was that there was evidence of all six meta-cognitive behaviors in both forms of online discussion.

Faculty Workload

Earlier in this chapter, reference was made to the United States Department of Education meta-analysis, which took note of the possibility that additional faculty and student time was a factor in student outcomes in blended courses. The issue of time and workload has been commented upon in a number of studies but rarely studied carefully. With a grant from the Australian Learning and Teaching Council (ALTC), Tynan, Ryan, Hinton, and Mills (2012) undertook a study to examine specifically workload issues at four Australian universities. The purpose of the study was to report on staff perceptions of increased workload and the strategies used to manage workload while maintaining quality, and to explore the implications of increased workload with regard to the future of university teaching.

A grounded theory approach was used that allowed for the generation of data about the impact of technologies on workload when teaching online or in blended modes. Grounded theory is an inductive research methodology that attempts to derive a theory from an activity, process, or interaction and is *grounded* in the views of the participants. To collect data, semi-structured interviews were conducted with a purposefully selected sample of 25 academic (faculty) and professional (support) staff at each of four universities: the University of New England (UNE), the Australian Catholic University (ACU), the University of Southern Queensland (USQ), and Central Queensland University (CQU). Three are predominantly distance education universities but with sizable on-campus numbers at several campuses; ACU is primarily campus-based but nationally-distributed and is moving rapidly to online delivery in order to combine small class size numbers at the various campuses.

A literature search was undertaken on workloads and costs associated with online-only and blended learning, drawing on US, Canadian, UK, and Australian peer-reviewed studies as well as "grey" or non-peer reviewed literature, including education media such as *The Chronicle of Higher Education.*

The research questions were as follows:

1) What research is available on how workload is allocated in online and blended learning environments through Workload Allocation Models (WAMs)?
2) How do staff perceive the validity of their institutional WAMs with respect to teaching time?
3) How do academic staff "manage" workload in online and blended teaching?

Interviewees were selected who had taught or were teaching in online and blended modes within a wide range of years of experience and differing levels of seniority. The 100 interviews produced 88 valid responses. A small number of the interviewees (3 out of 88) who had taught but were now designated as support staff were included, to give some perspective on how academics were managing their online delivery. Descriptive themes were analyzed using N-Vivo, and sub-themes were subsequently generated. The study provides rich descriptions of the findings for each of the research questions. Here is a sample from the interviews:

> One of the things about online is that people see it as a personal service. You say—yes, there's the Blackboard discussions and so on. That means that every day you go into it and you service that Discussion group—every day. If I'm running a lecture group—like face-to-face stuff—I'm not servicing those classes every day. And then of course students decide—oh well, they're a bit diffident about putting up a stupid question, so they email you or ring you.
>
> (Tynan et al., 2012, p. 78)

> I think it takes a lot longer for me to form a suitable reply online than it does for me to just spit out an answer. Because I spend a lot of time thinking 'how should I say it? Have I said that OK? Is someone going to take that the wrong way?' And I'll spend half an hour on a five minute question.
>
> (Tynan et al., 2012, p. 102)

> With 170 students, I'm probably spending in excess of 14 hours a week plus with the students, answering their queries. . . . I probably spend a good five to 10 hours the week before the semester starts.
>
> (Tynan et al., 2012, p. 104)

These quotes provide insights into the nature of the extra workload that might be engendered when teaching a course that has online components. The interview technique was most appropriate for collecting this type of descriptive data.

In general, the interviewees in this study overwhelmingly perceived their workload allocation as not sufficiently accounting for the additional time required by teaching in fully online or blended modes. This study did not attempt to quantify additional work hours in "e-teaching" although 1 of the 88 participants was prepared to estimate that blended learning added 20% to classroom instruction time, and another posited that it consumed double a face-to-face workload. Nevertheless, the study provided important insights into perceived additional workload as a direct result of the new technology tasks and communication modalities in teaching.

Scaling Up Blended Learning Research

Moskal and Cavanagh (2014) attempted to scale up and study faculty development courses across 20 institutions of higher education. In addition to findings on student and faculty satisfaction, the study also provided valuable insights into the difficulties encountered in conducting research across a number of institutions. Moskal and Cavanagh (2014) described the Next Generation Learning Challenges (NGLC) program as a collaborative, multi-year initiative created to address the barriers to educational innovation and tap the potential of technology to improve college readiness and completion in the United States. NGLC is led by EDUCAUSE in partnership with the League for Innovation in the Community College, the International Association for K–12 Online Learning (iNACOL), and the Council of Chief State School Officers (CCSSO), with funding provided by the Bill and Melinda Gates Foundation and the William and Flora Hewlett Foundation. The NGLC program consists of several "waves" of project funding, each with a slightly different focus.

In Wave 1 of the program, NGLC solicited proposals in four challenge areas designed to scale proven models to much wider student populations: Blended Learning, Open Educational Resources (OER), Learner Analytics, and Deeper Learning and Engagement. One of the Blended Learning projects was a collaboration between the University of Central Florida (UCF) and the American Association of State Colleges and Universities (AASCU) called *Expanding Blended Learning Through Tools and Campus Programs.*

In order to achieve the NGLC stated goal of scale, the UCF/AASCU project expanded the adoption of UCF's successful blended initiative to 20 participating AASCU member institutions by developing and disseminating a "Blended Learning Toolkit" based upon the proven best practices that had been successfully implemented by the University of Central Florida. Included in this Toolkit were strategies for blended course design and delivery, OER blended course models in English Composition and Algebra, assessment and data collection protocols, and "train-the-trainer" materials and workshops. AASCU recruited the 20 collaborating institutions and leveraged their networks and conferences to work with these institutions on blended learning implementation, while at the same time making the Toolkit and course models widely available to its entire 420 member institutions and systems. Each of the 20 partner institutions deployed one or more courses, either directly using the English Composition and Algebra templates or building other high-need courses by using the strategies and resources contained in the Toolkit.

The project connected the 20 participating AASCU institutions to a community of practice dedicated to curricular reinvention through technology. Faculty in these institutions worked with each other and with expert UCF faculty and staff to redesign the provided English Composition and Algebra courses needed. UCF's team of faculty, assessment, and blended learning experts worked with their peers at the participating institutions to create a "bottom up" buy-in of blended learning, using the toolkit and model courses to jump start adoption and rigorous assessment to prove efficacy.

The primary directive for the grant was to investigate whether blended learning could be scaled up to the 20 participating campuses. Across all 20 campuses, 79 unique blended courses were developed by 131 faculty who delivered 217 sections to 5,798 students.

To ensure that the evaluation was as straightforward as possible for participants, student and faculty surveys were developed and coded in Google Forms by UCF researchers. Faculty at each participating campus then received a request and reminders during the administration period near the end of the fall and spring semesters to encourage their students to participate.

Student grade data were de-identified and students' surveys were anonymous. This was a conscious decision on the part of the UCF evaluation staff. Having anonymous student data ensured that UCF's Institutional Review Board (IRB) classified the research as "exempt" from human subjects review. This made the process significantly easier for those responsible for assessment at the 20 participating schools in terms of obtaining IRB approval and handling student data. Even with this designation, several campuses required more information and were initially hesitant to release student data due to FERPA (Family Educational Right and Privacy Act) protection. These requests were handled individually by UCF's grant assessment coordinator who provided the necessary details to meet individual campuses' requirements for human subjects review. Having student identification would have greatly complicated this process, and would have hampered the ability to accomplish the evaluation in the 15-month grant time period. The result of not maintaining student identifiers was the loss of a possible comparison between grades and satisfaction while gaining quick access to the quality and quantity of data. In the researchers' experience, this was "a necessary sacrifice" (Moskal & Cavanagh, 2014, p. 48).

The results of the surveys completed by students enrolled in the blended learning courses yielded the following:

> 60% indicated that they were somewhat or very satisfied with the blended learning course;
> 43% indicated that time saving, convenience, and flexibility were what they liked most with the blended learning course;
> 17% indicated that technology issues, the instructor or other class characteristics were what they liked least about the blended learning course;
> 60% indicated that they would probably or definitely take another blended learning course.
>
> The results of the surveys completed by faculty teaching in the blended learning courses yielded the following:
>
> 74% indicated that they would teach a blended learning course again;
> 42% indicated that the most positive aspect of teaching a blended course was that it provided the best of both worlds (online and face-to-face), convenience, and the broad range of teaching materials;
> 28% indicated that blended learning does not work for students who lack discipline;
> 25% indicated that blended learning is a problem for students who are not computer savvy.
>
> Institutionally provided grade data for the blended learning courses indicated the following:
>
> 93% completed the blended learning course; completion rates were the same regardless of whether the students were from low-income households or not.
> 64% were successful (Received a grade of "A", "B" or "C"). Success rates for low-income students was 61% and 67% for non-low income students.
>
> (Moskal & Cavanagh, 2014, pp. 44–46)

Based on these findings, the authors concluded that student satisfaction, faculty satisfaction, and student outcomes were positive and indicative of a successful deployment of blended learning across the 20 participating institutions.

Before concluding their study, the authors reviewed some of the issues associated with conducting research on blended learning across multiple institutions. The authors of the study, because of time constraints and the possibility of having to seek IRB approvals at all 20 participating institutions, sought and received an exemption from human subjects review. This surely expedited and streamlined the evaluation but hindered the ability to do more in-depth analysis of student performance since they could not collect individual student identifiers. The authors lamented that a deeper investigation of student performance might have added significantly to their findings. The authors also indicated that the local institutional contexts varied in terms of technology support, faculty expertise with technology, course content, and grading practices. Lastly, the researchers indicated that coordination across institutions, local buy-in, and budget and time constraints hindered some of their original evaluation plans.

Future Research

We conclude this chapter by taking a brief look at several important issues for research on online education in the not too distant future. First, it is likely that as new online technology evolves, especially in areas such as adaptive learning, researchers will continue to study, evaluate, and compare new techniques and approaches. This has been going on for decades and there is little reason to assume that it will cease in the years to come.

Second, technology to support research is advancing rapidly. The era of big data and learning analytics is in its nascent stages. Avella, Kebritchi, Nunn, and Kanai (2016) in an extensive review of the literature concluded that big data and learning analytics were still emerging fields and that there were few studies reporting on empirical research. Nevertheless, the potential for these approaches to add significant new ways to study teaching and learning is real and will grow especially in the online education environment. Researchers will have at their disposal data on every instructional transaction undertaken by the student and teacher; this will allow for analysis at a very fine granular level. In fact, it is quite possible that big data will challenge many of our assumptions about quantitative research, statistical analysis, and significance. For example, a recent study by the Equality of Opportunity Project at Stanford University used data on 30 million college students to construct mobility report cards on students' earnings and their parents' incomes for each college in America. The analysis focused on how colleges shape children's prospects of upward mobility and how children climb the income ladder through higher education. Raj Chetty, one of the project's lead investigators indicated that with such large data sets, the concept of statistical significance has to be reconsidered (Equality of Opportunity Project, 2017).

Lastly, in addition to examining online education as an isolated object of study, it will be desirable to consider how it integrates with other issues facing education at all levels, especially in our colleges and universities. Public financing, cost-containment, education opportunity for low-income and minority students, student retention, and a changing labor market are critical issues that are challenging education leaders like never before. Online technology is frequently seen as a vehicle that can be part of the solution for addressing these. Undertaking case studies that illustrate how online education is being used as part of strategic planning and institutional initiatives to address larger education issues will be most beneficial to the educational enterprise (Dziuban & Picciano, 2015).

Summary

This chapter examined the research on online education. It started with a review of research paradigms used for studying online education and then examined and critiqued major studies of the field. It traced the nature of the research on online education over the past 20 years to demonstrate how it has evolved and changed. The chapter concluded with recommendations for continuation of this research and suggested areas in need of more study and investigation.

Further Reading/Case Studies

Readers may wish to refer to Appendix A—Case Studies in Online Education specifically to:

American Public University
University of Central Florida
University of Wisconsin—Milwaukee

References

Allen, I. E., & Seaman, J. (2013). Changing course: Ten years of tracking online education in the United States. *Babson Survey Research Group and Quahog Research Group, LLC.* Retrieved April 25, 2018 from: https://www.onlinelearningsurvey.com/reports/changingcourse.pdf

Avella, J. T., Kebritchi, M., Nunn, S. G., & Kanai, T. (2016, June). Learning analytics methods, benefits, and challenges in higher education: A systematic literature review. *Online Learning, 20*(2). Retrieved December 28, 2017 from https://olj.onlinelearningconsortium.org/index.php/olj/article/view/790/201

Baskin, P. (2017, October 2). Undergraduate research surges, despite uncertainties over best practices. *The Chronicle of Higher Education.* Retrieved October 3, 2017 from www.chronicle.com/article/Undergraduate-Research-Surges/241360?cid=at&utm_source=at&utm_medium=en&elqTrackId=2212b2e88332484b833275214f25eceb&elq=4cdbf3ecaa234c48aeb61197ba12d32b&elqaid=15875&elqat=1&elqCampaignId=6837

Bowen, W. G., Chingos, M. M., Lack, K. A., & Nygren, T. I. (2012). *Interactive learning online at public universities.* New York, NY: ITHAKA.

Chafkin, M. (2013, December). Udacity's Sebastian Thrun, godfather of free online education, changes course. *Fast Company.* Retrieved June 8, 2017 from www.fastcompany.com/3021473/udacity-sebastian-thrun-uphill-climb

Clark, R. (1983). Reconsidering research on learning from media. *Review of Educational Research, 53*(4), 445–459.

Clark, R. (1985). Evidence for confounding in computer-based instruction studies. *Educational Communications and Technology Journal, 33*(4), 249–262.

Clark, R. (1989). Current progress and future directions for research in instructional technology. *Educational Technology Research and Development, 37*(1), 57–66.

Collins, E. D. (2013, September). *Preliminary summary: SJSU and Augmented Online Learning Environment Pilot Project.* The Research and Planning Group for California Community Colleges (RP Group). Retrieved June 8, 2017 from www.sjsu.edu/chemistry/People/Faculty/Collins_Research_Page/AOLE%20Report%20Final%20Version_Jan%201_2014.pdf

Creswell, J. W. (2013). *Research design: Qualitative, quantitative, and mixed methods approaches* (4th ed.). Thousand Oaks, CA: Sage.

Crotty, M. (1998). *The foundations of social research: Meaning and perspective in the research process.* London: Sage.

Dziuban, C., Moskal, P., Cassisi, J., & Fawcett, A. (2016). Adaptive learning in psychology: Wayfinding in the digital age. *Online Learning, 20*(3). Retrieved June 8, 2017 from https://olj.onlinelearningconsortium.org/index.php/olj/article/view/972/223

Dziuban, C., & Picciano, A. G. (2015, June 17). The evolution continues: Considerations for the future of research in online and blended learning. *Research Bulletin.* Louisville, CO: ECAR. Retrieved June 10, 2017 from https://library.educause.edu/resources/2015/6/the-evolution-continues-considerations-for-the-future-of-research-in-online-and-blended-learning

Equality of Opportunity Project. (2017). *How can we improve education opportunity for our children?* Retrieved June 10, 2017 from www.equality-of-opportunity.org/

Fredericksen, E., Pickett, A., Shea, P., Pelz, W., & Swan, K. (1999a). Student satisfaction and perceived learning with online course: Principles and examples from the SUNY Learning Nework. *Journal of Asynchronous Learning Networks, 4*(2).

Fredericksen, E., Pickett, A., Shea, P., Pelz, W., & Swan, K. (1999b). Factors influencing Faculty satisfaction with asynchronous teaching and learning in the SUNY Learning Network. *Journal of Asynchronous Learning Networks, 4*(3).

Gladieux, L. E., & Swail, W. S. (1999). *The virtual university and educational opportunity.* Washington, DC: The College Board.

Haggard, S. (2013). *The maturing of the MOOC: Literature review of massive open online courses and other forms of online distance learning.* London, UK: Department for Business, Innovation and Skills.

Hattie, J. (2009). *Visible learning: A synthesis of over 800 meta-analyses relating to achievement.* London: Routledge/Taylor & Francis Group.

Ho, A. D., Chuang, I., Reich, J., Coleman, C. A., Whitehill, J., Northcutt, C. G., . . . Petersen, R. (2015, March 30). *HarvardX and MITx: Two years of open online courses Fall 2012–Summer 2014.* Retrieved May 18, 2017 from http://ssrn.com/abstract=2586847

Hoxie, A., Stillman, J., & Chesal, K. (2014). Blended learning in New York City. In A. G. Picciano, C. D. Dziuban, & C. R. Graham (Eds.), *Blended learning research perspectives* (Volume II, pp. 305–324). New York, NY: Routledge/Taylor & Francis.

Koumi, J. (1994). Media comparison and deployment: A practitioner's view. *British Journal of Educational Technology, 25*(1), 41–57.

Kozma, R. (1991). Learning with media. *Review of Educational Research, 61*(2), 179–211.

Kozma, R. (1994a). Will media influence learning? Reframing the debate. *Educational Technology Research and Development, 42*(2), 7–19.

Kozma, R. (1994b). A reply: Media and methods. *Educational Technology Research and Development, 42*(3), 11–14.

Kulik, J. A. (1984). Evaluating the effects of teaching with computers. In G. Campbell & G. Fein (Eds.), *Microcomputers in early education.* Reston, VA: Reston.

Kulik, J. A., Bangert, R., & Williams, G. (1983). Effects of computer-based teaching on secondary students. *Journal of Educational Psychology, 75*(1), 19–26.

Kulik, J. A., Kulik, C., & Bangert-Downs, R. (1984). Effectiveness of computer-based education in elementary schools. *Computers in Human Behavior, 1*(1), 59–74.

Kulik, J. A., Kulik, C., & Cohen, P. (1980). Effectiveness of computer-based college teaching: A meta-analysis of findings. *Review of Educational Research, 2*(2), 525–544.

Kulik, J. A., Kulik, C., & Schwab, B. (1986). The effectiveness of computer-based adult education: A meta-analysis. *Journal of Educational Computing Research, 2*(2), 235–252.

Lincoln, Y. S., & Guba, E. G. (1985). *Naturalistic inquiry.* Beverly Hills, CA: Sage.

Mackensie, N., & Knipe, S. (2006). Research dilemmas: Paradigms, methods and methodology. *Issues in Educational Research, 16.* Retrieved March 14, 2017 from www.iier.org.au/iier16/mackenzie.html

Mahesh, V., & Woll, C. (2007, July). Blended learning in high tech manufacturing: A case study of cost benefits and production efficiency. *Journal of Asynchronous Learning Networks, 11*(2), 43–60.

McCarthy, S. A., & Samors, R. J. (2009). *Online learning as a strategic asset.* Washington, DC: American Association of Public and Land-grant Universities.

Mertens, D. M. (2005). *Research methods in education and psychology: Integrating diversity with quantitative and qualitative approaches.* (2nd ed.). Thousand Oaks, CA: Sage.

Meyers, S., & Feeney, L. D. (2016, September). Examining interactive and metacognitive processes in student learning: Findings from a hybrid instructional environment. *Online Learning, 20*(3), 110–125.

Moskal, P., & Cavanagh, T. (2014). Scaling blended learning beyond the university. In A. G. Picciano, C. D. Dziuban, & C. R. Graham (Eds.), *Blended learning research perspectives* (Volume II, pp. 34–51). New York, NY: Routledge/Taylor & Francis.

Perna, L. W., Ruby, A., Boruch, R. F., Wang, N., Scull, J, Seher, A., & Evans, C. (2014, December). Moving through MOOCs: Understanding the progression of users in massive open online courses. *Educational Researcher, 43*(8), 421–432.

Phipps, R., & Merisotis, J. (1999). *What's the difference: A review of contemporary research on the effectiveness of distance learning in higher education.* Washington, DC: The Institute for Higher Education Policy.

Picciano, A. G., & Seaman, J. (2007). *K–12 online learning: A Survey of U.S. School District Administrators.* Needham, MA: The Babson Survey Research Group and The Sloan Consortium.

Pring, R. (2000). *Philosophy of educational research.* London: Continuum.

Staff. (2015). *2015 training industry report.* Retrieved January 30, 2017 from http://pubs.royle.com/publication/?i=278428&p=22

Staker, H., & Horn, M. B. (2014). Blended learning in the K–12 education sector. In A. G. Picciano, C. D. Dziuban, & C. R. Graham (Eds.), *Blended learning research perspectives* (Volume II, pp. 287–303). New York, NY: Routledge/Taylor & Francis.

Taylor, P. C., & Medina, M. N. D. (2013). Educational research paradigms: From positivism to multiparadigmatic. *The Journal of Meaning-Centered Education, 1,* Article 2. Retrieved July 30, 2014 from www.meaningcentered.org/journal/volume-01/educational-research-paradigms-from-positivism-to-multiparadigmatic

Trochim, W. (2006). *Research methods knowledge base.* Stamford, CT: Cengage Publishing. Retrieved March 14, 2017 from www.socialresearchmethods.net/kb/positvsm.php

Tynan, B., Ryan, Y., Hinton, L., & Mills, A. L. (2012). *Out of hours: Final report of the project e-teaching leadership: Planning and implementing a benefits-oriented costs model for technology enhanced learning.* Australian Learning and Teaching Council.

U.S. Department of Education (U.S. ED). (2010). Office of planning, evaluation, and policy development. *Evaluation of evidence-based practices in online learning: A meta-analysis and review of online learning studies.* Washington, DC. Retrieved from www2.ed.gov/rschstat/eval/tech/evidence-based-practices/finalreport.pdf

Wiebe, E., Thompson, I., & Behrend, T. (2015, May). MOOCs from the viewpoint of the learner: A response to Perna et al. (2014). *Educational Researcher, 44*(4), 252–254.

Section II

Planning and Pedagogy

Chapter 5

Planning for Online Education

A Systems Model

Michael Crow is the president of Arizona State University (ASU). Prior to his appointment at ASU, he was a professor and administrator at Columbia University where he was involved with the Fathom online education program. William Dabars is a Senior Research Fellow and Director of Research for the New American University in the Office of the President at ASU. He is also an associate research professor in ASU's School of Historical, Philosophical, and Religious Studies. In 2015, they co-authored *Designing the New American University*, which provided readers with insights into the practices, approaches, and policies that have moved ASU to become the largest research university in the country. Many think that the ASU model portends the future of the American university but Crow and Dabars caution that no single approach is appropriate for all of education.

> There is no single codified model for the American research university,. . . and there would appear to be a number of variants . . . The model for the New American University that we delineate is intended to complement the set of highly successful major research universities and is only one among many possible models.
>
> (Crow & Dabars, 2015, p. 7)

Crow and Dabars also commented that each institution must plan according to its own unique situation determined by:

> its mission and setting; the characteristics of its academic community; the scope of its constituent colleges, schools and departments; and the extent of its willingness to undertake commitment to public service and community engagement.
>
> (Crow & Dabars, 2015, p. 8)

Emphasis was placed on how the constituents of ASU re-examined their mission and goals and redefined them as follows:

> The university's four major objectives are to demonstrate leadership in academic excellence and accessibility; to establish national standing in academic quality; to establish ASU as a global center for interdisciplinary research, discovery, and development 2020; and to enhance local impact on social embeddedness.
>
> (Crow & Dabars, 2015, p. 61)

Crow and Dabars go on to comment extensively on how online education and other technologies are enabling them to achieve their goals and objectives. What is critical in their recommendations is that online education was not the goal but it enabled them to achieve their broader goals and objectives. More succinctly, technology is the enabler for change. While they use a good deal of technology, theirs is not a techno-centric view of the future of higher education, but a holistic one. Nor does it provide a quick fix. They state that it takes time to plan and as much as "a decade to operationalize" (Crow & Dabars, 2015, p. 17). In sum, they advise that education administrators must first understand what their institutions are, what their missions are, who their faculty and students are, and then use the appropriate technology to meet these needs.

The ASU case serves as an example of where online education fits in institutional planning. Allen and Seaman (2014), who have been surveying online learning in American higher education since 2002, indicate that almost 70% of chief academic officers consider online education as critical to their long-term strategic planning. The purpose of this chapter is to revisit the basic principles of planning as related to online education.

One of the most fully studied topics in educational administration is planning. Numerous books, articles, and guides have been written on how to plan and whom to involve in educational planning. Journals devoted entirely to issues of planning are available that enable administrators to keep up-to-date with the most current thinking. Consultants abound at conferences where sessions are routinely dedicated to planning, its theories, and practices. Professional organizations such as EDUCAUSE, the Online Learning Consortium, iNACOL, and United States Distance Learning Association also provide planning and implementation resources on their websites. This chapter will not provide a review of this extensive literature, but will instead provide a framework for planning as applied to online education.

The first part of this chapter will focus on a conceptual framework for planning related to technology, followed by a discussion of practical examples which highlight the model's use in online education. The chapter will conclude with an integration of the ideas presented, especially the need for purposeful planning rather than unplanned and potentially negative disruption or radical transformation.

Defining Planning

A generally accepted definition of planning is elusive. In one extensive review of the literature, Adams (1987) provided at least seven different definitions, all of which he considered incomplete. One obvious reason is that planning means different things to different people and is done for different purposes. However, elements common to any definition involve individuals thinking about and developing strategies to prepare their organizations for the future. It is also understood that planning goes on in all organizations although it may take on different characteristics. Planning can be structured, formal, top-down, and non-participatory in some cases; or unstructured, informal, bottom-up, and highly participatory in others. It can also involve complex social and administrative phenomena related to financial resources, personalities, and individual and departmental needs. Schools, colleges, and universities are social systems that in the course of their activities—including planning—usually consider the social needs of students, teachers, administrators, and communities within the context of the larger social environment. The redirection of the various definitions of planning to these common elements will serve to define and describe planning for purposes of this chapter. This approach may be considered an oversimplification of a very complex topic; however, it recognizes and respects a variety of existing situations.

The Systems Model

Various theories and models have been developed to describe and explain the way education institutions operate in our society. Most of them stem from general organization theory and development. The writings of classical organizational theorists such as Chester Barnard (1964),

Herbert Simon (1960, 1982), Talcott Parsons (1958), and Amitai Etzioni (1961) are cited in basic administration courses and form the foundation of some of our knowledge in this area. More modern organization theorists such as Christensen (1997; Christensen & Eyring, 2011), Senge (2006), Fullan (2001), and Wenger (2000) have expanded on earlier theories and applied them to modern organizations that are dealing with societal and cultural shifts, globalization, and technology. The literature in educational administration deals with topics such as organizational culture, strategic planning, environmental scanning, transformation, disruptive change, and shared decision making. The common thread underlying this material is the assumption that schools and colleges operate as part of their larger societies. Faculty, students, and administrators interact with each other and also interact individually and collectively with their communities and larger societies. Joseph A. Aoun (2017), president of Northeastern University, in a recent book titled *Robot Proof: Higher Education in the Age of Artificial Intelligence* lays out a framework for the future of education in a technology-dominated world. A fundamental aspect of his framework, which he names *humanics*, is a recognition that systems thinking is critical to the process of examining any society, corporation, or school holistically, in order to make connections among its different functions in an integrative manner.

Based on this, a social systems model (see Figure 5.1) of planning for technology is recommended. This model can be used for many types of organizations (university, K–12 school district, non-profit agency, corporation). In this chapter, the model (see Figure 5.2) and examples presented will reflect a college/university environment. Figure 5.2 shows planning for technology as proceeding from values defined by the environment and the institution toward goals and objectives formulated primarily at the college/university. Typically values are documented and modified in a mission statement. To achieve goals and objectives, technology applications are identified as the main courses of action that in turn require hardware and software, staff, facilities, finances, and policies to be implemented or provided for at the local college/university

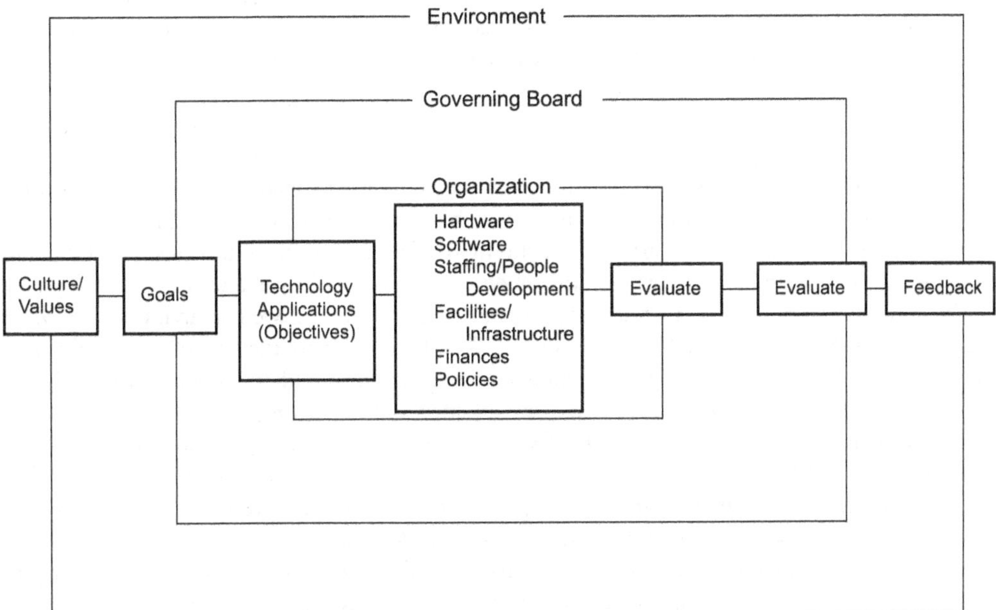

Figure 5.1 Planning Model for Technology

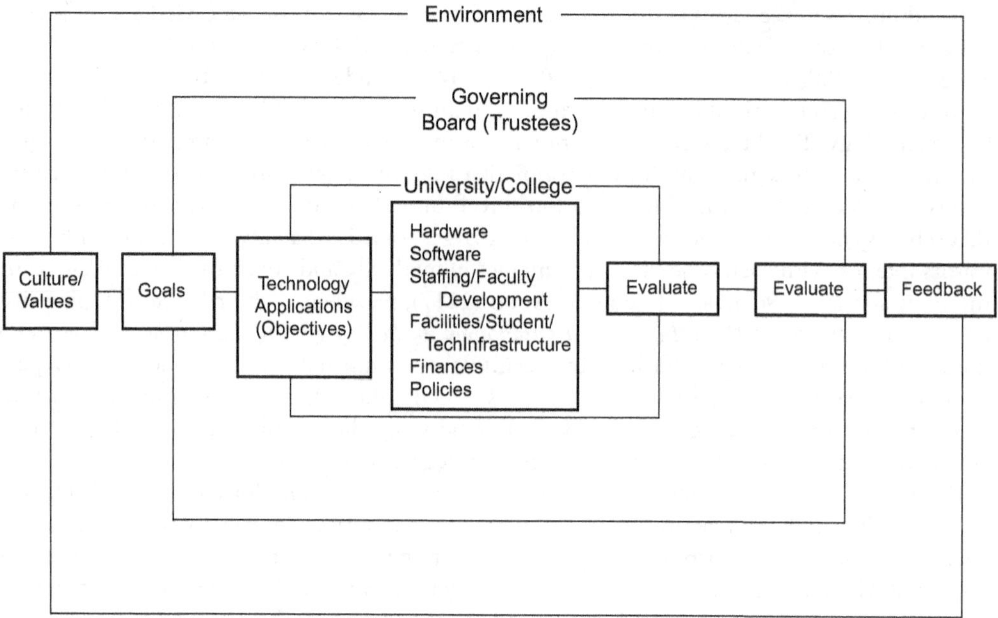

Figure 5.2 Planning Model for Technology Adopted for a University/College

level. Once in place, they are subsequently evaluated, and feedback is provided to the planning process for establishing new goals, objectives, and applications and for revising existing ones. The model requires a good deal of information gathering and idea sharing, which may be done formally through committees as well as informally through ad hoc discussions, observations, field visits, and reading the literature. This model should be integrated with other planning activities at the college or university.

An important feature of this model is that it incorporates *environmental scanning*, which simply means engaging in activities that provide information about the community, state, and society for planning purposes. In addition to understanding societal and community values, environmental scanning is critical for comprehending changes in technology. The fundamental nature of technology involves change—in the field of digital communications, rapid change. In a global, high-tech world, organizations need to be fluid, inclusive, and responsive (Kanter, 1999). For those involved in technology, this can be frustrating as well as invigorating. Based on a study in seven countries, Collis and van de Wende (2002) provided excellent insights into the nature of the types (i.e., systemic, gradual, changing the mold) of organizational change that occur when colleges and universities implement technology projects.

Monitoring trends in hardware and software development enables planners to avoid technology that might soon become obsolete. Successful environmental scanning also involves establishing and developing contacts with experts in the community, professional organizations, and private businesses. A basic component of this model is an administrator(s) who provides the necessary leadership in converting environmental values and conditions into college/university-wide goals and objectives. However, the model assumes stakeholders (faculty, students, alumni, community members) are involved with the process of converting values into goals and objectives as well.

A good plan covers a specific period of time, frequently from 5 to 7 years, allowing for more inclusion than exclusion. Administrators should attempt to be equitable in distributing resources among competing stakeholders. If resources are severely limited, then a major goal of the planning participants should be securing more funds before developing applications. The participation of alumni and community representatives may help identify and develop financial support from external sources including governmental (federal, state, local) and private agencies.

A pivotal step in using the technology planning model is the development of an articulated plan. The purpose is to provide a clear framing of the specifications to all participants. Just as information flow is critical in the formative stages of planning, a written summary of what has been discussed and agreed upon is essential for implementing the plan. Participants and others such as board members, administrators, faculty, students, and alumni need to understand what the goals are and what their responsibilities are in achieving them.

Evaluation and feedback are critical for continuing planning activities from year to year and from planning cycle to planning cycle. Participants need information on how well technology applications are achieving objectives. This can only be provided if mechanisms are established for evaluating applications and generating feedback.

Planning for Online Education

The following sections of this paper will focus on planning for online education as an example of the systems model in operation. It is important to bear in mind that online education would be one of the applications being considered within an overall technology plan. Other applications related to administration or other areas of instruction (digital research equipment, modernizing access to library databases, integrating technology into the curriculum) not necessarily related to online education would be part of the overall campus technology plan as well.

Environmental Scanning

Understanding the environment is a beginning point for any planning activity including the development or enhancement of online education applications. Participants at any level can be of assistance in this aspect of planning. Governing boards and trustees, for example, are appointed specifically from outside the university or college to provide guidance on matters of mission, policy, funding, and future directions. College administrators can consult with and seek guidance from trustees in identifying external developments that might affect the university. Administrators should also seek assistance from those within the university (institutional research, external affairs, faculty) in identifying developments in the community, region, and beyond that might be of importance. The ubiquity of the Internet has facilitated environmental scanning at all levels. At the same time, because of its dynamic nature, technology itself should be monitored on a regular basis especially in an area such as online education.

In scanning the online education environment, it is safe to say that we are well beyond the beginning stages. As was presented in Chapter 2, online education via the Internet developed 20 years ago in the early and mid-1990s. The leaders of this development were distance education providers in both the non-profit and for-profit sectors of higher education. The focus at that time was on harnessing online technology to deliver instruction to distant student populations, most of whom were relying on slow-speed communications equipment. The fully online, asynchronous course became the fundamental method of choice. By the end of the 1990s, mainstream higher education started to consider online learning as part of its mission and began developing models based on their pedagogical benefits rather than serving distant student populations. Institutions began to integrate online with face-to-face delivery in a myriad of blended formats that took advantage of the best of both worlds. At the present time, while many distance education providers such as the Penn State World Campus, the University of Maryland—University College, and the University of Phoenix continue to use a mostly asynchronous, fully online model, mainstream higher education is pursuing a reconciliation of the pedagogically rich blended model and the cost-effective MOOC model. In addition, social media, big data/learning analytics, adaptive learning, mobile computing, competency-based learning, and gaming are also being integrated into online education.

Other significant higher education trends indirectly related to the role that technology and online education play in responding to the environment include:

1. *expanding enrollment*—the number of students seeking a higher education continues to expand at all levels;
2. *life-long learning*—students are seeking more advanced degrees as well as other higher credentials and no longer see higher education as strictly for 18 to 21 year-old traditional students;
3. *retention/attrition*—student attrition has evolved as a major issue for higher education especially at open admissions and less-selective colleges;
4. *rising tuition*—continues and has surpassed state funding as the main revenue source in public higher education;
5. *student loan debt*—continues to rise;
6. *government oversight*—the US. Department of Education has initiated a number of proposals to foster greater accountability for colleges and universities; and
7. *commoditization*—higher education is increasingly being seen and pursued as a personal benefit rather than as a public good.

Colleges and universities should contemplate where they see themselves in terms of these issues and should consider whether online education has a role to play in addressing them. Where does it fit in their plans? Where does the institution fit within the evolution of online education? Are they at the beginning or at an advanced stage? Do they need to refine or modify what they are already doing or do they need to make a major leap forward? This last question is most important and the answer depends upon an institution's mission, culture, and goals. If the reader is not familiar with these issues, a book titled *Lesson Plan: An Agenda for Change in American Higher Education* (Bowen & McPherson, 2016) reviews them well.

Developing Goals—Colleges Are Not All the Same

Colleges and universities have different missions and goals, serve different constituents, and will approach online education in different ways. The Carnegie Classification of Institutions of Higher Education starts with six basic categories: Associate Degree Colleges, Baccalaureate Colleges, Masters Colleges and Universities, Doctoral-Granting Universities, Special Focus Institutions, and Tribal Colleges. This classification expands considerably depending upon the nature of the academic programs, size of the student body, locale, non-profit or for-profit status, and level of research. Community colleges, for example, provide access to higher education as their primary goal. They generally serve local commuter student populations by offering a range of academic programs designed to enhance employment opportunities or to enable students to transfer to a four-year institution. Private four-year liberal arts colleges focus on providing a high-quality undergraduate experience for their largely residential students. Social life and campus experiences at a private liberal arts college are as important as the academic programs. Research institutions offer a variety of undergraduate and graduate programs and are quite active in securing grants, corporate contracts, and other external funding. Faculty at these institutions see research, scholarship, and grantsmanship as primary responsibilities. As a result, how these institutions approach online education will differ. A community college might seek to use fully online courses and programs as vehicles to broaden student access or to help enrolled students to remain in their programs when family, financial, and other responsibilities might pressure them to withdraw. The four-year liberal arts college might prefer to take advantage of the pedagogical benefits of blended learning applications that can be integrated into traditional classrooms. Research institutions might use online education to extend graduate expertise or to brand their programs nationally or globally.

If you examine institutions that have been successful in developing online education applications, most derive their success from applications that relate directly to their missions and goals. Most did not try to use online education to remake themselves into something totally different from their fundamental missions. There have been exceptions such as Southern New Hampshire University and Rio Salado Community College, both of which launched substantial new online programs enrolling tens of thousands of students. However, not all colleges seek to, or are able to, replicate this type of success. Colleges and universities should develop goals for online education just as they develop goals for any other activity appropriate to their mission. Participation in planning by stakeholders—especially faculty—is important. In sum, the goals for online education should fit the institution's mission and culture.

Online Education Applications

Online education applications are growing substantially every year. Converting what have historically been considered traditional, face-to-face courses into fully online courses has become commonplace. The development of completely online programs is being done on a more regular basis. Once a college or university has successfully developed a fully online course or program, the tendency is to develop more courses and programs until they have reached a saturation point. While student interest and demand can support online courses in just about any academic discipline, the same is not necessarily true for entire degree programs. Career-oriented subject areas such as business, computer science, and education generally are the more popular.

In addition to the fully online modality, there has been a clear and substantive acceptance of blended learning, particularly in traditional or mainstream higher education. The blended learning modality is perceived as the best of both learning modalities—face-to-face and online. Administrators, faculty, and students are generally supportive of initiatives in the blended format. In 2014, the results of a survey of American college presidents commissioned by *The Chronicle of Higher Education* indicated that an overwhelming majority of presidents—three quarters at private institutions and almost 80% at public campuses—believed blended courses that contain both face-to-face and online components will have a positive impact on higher education (Selingo, 2014). However, blended learning has a nebulous quality because it defies any simple definition and comes in so many different forms and styles. The name "blended" is not universally accepted and we see the terms "hybrid," "mixed-mode," "web-enhanced," "mini-MOOC," and "flipped" to mean the same thing or some variation thereof. After the MOOC-hype subsided, the blended model was seen by some as their savior. As mentioned in Chapter 2, Daphne Koller, the founder of MOOC provider, Coursera, commented at the Sloan Consortium's International Conference on Online Learning that MOOC companies should consider the development of more pedagogically sound course materials that can be used in blended online formats rather than fully online formats. In a sense, she was suggesting that Coursera and other MOOC providers might rebrand themselves as producers of high-quality content that gives faculty the option as how to best use their materials, rather than as fully online course providers and developers (Koller, November 2013).

In addition to developing new online and blended programs and courses, additional online education applications might include:

1. Adding learning analytics software to a course management system to develop a student alert system;
2. Making greater use of social media software (blogs, wikis, Facebook, twitter) in existing online courses and programs;
3. Integrating mobile technologies into existing online courses and programs;
4. Creating or supporting a specific genre of courses (i.e., large lecture sections) with blended or "flipped" learning;
5. Adding adaptive learning software to a course management system to develop more personalized instruction environments;
6. Insuring that all online education materials are ADA (Americans with Disabilities Act) compliant;
7. Undertaking a blended learning initiative to support certain academic subject areas such as STEM or health sciences that have specific or more complex pedagogical needs.

It should be obvious that applications can vary significantly depending upon academic program needs, existing online education development, teacher readiness, student readiness, and instructional and student support services.

The Major Components of an Online Education Application

The major components of technology applications including online education are: hardware, software, staffing/faculty development, facilities/student/tech support infrastructure, finances, and policies. These components are fundamental to every technology initiative and need to be considered if an online education application is to be successful. It is not feasible to cover each of these components in depth in one chapter. In the following paragraphs, several current and important issues with respect to each component will be presented.

Hardware

The fundamental hardware required for online education applications is not particularly complex but should be consistent with the strategic plan. Essentially it consists of servers that can support a network size appropriate for the institution. The network must also integrate with the hardware used for the institution's database management system as well as some type of course or learning management system. The vast majority of colleges and universities have established such a hardware facility in house or have contracted out with a service or cloud provider.

The hardware that the faculty and others involved with the online education application will have available to them also needs to be considered. Desktop computers are common but increasingly, the world has moved to mobile technology (i.e., laptops, tablets, smartphones). When launching an online education application, some thought should be given to supporting faculty acquisition of laptops. In many cases, faculty members already own laptops but it would be beneficial to make sure of this, and that the equipment is relatively up-to-date as well. In the earlier days of online education, it was quite common to incentivize faculty to use online technology by providing them with a free computer. For institutions that are just making the move to online education, this approach should be considered.

Software

The critical software for an online education application is a course management system (CMS)—also known as a learning management system (LMS). Many colleges have already acquired a CMS/LMS or have contracted with a vendor to host their applications. Blackboard, Canvas, and Desire2Learn are three dominant providers of this type of software. Moodle, a free, open source software platform, is also used by a number of colleges as their CMS/LMS. Regardless of the CMS/LMS a college chooses, it will require a good level of programming and systems support if installed in-house. A CMS/LMS needs to be integrated with the college's databases to allow for a graceful and efficient transfer of pertinent course and student data. It is critical that the CMS/LMS has a stable software environment and maybe a backup system since any serious or lengthy disruption can be disastrous for students and faculty.

An alternative to acquiring a CMS/LMS and developing online courses in-house is outsourcing course development to a third party vendor (also referred to as an online program manager or OPM). Companies such as Pearson's Embanet—Compass Knowledge Group, Bisk Education, and Colloquy provide a variety of support services including online course and program development. Several MOOC providers are also providing these services. While this might be an administratively easy way for a college or university to get started in online education, the costs can be significant. Before taking this approach, a careful cost-benefit analysis needs to be undertaken. An article titled "Colleges Finding Partners for Online Courses" that appeared in *University Business* provides a good overview of the issues associated with outsourcing online course development (Finkel, 2013).

In addition to a basic CMS/LMS, specialized software for assessment, adaptive learning, learning analytics, and gaming might also be considered.

Staff/Faculty Development

A most significant issue in developing or expanding online education is the readiness and commitment of staff and faculty. Faculty "buy in" is particularly critical. In many colleges and universities, adjunct faculty teach the online courses because full-time faculty are unwilling or unable to do so. This is not the most desirable situation. Faculty resistance has been observed. Allen and Seaman (2012) in a national study of faculty attitudes commented:

> Faculty report being more pessimistic than optimistic about online learning. Professors, over all, cast a skeptical eye on the learning outcomes for online education. Nearly two-thirds say they believe that the learning outcomes for an online course are inferior or somewhat inferior to those for a comparable face-to-face course.
>
> (p. 2)

In 2016, *Inside Education* in a survey of faculty found similar results.

> Faculty members are most likely to see online education as inferior to in-person instruction for the following course tasks or objectives: interacting with students during class (83 percent), ability to reach "at-risk" students (78 percent), ability to maintain academic integrity (64 percent) and ability to rigorously engage students in course material (64 percent).
>
> (Jaschik & Lederman, 2016, p. 21)

There is no silver bullet that will automatically change faculty attitudes. However, administrators need to engage and involve faculty in any plans and decisions that are important to the institution, including the development of online and blended learning. In some institutions, more and more faculty are teaching online, especially in blended formats, and there is no reason that an open discussion cannot be held about online education. In fact, in the same *Inside Education* survey cited earlier:

> Thirty-nine percent of faculty members say they have taught an online course for credit, and 43 percent have taught a blended or hybrid course that combines in-person and online teaching. Most faculty who have taught online courses, 79 percent, say the experience has helped them develop skills and practices that have improved their teaching in the classroom as well as online.
>
> (Jaschik & Lederman, 2016, p. 7)

So it appears that with proper training and engagement with faculty, online learning can be seen as a positive experience for faculty for their traditional as well as online teaching.

A fundamental characteristic of technology is that it changes, sometimes rapidly, and those using it will need on-going development if they are to be successful in its applications. While generic workshops and other training activities may suffice to initiate a professional development program, activities geared to certain types of instructional applications (i.e., large lecture sections, laboratory courses, math-based instruction) or disciplines may prove most beneficial in the long run. It is well recognized, for example, that how one teaches English literature is different from how one teaches chemistry or how one teaches social work. The pedagogical approaches are different as are the skills necessary to be successful teachers. Faculty, for example, who teach English literature may be excellent readers and writers with little facility for calculus. The opposite might be true of those who teach a laboratory science where a command of mathematical principles might be more beneficial if not necessary. A recognition of the differences in teaching approaches, styles, and required skills should be considered as part of the planning for professional development. Shulman (1986) developed the *Technological Pedagogical Content Knowledge* framework that focuses on the need for the integration of the relationships among technology, pedagogy, and content knowledge to implement effective instructional technology applications. Readers might want to refer to Mishra and Koehler (2006) for a review of this framework that is appropriate for the development of online education applications.

Characteristics of effective professional development include:

Pedagogical principles—start with the assumption that good pedagogy (i.e., social construction of knowledge, student interaction, instructor responsiveness) drive online learning technology;

Hands-on activities—participants need to use equipment and be allowed to experiment and make mistakes;

One-on-one coaching—group work is a good start but at some point faculty will need one-on-one assistance as they try different features;

Train the trainers—identify faculty in departments who have an interest in helping other faculty and provide them with assistance and release time so that they can be available to help other faculty;

Making sure that faculty have proper equipment—online education will require faculty to be available for student inquiries. While desktop computers are fine, laptops are far more convenient for teaching online;

Provide incentives—faculty new to online teaching deserve rewards for taking the time and effort to do so. Without a doubt, teaching online takes more time in preparation and teaching, especially for beginners;

Start with smaller modules—developing a fully online course may be daunting for someone who has never done so. It might be better to start with smaller modules rather than the entire course.

A good instructional design team is also critical for professional development and needs to be at the forefront of any faculty development effort. Investing in instructional design support services becomes a requirement for successful online and blended learning courses and programs.

Facilities/Student/Tech Infrastructure

In the early days of central computer centers, discussions of facilities and infrastructure generally referred to a single physical facility and the technical staff assigned to maintain it. The concept has changed considerably with the ubiquity of Internet technology. Faculty and students expect Wi-Fi service throughout a campus with "help desk" support available online. When developing online education applications, the concept of the help desk extends to all engaged faculty and students regardless of where they are. For online and blended learning courses, providing this support means assisting faculty in the development of online materials and assisting faculty and students using a CMS/LMS.

For fully online programs, the level of support infrastructure increases considerably. If a college expects to attract a wide audience or student base for fully online programs, then it must invest in a full gamut of academic, library, marketing, and student support services. Academic advisement, admissions, financial processing, registration, library databases, and student counseling must be provided from afar via online and telephone help facilities. This can be a daunting proposition for colleges and universities launching their first fully online programs. In fact, providing these services may be a more difficult undertaking than the development of the academic program. There are many cases where colleges have invested significantly in online program development only to find that the necessary support services have not been fully considered, resulting in significant delays in implementation. If students are recruited across time zones, many of these services need to be provided on a 24-hour, 7-days-a-week schedule. While some colleges provide these services themselves, others are increasingly contracting with private companies for some or all of them. Successful fully online programs without a doubt need good and reliable academic and student support services.

One of the most significant issues regarding facilities/infrastructure is the organizational placement of online education programs. This is especially the case with fully online programs. Generally, the choices come down to:

1. Centralizing online education in one specific department that takes on responsibility for development of programs, providing support services, contracting with faculty, recruitment, admissions, and registration, etc.; or
2. Integrating online education into existing academic department structures with coordination and oversight provided by an administrative officer.

Both approaches have been used and can be successful. The decision to centralize or not is similar to organizational decisions regarding for-credit adult and continuing education programs. Administrators need to consider carefully where fully online programs fit best in their organization. Regardless of which administrative avenue is chosen, individual online courses and blended learning courses generally are developed and maintained in existing academic departments.

Finances

The enthusiastic and creative discussions that take place in many planning processes center on the consideration of goals, objectives, and applications. However, the hard reality of finance can sometimes temper much of this enthusiasm. Online education initiatives require funding, and for institutions just embarking on them, the investment in software and support services can be significant. With the exception of colleges and universities with substantial endowments, much of higher education finds itself under serious financial constraints. Private colleges that are tuition-driven struggle to control costs and to maintain an affordable tuition rate. Publicly funded institutions increasingly are relying on student contributions via tuition and fees as many states have significantly reduced if not abandoned their commitment to higher education. The U.S. General Accounting Office (2014) issued a report stating that an important milestone had been reached in 2012 when, for the first time in the history of our country, student tuition surpassed state appropriations for the financing of public higher education. In this section, several important financial considerations will be discussed.

First, an online education initiative may constitute a bold new program that addresses a specific need or an enhancement to an existing program. While the former case will likely require major new funding, the latter might be accomplished at modest incremental costs. In all cases, the newness, size, and scope of the initiative needs to be reviewed to determine its funding requirements. Each of the components (hardware, software, staff/faculty development, facilities/infrastructure, etc.) of the planning for a technology system's model should be considered. This is just part of good basic planning and not unique to online education.

Second, administrators should exercise caution if thinking about online education primarily as a way to substantially improve financial positions. While some colleges and universities have been able to realize significant profits from online education programs, many have not. In most cases, the revenue generated offsets costs. Colleges and universities that have made significant profits, and this includes for-profit colleges, have done so by using large numbers of adjunct faculty to teach in their online programs rather than full-time faculty. The possibility that offering fully online programs will create savings in brick and mortar facilities might also be tempting to some, but the number of documented cases—especially for colleges and universities that already have substantial physical campuses—are few and far between. On the other hand, institutions that rent off-campus centers for continuing, adult, and other types of special programs might find an online education program to be a cost-beneficial way to offer services without paying part of or all of the fees related to rent or leasing costs.

Third, for those institutions planning on contracting out for online program management (OPM) for hosting, course/program development, or support services, a careful analysis must be undertaken. Finkel (2013) references the experiences of Goodlett McDaniel, associate provost of distance education at George Mason University, which contracted with Colloquy to develop an online MBA program. In McDaniel's experience, vendors will sometimes "over-promise and under-deliver" results to administrators who don't have significant business world experience.

> "There can be a natural tendency to be excited and think that all of their problems will be solved by the contract." Administrators should check companies' references, pay close attention to the revenue split, and make sure the length of the contract seems right, with an "out-clause" if the school thinks it might need one.
>
> (Finkel, 2013)

This sound advice should be heeded. Contract services are not panaceas that will make "all the problems" go away, so the costs and benefits of this approach will require careful analysis.

Fourth, in order to incentivize academic departments and full-time faculty to become active players in the development of online education, especially fully online programs, administrators might consider establishing a revenue sharing policy in which a percentage of the income derived from the online program is returned to the academic departments. This has worked successfully in a number of institutions. On the other hand, it opens up a number of issues related to precedence that many administrators would rather avoid. This is especially true in public institutions where budget and revenue processes may need to comply with state policies. It can, however, work well where self-supporting activities are allowed (as in the case of private and for-profit institutions).

Lastly, colleges and universities could also consider instituting an additional fee per credit hour to offset costs associated with developing and supporting online courses. Precedents for this were set in the 1980s and 1990s when a number of colleges established student technology fees to fund instructional hardware, software, and support services.

Policies

The last component of an application is the consideration of any policy issues that may arise as a result of a new or substantial expansion of online education. Existing bylaws, governance documents, and collective bargaining contracts need to be reviewed to insure that institutional policies related to curriculum approval, workload, intellectual property, accreditation compliance, faculty observations, and evaluation are not being bypassed or infringed upon. If a college has already developed a substantial online program, many of these policy issues may have already been addressed. Those colleges mounting new initiatives would be wise to consult their legal, procurement, and personnel offices for a review of policies that might relate to online education.

Where there are strong faculty governance bodies and/or collective bargaining agencies, administrators would be wise to understand their prerogatives in mounting online education initiatives. In many cases, the mounting of such programs falls into grey areas. The rollout of MOOC courses at San Jose State University provides a good example. (Collins, 2013). After the announcement of a contract award to Udacity for the development of MOOC courses, faculty governance leaders raised a number of objections and concerns. As described in *The Chronicle of Higher Education*, faculty governance leaders passed a resolution asking the chancellor of the California State University system to review governance policies at the university because of the way the contract was awarded and because of a number of "communication and transparency issues." In addition, San Jose's Academic Senate developed a policy proposal to clarify the rules governing the development of "technology intensive, hybrid, and online courses and programs" at the university (Kolowich, 2013). As a result, in July 2013, San Jose State University put the entire MOOC initiative with Udacity on hold. (Chafkin, 2013). Without going into all of the details of the MOOC experiment at San Jose State University, it appears that consultation with the Academic Senate on the awarding of the contract was minimal or non-existent. The Academic Senate reacted strongly against the administration, citing policy issues related to consultation. The experience at San Jose is an excellent policy lesson and one that should be studied by college administrators who are tempted to bypass faculty governance when developing academic initiatives.

In addition to in-house policies, institutions need to be aware of external compliance issues. Section 504 of the Rehabilitation Act of 1973 and the Americans with Disabilities Act (ADA) of 1990 are major federal legislative policies designed to protect the civil rights of individuals with disabilities. The intent of these two laws is to prevent any form of discrimination against individuals with disabilities. Section 504 applies to entities that receive federal funds, and the ADA applies to virtually every entity except churches and private clubs. In designing online education material, there needs to be an awareness that the designs are in compliance with Section 504 and the ADA. Most major course management systems make provisions for this compliance, but administrators should be aware that they exist and that instructional design staff and faculty are aware also. The National Center for Accessible Instructional Materials (see: http://aim.cast.org/learn/post-secondary/higher_ed#.VLEH9nt9ZbA) provides excellent resources regarding compliance issues with Section 504 and ADA.

Special accreditation requirements, especially for fully online programs, may be needed depending upon the college or university accrediting body. Administrators should consult with their regional accreditor to determine its requirements for fully online programs. For example, the Middle States Commission on Higher Education has published a guide, *Distance Education Programs: Interregional Guidelines for the Evaluation of Distance Education (Online Learning)* that outlines standards for accreditation of online education programs. It is available online at: www.msche.org/publications/Guidelines-for-the-Evaluation-of-Distance-Education-Programs.pdf

Lastly, a review of copyright infringement laws are in order when developing or expanding online education. The facility with which the Internet makes it possible to copy and paste and to download files and media have made many institutions vulnerable to copyright infringement. In addition, having materials online and open to the public also makes it easier for infringement to be detected by copyright owners. Instructional designers and faculty need to be aware of what is allowed before a copyright infringement occurs and to make sure that online materials are in compliance. For further information, New York University's Faculty Resource Network has an excellent paper on copyright issues related to online education and can be accessed at: www.nyu.edu/frn/publications/millennial.student/Copyright.html

Evaluation

Evaluation and feedback are critical for continuing planning activities from year to year and from planning cycle to planning cycle. All planning participants need to know if and how well the online education applications are achieving objectives. Several principles of good evaluation in general are worth a discussion.

First, evaluation criteria that relate to the goals and objectives of the online education application must be established. For example, if a goal or objective was to improve teaching and learning, then criteria appropriate to evaluating instruction such as student assessments are appropriate. If a goal or objective was to increase student engagement, then student satisfaction criteria are appropriate. If a goal or objective was to provide greater access to an education, then enrollment patterns and retention criteria are appropriate.

Second, the data capture capabilities of online and blended learning have opened up entire new areas of evaluation that can focus not only on common instructional criteria (tests, grades, retention, student and faculty satisfaction) but also on the uniqueness and subtlety of a course or program. Because so many instructional transactions are captured electronically on discussion boards, blogs, and wikis, a plethora of data is available for evaluation and analysis. Discourse and content analysis of student transactions and course postings can delve much deeper into what students are doing and learning in an online class than is possible in the face-to-face modality. Simply put, the data is there in electronic form and ready for analysis. One caution is that attention should be paid to any possible infringement to the Family Educational Rights and Policy Act (FERPA) which was enacted by Congress to protect the data privacy of students. In addition, the European Union has established a series of regulations designed to protect all EU citizens from privacy and data breaches in an increasingly data-driven world. These regulations (General Data Protection Regulation—GDPR), went into effect in May 2018 (see Appendix E). They will have serious ramifications for all organizations (businesses, government agencies, and educational institutions) that maintain data on EU citizens. Distance and online education providers that enroll EU citizens will have to comply with these regulations. GDPR regulations are also spurring discussion about similar data protection policies for individual in the United States and other countries.

Third, evaluation should not be strictly summative or occur only at the end of an activity but should be formative and allow for improvements and adjustments as needed. Evaluation benchmarks should be included in the plan at appropriate points so as to refine the development process.

Fourth, evaluation provides feedback in an iterative, continuous planning process and should not serve as the process's endpoint. Evaluation results inform future planning activities. Successes as well as problems in the planning activity development should be documented and shared. In this way, evaluation is a beginning and can help initiate the next planning cycle's activities.

A Quality Framework

The Online Learning Consortium (formerly The Sloan Consortium) has invested considerable time and effort in developing a quality framework designed to evaluate and measure the effectiveness of online education initiatives. Specifically this framework consists of five interrelated *pillars*:

- learning effectiveness;
- access;
- faculty satisfaction;
- student satisfaction; and
- scale.

The specific intent of this quality framework has been to help institutions identify goals appropriate for online education and measure progress in achieving them. A brief examination of each of these pillars provides a bit more depth and nuance to their use in evaluating online education initiatives.

Learning effectiveness is concerned with ensuring that online students are provided with a high quality education. This means that online students' learning should at least be equivalent to that of traditional students. This does not necessarily mean that online learning experiences should duplicate those in traditional classrooms. Rather it means that instructors and course developers should take advantage of the unique characteristics of online environments to provide learning experiences that represent the distinctive quality of the institution offering them. Effective practices that support learning effectiveness can include evaluating and collecting data on: course design, learning resources, faculty development, learner characteristics, pedagogical awareness, interaction (i.e., with content, faculty, other students; development of learning communities, etc.), assessment, and learning outcomes (i.e., student satisfaction, retention, achievement, performance, etc.).

Access provides the means for all qualified, motivated students to complete courses, degrees, or programs in their disciplines of choice. The goal is to provide meaningful and effective access throughout the student's entire life cycle. Access starts with enabling prospective learners to become aware of available opportunities through effective marketing, branding, and basic program information. It continues with providing program access (for example, quantity and variety of available program options, clear program information), seamless access to courses (i.e., readiness assessment), and appropriate learning resources. Access includes three areas of support: academic (such as tutoring, advising, and library); administrative (such as financial aid, and disability support); and technical (such as hardware reliability and uptime, and help desk). Effective practices for measuring increasing accessibility may analyze and apply the results of student surveys, narrative or case study descriptions, focus groups, or other means of gathering student feedback.

Faculty satisfaction means that instructors find the online teaching experience personally rewarding and professionally beneficial. Personal factors contributing to faculty satisfaction with the online experience include opportunities to extend interactive learning communities to new populations of students and to conduct and publish research related to online teaching and learning. Institutional factors related to faculty satisfaction include several categories: support, rewards, and institutional study/research. Faculty satisfaction is enhanced when the institution supports faculty members with a robust and well-maintained technical infrastructure, training in online instructional skills, and ongoing technical and administrative assistance. Faculty members also expect to be included in the governance and quality assurance of online programs, especially as related to curricular decisions and development of policies of particular importance to the online environment (such as intellectual property, copyright, royalties, collaborative design, and delivery). Faculty satisfaction is closely related to an institutional reward system that recognizes the rigor and value of online teaching. Satisfaction levels increase when workload assignments/assessments reflect the greater time commitment in developing and teaching online courses and when online teaching is valued on par with face-to-face teaching in promotion and tenure decisions. A final institutional factor—crucial to recruiting, retaining, and expanding a dedicated online faculty—is commitment to ongoing study and enhancement of the online faculty experience. Institutions should consider rewards (i.e., promotion, tenure, recognition, course releases for new course design and development, and opportunities for research and publication).

Student satisfaction reflects the effectiveness of all aspects of the educational experience. The goal is that all students who complete a course express satisfaction with course activities, with professor and peer interaction, and with support services. Online students put a primary value on appropriate, constructive, and substantive interaction with faculty and other students. Effective professors help students achieve learning outcomes that match course and learner objectives by using current information and communications technologies to support active, individualized, engaged, and constructive learning. As consumers, students are satisfied when provider services—learning resources, academic and administrative services, technology and infrastructure support—are responsive, timely, and personalized. Effective practices may analyze and apply the results of student and alumni surveys, referrals, testimonials or other means of measuring perceived satisfaction with learning communities.

Scale is the principle that enables institutions to offer their best educational value to learners and to achieve capacity enrollment. Institutional commitment to quality and finite resources require continuous improvement policies for developing and assessing cost-effectiveness measures and practices. The goal is to control costs so that tuition is affordable yet sufficient to meet development and maintenance costs—and to provide a return on investment in startup and infrastructure. Metrics may compare the costs and benefits of delivery modes by discipline and educational level; faculty salary and workload; capital, physical plant and maintenance investments; equipment and communications technology costs; scalability options; and/or various learning processes and outcomes, such as satisfaction levels and retention rates. These types of comparison enable institutions to: develop better strategic plans for market demand and capture; achieve capacity enrollment; develop brand recognition; and secure long-term loyalty among current and prospective constituents. Practices for scale help to leverage key educational resources while offering new online learning opportunities to students and faculty. Practices for scale help to leverage key educational resources while offering new online learning opportunities to students and faculty.

The Online Learning Consortium has developed a number of evaluation criteria derived from these five pillars. These can be found in Appendices B, C, and D (OLC Quality Framework, 2017, https://onlinelearningconsortium.org/about/quality-framework-five-pillars/).

Planning Versus Disruption

It should be obvious that this chapter's emphasis on careful deliberate planning is counter to the notion that higher education needs disruption and radical transformation. Clayton Christensen (1997), who is credited with coining the term "disruptive innovation," originally applied the concept to corporate America. He has applied the term to non-profit entities including higher education (Christensen & Eyring, 2011) and K–12 education (Christensen, Horn, & Johnson, 2008). However, corporate America has a very different culture based on profit-motive and intense competition. It is an environment encompassing in excess of 18 million companies incorporated in the United States alone according to DMDatabase.com (see http://dmdatabases.com/databases/business-mailing-lists/how-many-businesses). American higher education includes no more than 5,000–6,000 postsecondary institutions including many small proprietary colleges. American K–12 education includes about 13,000-plus school districts. The culture of education at many levels is not profit driven nor is it based on intense competition. The disruption approach is not needed and in fact, may do more harm than good. There is also concern that the term has become a rallying cry for neoliberal ideologues who feel they must disparage an institution in order to promote radical change. David Harvey (2005)—in his seminal work on the history of neoliberalism—cautioned that a common tactic within this movement has been what he calls "creative destruction" that builds a narrative that calls for destroying institutional frameworks and values in order to make way for a market mentality based on competition and profit maximization. It would not be beneficial for the majority of colleges and schools to change their values for the sake of increasing revenue nor do they have to in order to adopt or expand online education.

Bynre (2014), in an article titled *Why Clayton Christensen is Wrong (and Michael Porter is Right)?*, reaches a similar conclusion with respect to the online education initiatives of the Harvard Business School. There are many fine online and blended learning initiatives throughout higher education that are exemplars of good planning and implementation including the Penn State World Campus, the University of Central Florida, the University of Illinois—Springfield, the City University of New York School of Professional Studies, the State University of New York Learning Network (now Open SUNY), the University of Wisconsin—Milwaukee, the University of Nebraska, and others. The online education programs in these schools evolved over a number of years and did not require or cause massive or sudden disruption in the institution's normal planning processes.

The United States has had the highest ranked higher education system in the world for a number of years according to several organizations such as the Times Higher Education World Ranking System and Universitas (based in the United Kingdom). While education ranking systems can be questioned, they do provide some indication that things are not all wrong in American colleges and universities and are possibly quite good. Nevertheless, other countries are pouring significant resources into their higher education systems at a time when the United States is withdrawing its support. For the first time in its history, the majority of funding for public higher education in this country comes not from states but from student tuition. In addition, the private non-profits, especially those that are tuition-driven with limited endowments, are already beginning to compete rigorously for students. This competition will accelerate in the years to come. President Barack Obama's proposal in January 2015 calling for free tuition to community college students, has had some ramifications for our colleges and universities. Several states including New York and Tennessee have initiated free tuition policies for its public universities and colleges. For American higher education to maintain its prominence in the world community, it will need to continue to evolve and develop its academic programs and services to its students, communities, and society. Its evolution will be dependent upon careful purposeful planning. Instructional technology and online education have a definite and important role to play in this endeavor.

Summary

The purpose of this chapter was to examine the basic principles of technology planning as applied to online education initiatives. While not meant to be an exhaustive treatment of the topic, the chapter focused on the development, integration, and expansion of online education as part of education planning activities. The chapter presented a systems model that promotes purposeful planning as key to the successful implementation of online education as opposed to disruption or radical transformation that may be damaging to an institution's culture.

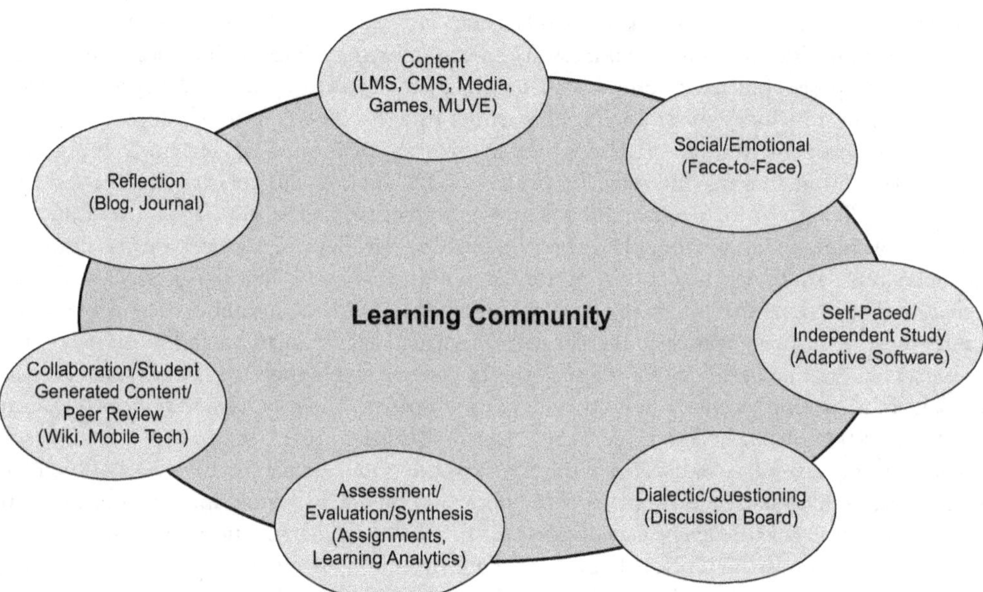

Plate 1 Multimodal Model for Online Education

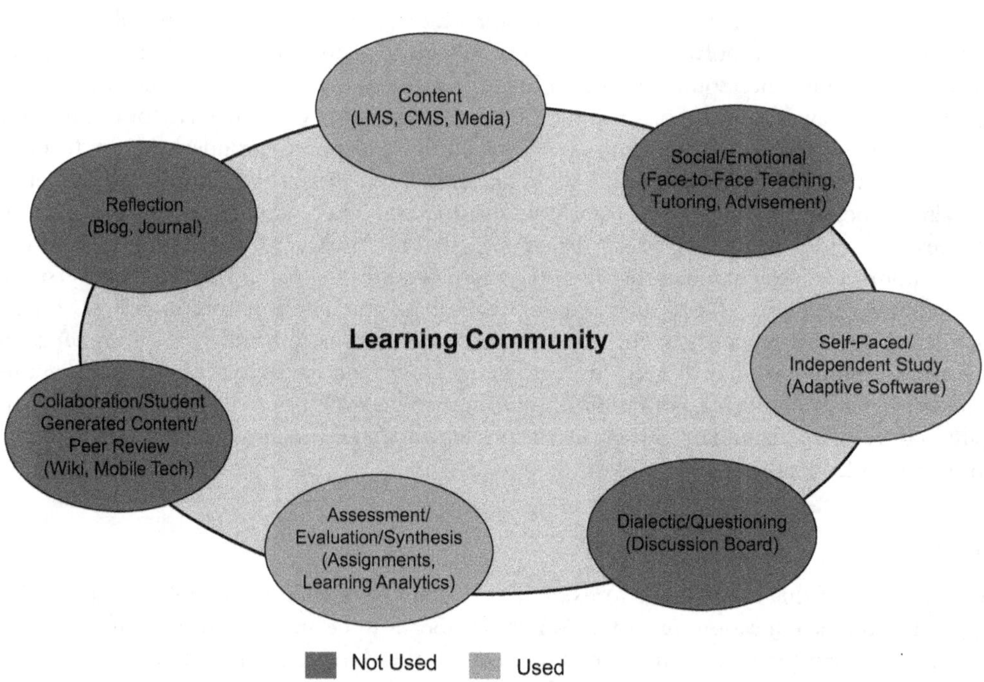

Plate 2 Example of a Distance Education Course

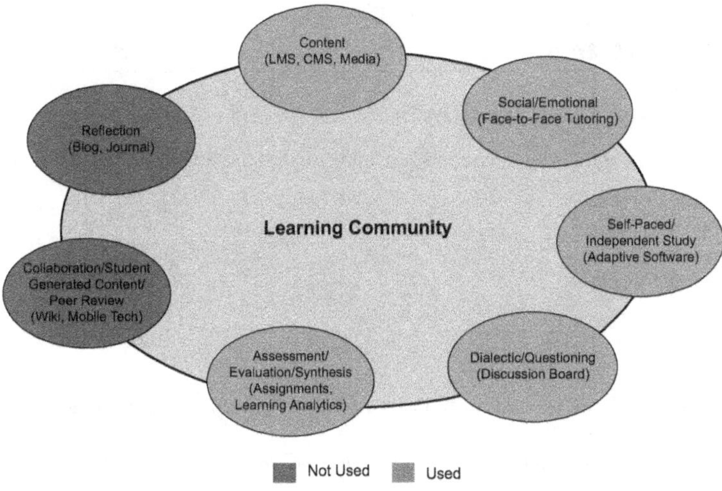

Plate 3 Example of a Modified Distance Education Course

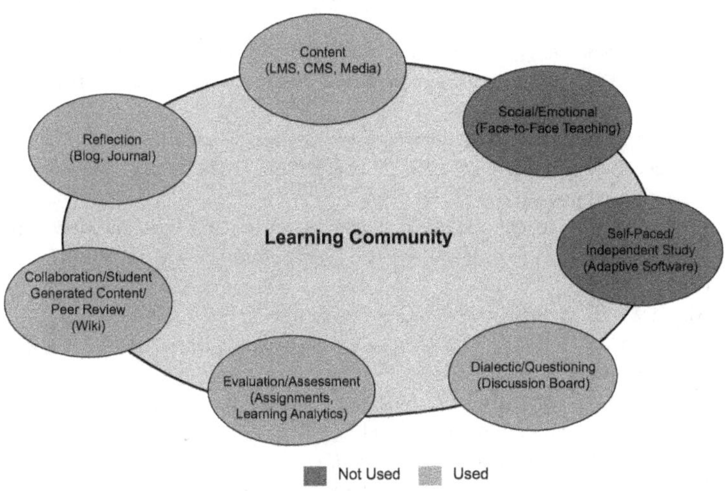

Plate 4 Example of a Teacher-Led Fully Online Course

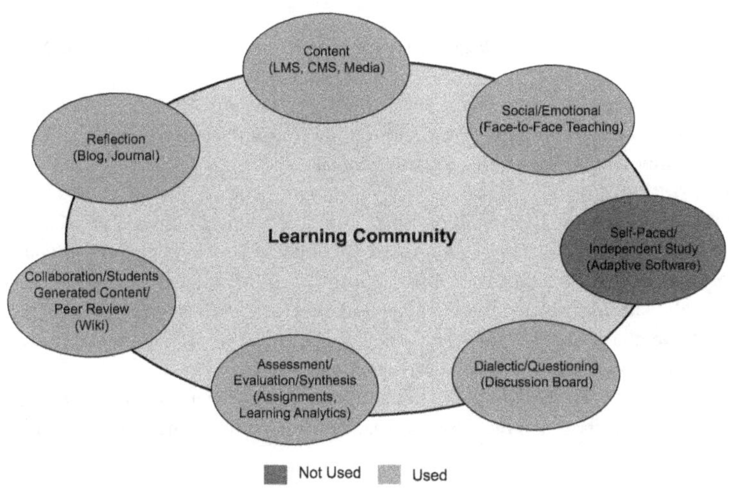

Plate 5 Example of a Mainstream Blended Course

Further Reading/Case Studies

Readers may wish to refer to the Appendix A—Case Studies in Online Education specifically to:

Apex Learning Virtual School
California Community Colleges
Rio Salado Community College
University of Central Florida

References

Adams, D. (1987). Paradigmatic contexts of models of educational planning and decision making. *Educational Planning, 6*(1), 36–47.

Allen, E., & Seaman, J. (2012). *Conflicted: Faculty and online education.* Needham, MA: Babson College Survey Research Group.

Allen, E., & Seaman, J. (2014). *Grade change: Tracking online education in the United States.* Needham, MA: Babson College Survey Research Group.

Aoun, R. E. (2017). *Robot proof: Higher education in the age of artificial intelligence.* Cambridge, MA: The MIT Press.

Barnard, C. I. (1964). *The functions of the executive.* Cambridge, MA: Harvard University Press.

Bowen, W.G., & McPherson, M.S (2016). *Lesson plan: An agenda for change in American higher education.* Princeton: Princeton University Press.

Bynre (2014, June 14). Why Clayton Christensen is wrong (and Michael Porter is right)? *Poets & Quants.* Retrieved March 20, 2015 from www.beatthegmat.com/mba/2014/06/14/why-clayton-christensen-is-wrong-and-michael-porter-is-right

Chafkin, M. (2013, December). Udacity's Sebastian Thrun, godfather of free online education, changes course. *Fast Company.* Retrieved December 1, 2014 from www.fastcompany.com/3021473/udacity-sebastian-thrun-uphill-climb

Christensen, C. M. (1997). *The innovator's dilemma.* New York, NY: HarperCollins.

Christensen, C. M., & Eyring, H. J. (2011). *The innovator's university: Changing the DNA of higher education from the inside out.* San Francisco, CA: Jossey-Bass.

Christensen, C. M., Horn, M. B., & Johnson, C. W. (2008). *Disrupting class: How disruptive innovation will change the way the world learns.* New York, NY: McGraw-Hill.

Collins, E. D. (2013, September). *Preliminary summary: SJSU and Augmented Online Learning Environment Pilot Project.* The Research and Planning Group for California Community Colleges (RP Group).

Collis, B., & van der Wende, M. (Eds.). (2002). *Models of technology and change in higher education: An international comparative survey on the current and future use of ICT in higher education.* Enschede: The Netherlands, Center for Higher Education Policy Studies, University of Twente. Retrieved from http://doc.utwente.nl/44610/1/ictrapport.pdf

Crow, M. M., & Dabars, W. B. (2015). *Designing the New American University.* Baltimore, MD: Johns Hopkins Press.

Etzioni, A. (1961). *A comparative analysis of complex organizations.* New York, NY: Free Press.

Finkel, E. (2013, June). Colleges finding partners for online coursed. *University Business.* Retrieved January 8, 2015 from www.universitybusiness.com/designingdigital

Fullan, M. (2001). *Leading in a culture of change.* San Francisco, CA: Jossey-Bass.

Harvey, D. (2005). *A brief history of neoliberalism.* New York, NY: Oxford University Press.

Jaschik, S., & Lederman, D. (2016). *The 2016 Inside Higher Education Survey of faculty attittudes on technology: A study by Gallup and Inside Higher Education.* Washington, DC: Inside Higher Education and Gallup.

Kanter, R. M. (1999). The enduring skills of change leaders. *Leader to Leader, 13*(Summer), 1522.

Koller, D. (2013, November). *Online learning: Learning without limits.* Keynote presentation at the 19th Annual Sloan Consortium Conference on Online Learning, Orlando, FL.

Kolowich, S. (2013, November 19). Citing series of conflicts, San Jose State U. asks for governance review. *The Chronicle of Higher Education.* Retrieved January 10, 2015 from http://chronicle.com/blogs/wiredcampus/

citing-series-of-conflicts-san-jose-state-u-asks-for-governance-review/48427?cid=wc&utm_source=wc&utm_medium=en

Mishra, P., & Koehler, M. J. (2006). Technological pedagogical content knowledge: A framework for teacher knowledge. *Teachers College Record, 108*(6), 1017–1054.

Parsons, T. (1958). Some ingredients of a general theory of formal organization. In A. W. Halpin (Ed.), *Administrative theory in education* (pp. 40–72). Chicago, IL: University of Chicago Press.

Selingo, J. J. (2014). The innovative university: What college presidents think about change in American higher education. *The Chronicle of Higher Education.*

Senge, P. (2006). *The fifth discipline: The art and practice of the learning organization.* New York, NY: Doubleday.

Shulman, L. S. (1986). Those who understand: Knowledge growth in teaching. *Educational Researcher, 15*(4).

Simon, H. A. (1960). *The new science of management decision.* New York, NY: Harper & Row.

Simon, H. A. (1982). *Models of bounded rationality.* Cambridge, MA: MIT Press.

U.S. General Accounting Office. (2014, December). State funding trends and policies on affordability: Report to the Chairman, Committee on Health, Education, Labor, and Pensions, United States Senate. *Report No. GAO-15–151U.* Retrieved January 8, 2105 from www.gao.gov/assets/670/667557.pdf

Wenger, E. (2000). *Communities of practice: Learning, meaning, and identity.* Cambridge: Cambridge University Press.

Chapter 6

Designing Instruction for Online Environments

Franco Zeffirelli is a world-renowned producer and director of opera, film, and theater whose productions have won almost every possible award. When the curtain goes up on a Zeffirelli opera, the beauty and magnificence of his set designs provoke "oohs", "aahs", and even applause from normally reticent and critical audiences. He has worked with many of the greatest performers of the past 50 years including Maria Callas, Luciano Pavarotti, and Placido Domingo. During a lecture at the Metropolitan Opera in New York City, he was asked this question: How does he start a new production: with the music, the story, the performers, or the sets? He immediately responded that he starts with the audience, which he visualizes as an "ensemble" of individuals each with unique expectations and needs when coming to his production. His production becomes a struggle to address these individual expectations (Zeffirelli, 1998).

In developing and designing online programs and courses, instructors should perhaps not start with the curriculum, or the course materials, or the technology, or the delivery mechanisms, but with the individual needs of students. Faculty and instructional designers would do well not to think of students as a singular group or class but as individuals with individual needs and expectations. In an online course, where most students will participate in the privacy of their homes or offices, designing courses that meet individual needs becomes important. Faculty should visualize their online courses through the eyes of individual students whose basic interactions may be through a laptop computer or a mobile device. The challenge in creating online learning environments is to determine what students need and to accommodate these needs as reasonably as possible.

This chapter focuses entirely on the design of instruction for online education. It refers to some of the ideas and material presented in Chapter 3. Readers may want to review the discussion of learning theory in that chapter, especially the work of Benjamin Bloom (1956) and Robert Gagné (1977). Bloom developed a taxonomy of key elements in instructional design. Gagne emphasized nine events in instruction that drive the definitions of objectives and strategies for presentation of material, activities, and assessment. This chapter will take theory and apply it to the real world of instructional design for online education. The principles outlined in the chapter can apply to entire academic programs, courses, or course modules. It will conclude with scripts for several different models of online education courses.

Instructional Development and Design

Instructional development occurs at many levels and takes many shapes and sizes. When teachers design simple lesson plans with goals, objectives, activities, materials, and student assessments, they are engaging in instructional development. A single faculty member might comprise the

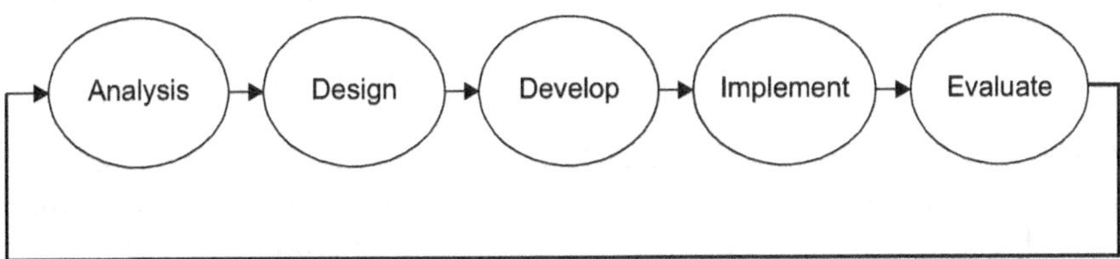

Figure 6.1 ADDIE Instructional Design Model

entire development team. On the other hand, instructional development that occurs for large projects such as entire new academic programs requires a more formal, organized approach. Large projects can involve specialists in content, media development, and technology. Regardless of the scope of the project, knowledge of instructional development is a must. The generic ADDIE Model (analyze, design, develop, implement, evaluate) originally developed in the 1970s, is highly regarded (see Figure 6.1) and will be used to illustrate a design framework. Major contributors to this field such as Dick, Carey, and Carey (2014) and Kemp and Smellie (1989) have based their models on ADDIE.

Analyze

In the Analyze stage, faculty and instructional designers consider objectives of the program, course, or module. For example, two common objectives are:

1. providing content knowledge and
2. developing skills.

These broad objectives are customized for the specific instructional development project (program, course, module) at hand. For example, in basic foundation and introductory courses, a good deal of content is provided in the form of varying media with text (books, articles) and digital video being the most popular. In online education, electronic media increasingly are becoming more popular for presentation of content. The common lecture that has been a staple of instruction for centuries is still popular and alive but increasingly is being provided entirely electronically or supplemented with digital video. Furthermore, digital media have built-in accommodations that allow students to go at their own pace, to assess their knowledge, and to review again and again what they see and hear.

Developing communications skills, especially writing, has become a common goal in many online course activities. Critical thinking is one of the more important skills that integrates well into online course environments where students can critique ideas and easily exchange commentary with other students. Engaging in collaborative activities is a skill important in many professional programs and can be gracefully accomplished in online environments. In the past decade, there has been much discussion about *21st century skills development*. Unfortunately, the term suffers because of a lack of a specific definition and has been used in a number of different contexts. As stated in *The Glossary of Education Reform:*

> It should be noted that the '21st century skills' concept encompasses a wide-ranging and amorphous body of knowledge and skills that is not easy to define and that has not been officially codified or categorized. While the term is widely used in education,

> it is not always defined consistently, which can lead to confusion and divergent interpretations.
>
> (*The Glossary of Education Reform*, 2016)

Tony Wagner, Co-Director of the Change Leadership Group at the Harvard Graduate School of Education, has written extensively on the need for students to master seven skills in order to thrive in the new world of work and to enable them to become productive citizens who contribute to solving some of the most pressing issues of the 21st century. He identifies these skills as follows:

1. Critical Thinking and Problem Solving
2. Collaboration and Leadership
3. Agility and Adaptability
4. Initiative and Entrepreneurialism
5. Effective Oral and Written Communication
6. Accessing and Analyzing Information
7. Curiosity and Imagination

(Wagner, 2008)

Many educators have begun to integrate these or similar skills into the curricula at all education levels. It has been recognized that skills such as collaboration, accessing and analyzing information, and written communication are facilitated in online environments. As a result, instructors seeking to integrate these skills into their courses find the online environment convenient and effective.

In the Analysis stage, consideration also is given to the students who are expected to enroll in the programs or courses. At the college level, this is especially of concern because of the large diversity within and among student populations, especially the number of adult learners attracted to online courses. Increasingly, colleges and universities are profiling, for all of the right reasons, the characteristics of students including demographic, motivational, academic preparedness, and access to resources. Box 6.1 provides a list of student characteristics that designers might consider in designing online course materials. These characteristics are not all inclusive but provide a general framework for profiling a student population. In K–12 education, student profiling takes on a different dimension since certain demographic characteristics such as age are more homogenous. Also whether desirable or not, many K–12 schools group students according to academic ability.

Box 6.1 Student Profile Characteristics

Demographic Characteristics

What are the age, gender, ethnicity, race, primary language spoken, family responsibilities, disabilities, and occupations of potential students?

Motivational Characteristics

What are the student educational goals and objectives?

What are student career goals and objectives?

Why might students be interested in an online course or program over a traditional face-to-face learning environment?

Academic Preparedness

What is the student educational achievement level (primary, secondary, community college, four-year college, graduate school)?

What are the student skill levels (reading, writing, basic mathematics, technical where appropriate)?

What formal background do the students have with the subject matter of the course or progam?

What are their personal interests and experiences that relate to the subject matter?

What prior experiences do students have with online learning?

Resources

How will students pay for tuition and fees?

How much time will students be able to devote to online learning?

What access do students have to media and technology?

Where and how do students access the Internet?

As part of the analysis, consideration is given to the resources and materials available for the project. For example, is an instructor designing the course by him or herself or will there be an instructional design team available to assist? The latter becomes very important in designing media. Even something as straightforward as creating the video of a lecture requires experience and expertise that might be problematic for an instructor who has never done it before. The professional appearance of media is important and is dependent upon resources. Integrating questions or formative assessment adds to the complexity of the project as well. Another consideration is the availability of funds to purchase curriculum material from outside vendors and instructional software providers. Increasingly, instructional designers consider what might already be available either free or for a fee rather than beginning from scratch. Certain disciplines such as the sciences might benefit greatly through the purchase of simulation software available from an outside source. There are also increasing amounts of instructional software available on the Web that is free or low cost.

Design

In the Design stage, faculty and instructional designers consider the program, courses, and modules to be developed that will meet the goals, objectives, and resource availability specified in the Analyze stage. A determination is made as to whether courses will be totally online or offered in blended formats. Modularization of courses into manageable segments is critical. A course outline helps determine the nature and sequencing of each module. Important consideration has to be given at this stage as to whether it will be necessary to scaffold course materials. In scaffolding, the material in one module has to be mastered in order to understand the material in subsequent modules. Once determined, the proper sequencing of modules is made.

An important decision during the Design stage is which materials can be acquired or have to be developed anew. Are there courses, modules, or other materials available that will meet the goals and objectives? If materials are available, what are their costs? A good deal of free material (open source) is available on the Internet and should be considered if it meets objectives.

Pedagogical approaches related to how material will be presented and used in a course or module are considered. Well-established techniques such as dialectic questioning (Socratic Method), reflection activities, and collaboration are evaluated for their appropriateness for each module. Consideration is also given as to how students will engage with material: in a self-paced, individual mode, or a group mode.

In the end, a plan is developed that outlines program and course objectives and the mechanisms and tools that will be used to achieve these objectives. Courses are also organized into modules, each of which has objectives and design considerations. Each module will also have an assessment activity to assist in determining if an objective(s) is met. A common question with regard to the design plan is how much detail is required. This depends upon the nature of the module as well as the time of faculty and instructional designers to commit to the project. Box 6.2 provides an excerpt from a design plan for a history module on the United States Supreme Court's *Brown v. Board of Education* decision of 1954.

Box 6.2 Excerpt From a Module for an Asynchronous Online Learning Course

This module is taken from a class on the United States Supreme Court's *Brown v. Board of Education* decision in 1954. This class is conducted entirely online using asynchronous communication. Students access all material and interact online. Each module is from one to three weeks long. This particular module last three weeks.

Lesson Objectives

1. To study the checks and balances system in the American governmental system.
2. To analyze how a democracy responds to crisis.
3. To explain key aspects (background, rationale, importance) of the *Brown v. Board of Education* decision.
4. To explain and consider the aftermath of the *Brown* decision.

Key Questions

1. Why is the *Brown v. Board of Education* decision regarded as one of the most significant decisions of the U.S. Supreme Court during the 20th century?
2. What was the reaction to the *Brown* decision on the part of various segments of American society?
3. What has been the effect of the *Brown* decision on American society in general?

Synopsis of the Case

In the early 1950s, de jure (by law) segregation in public schools was well-established in 17 states and Washington, D.C.

In Topeka, Kansas, a black third-grader named Linda Brown had to walk one mile through a railroad switch yard to attend her black elementary school, even though a white elementary school was only seven blocks away. Linda's father, Oliver Brown, tried to enroll her in the white elementary school but the principal of the school refused. Brown went to McKinley Burnett, the head of the Topeka branch of the National Association for the Advancement of Colored People (NAACP) and asked for help. Other black parents joined Brown, and in 1951, the NAACP requested an injunction that would forbid the segregation of Topeka's schools. The U.S. District court for the District of Kansas heard the Brown case on June 25–26, 1951. At the trial, the NAACP argued that segregated schools sent the message to black children that they were inferior to whites; therefore, the schools were inherently unequal.

The Board of Education's defense was that, because segregation in Topeka and elsewhere pervaded many other aspects of life, segregated schools simply prepared black children for the segregation they would face during adulthood. The Board also argued that segregated schools were not necessarily harmful to black children; prominent African Americans such as Frederick Douglas and George Washington Carver had attended segregated schools and made significant achievements during their lives.

The request for an injunction put the Court in a difficult position. On the one hand, the judges agreed with witnesses; in their decision they wrote: "Segregation of white and colored children in public schools has a detrimental effect upon the colored children . . . A sense of inferiority affects the motivation of a child to learn."

On the other hand, the precedent of *Plessy v. Ferguson* (1896) allowed for "separate but equal" public facilities including school systems for blacks and whites, and no Supreme Court ruling had overturned Plessy. Because of the precedent of *Plessy v. Ferguson*, the District Court felt "compelled" to rule in favor of the Board of Education.

Oliver Brown and the NAACP appealed to the U.S. Supreme court on October 1, 1951 and their case was combined with other cases that challenged school segregation in South Carolina, Virginia, Delaware, and the District of Columbia. The U.S. Supreme Court first heard the case on December 9, 1952, but failed to reach a decision. In the re-argument, heard on December 7–8, 1953, the Court requested that both sides discuss "the circumstances surrounding the adoption of the Fourteenth Amendment to the Constitution adopted in 1868."

On May 17, 1954 Chief Justice Earl Warren read the unanimous decision (Brown I):

> We come then to the question presented. Does segregation of children in public schools solely on the basis of race, even though the physical facilities and other "tangible" factors may be equal, deprive children of the minority group of equal educational opportunities? We believe that it does . . . We conclude that in the field of public education the doctrine of "separate but equal" has no place. Separate educational facilities are inherently unequal. Therefore, we hold that the plaintiffs and others similarly situated for whom the actions have been brought are, by reason of the segregation complained of, deprived of the equal protection of the laws as guaranteed by the Fourteenth Amendment.

With this decision, the U.S. Supreme Court struck down the "separate but equal" doctrine of *Plessy v. Ferguson* and ruled in favor of the plaintiffs. One year later, the U.S. Supreme Court issued its implementation decree ordering all segregated school systems to desegregate (Brown II).

Major Personalities

Oliver Brown—father of Linda Brown
Thurgood Marshall—lead attorney for the case for the NAACP Legal Defense Fund
John W. Davis—lead attorney for the defense
Kenneth Clark—social scientist and expert witness in the case
Charles Houston—dean of Howard University's School of Law
Earl Warren—Chief Justice of the U.S. Supreme Court

Aftermath of the *Brown* Decision

1. Integration of Central High School in Little Rock, Arkansas (1950s)
2. School Decentralization and Community Power in New York City (1960s)
3. Busing as a Remedy for Segregated Schools in Boston (1970s)

Legacy of the *Brown* Decision

1. Provided the Legal Foundation for the American Civil Rights Movement
2. Catalyst for Federal Legislative Initiatives and Entitlement Programs (i.e., Civil Rights Acts)
3. Established the Legal Precedence for other Groups on Constitutional Issues of Equality

Readings/Media

1. Blackside/PBS Video *Eyes on the Prize: America's Civil Rights Years 1954–1965*. (Selected Video Clips).
2. Kluger, R. (1976). *Simple justice: The history of Brown v. Board of Education and black America's struggle for equality*. New York: Alfred A. Knopf (Selected Chapters).
3. Holder, R. (2014). *Commemorating the 60th Anniversary of* Brown v. Board of Education *and Continuing the March Toward Justice*. https://obamawhitehouse.archives.gov/blog/2014/05/16/commemorating-60th-anniversary-brown-v-board-education-and-continuing-march-toward-j

Assignment

On its 60th anniversary in May 2014, Attorney General Eric Holder gave a commencement speech commemorating the Brown v. Board of Education Decision. At one point, he stated:

> our nation did not automatically translate the words of Brown into substantive change. The integration of our schools was a process that was halting, confrontational, and at times even bloody. And, for all the progress our nation has seen over the last six decades, this is a process that continues, and a promise that has yet to be fully realized, even today.
>
> While the number of school districts that remain under desegregation court orders has decreased significantly in just the past decade, the Department of Justice continues to actively enforce and monitor nearly 200 desegregation cases where school districts have not yet fulfilled their legal obligation to eliminate segregation "root and branch." In those cases, the department works to ensure that all students have the building blocks of educational success—from access to advanced placement classes, to facilities without crumbling walls and old technology, to safe and positive learning environments.

Write a brief (1000–1200 word) essay on whether the *Brown* decision still matters in the present day. In explaining your position, cite examples from your personal life or from publicized events to support your position(s). Be prepared to present a synopsis of your paper on our course discussion blog.

Develop

Once the design of a course has been completed, the task of actually acquiring the materials and developing the lessons and assessments begins. A good starting place is to examine what already exists in the same or similar courses offered in traditional face-to-face or in other online courses at the school or college. Online education is more than 20 years old and maybe a good deal of digital course material already exists within the institution. By the Development stage, resources in the form of an instructional designer and/or faculty time should be identified as well as a budget for any software or media acquisition. Once resources are in place each module is developed according to design team specifications.

It is very desirable to test module(s) as they are developed. Securing student feedback during testing allows for adjustments and fine tuning the module. The clarity of course instructions and ground rules for participation in an online course should be subject to a review by students. Simple items such as the efficacy of an instructor's question(s) to spur an online course discussion should be tested. The effectiveness of assessments also can be evaluated. At this stage, soliciting student feedback does not have to be formal but can occur informally.

Implement and Evaluate

The two stages Implement and Evaluate are presented together because evaluation should begin immediately and be conducted as part of the implementation process. Implementation occurs when a course is offered formally to students. It is also possible to test modules before an entire course has been developed assuming similar courses are being offered in other modes. Instructors should immediately begin making notes about what appears to be working well or not. This should take place throughout the course. More formal evaluation should also take place that allows for feedback from students as well as instructors. While most understand the importance of student feedback, faculty feedback is just as important. Essentially, faculty have to be pleased with the design, development and implementation of a new online course. Faculty insights can prove valuable in determining what has worked well or not and why. It is also important to solicit from them their satisfaction with the course and whether the new online course development was worth their time and effort. In soliciting faculty feedback, attention should be paid to faculty comments about the time it is taking them to teach in an online format. Many faculty report concerns about the additional time it takes to teach online. A qualitative study by Tynan, Ryan, Hinton, and Mills (2012) mentioned in Chapter 4 provides very interesting insights into the issue of faculty workload. For example, the simple task of responding to a student question might take more effort online than in a face-to-face classroom. This has evolved as a common issue especially with new online instructors and should not be ignored. Faculty satisfaction with their teaching is important regardless of the modality and good online course design and development takes this into consideration.

Students have been asked to evaluate classes formally and informally for decades. The end of semester course evaluation has become standard in many schools and colleges. Most of these standard evaluations are based on students' perceptions of what they have learned, their perceived quality of the course, and their engagement with the instructor, other students, and the material. The last becomes especially important if course material is integrated into software such that students are allowed to adapt and navigate through material at their own pace and interest. End of semester student evaluations should be expanded or modified to address online learning activities.

While faculty and student perceptions of a course are important, the critical evaluation criteria is the extent to which course goals and objectives have been met. An evaluation of assessment results will provide valuable guidance in this respect. A study conducted by this author titled *Beyond student perceptions: Issues of interaction, presence, and performance in an online course* provides insight into this issue. The study concluded that student satisfaction does not necessarily equate to performance (Picciano, 2002).

In sum, the results of the evaluation provide critical feedback that can be used by the instructor as well as by others who might teach or develop the same or a similar course. The evaluation also provides input into the analysis of a new course development cycle.

Communications and Interactivity

Fundamental to successful instruction is the ability to communicate and interact. In preparing a lesson, a teacher attempts to provide mechanisms and activities through which he or she communicates with students and shares ideas about a topic. If students do not understand some aspect of a lesson, they ask questions and receive appropriate responses. In a traditional, face-to-face classroom, this model of instruction is well-established and familiar to both teacher and student. Even in laboratory and studio classes where students are engaging in experiential activities designed to help them learn by handling and manipulating materials, the ability to ask the teacher a question and to receive feedback is critical to student success. In designing an online course or module, communication and interactivity are likewise fundamental to the design and development of instructional activities. However, the online environment affords alternate forms of communication and interactivity. These forms such as blogs, discussion boards, interactive media, and adaptive learning modules provide opportunities that should be taken advantage of in designing instruction.

Synchronous Versus Asynchronous Communications

In a traditional classroom most interactions are synchronous; that is, occurring at the same time and place. In an online learning environment, communications can be synchronous or asynchronous. Synchronous Web conferencing software facilities such as Zoom, GoToMeeting, Eluminate, and ADOBE Connect have developed to the point where they are stable and can be easily used on many types of digital equipment (desktops, laptops, tablets, etc.). This type of synchronous communication most closely simulates the traditional classroom and can function well in an online learning environment. One caution involves large classes. Too many students trying to log into a class session might cause technical and logistical problems. Pre-implementation testing is suggested.

Asynchronous forms of communication such as blogs, wikis, discussion boards, voice threads, and group email facilities are very popular in online education. These facilities are easy to use and are very familiar to faculty and students alike. Boxes 6.3 and 6.4 provide comparisons (advantages and disadvantages) of asynchronous versus synchronous communication in online learning environments.

Box 6.3 Asynchronous Communications

Advantages

- Available anytime;
- Available anyplace;
- Can incorporate a variety of media;

- Can be used for one to one communication and one to many communication;
- More time for reflection;
- Contribution to discussion can be more evenly distributed; and
- More opportunity for students to share multiple perspectives.

Disadvantages

- No immediate feedback;
- Difficult to keep track of collaboration (postings overload);
- Class activities must be well-organized;
- Can lack a true 'social presence';
- Learner may feel less engaged due to lag in response time to forum posts or questions; and
- Irregular or inconsistent contribution by individuals can affect the richness of discussion and learning.

Box 6.4 Synchronous (i.e., Web Conferencing) Communications

Advantages

- Real-time collaboration;
- Immediate response and feedback;
- Most useful for smaller class sizes;
- Video/web conferencing allow for body language and tone of voice; and
- Increased social presence.

Disadvantages

- If technology fails the collaboration session is not possible;
- Lack of reflection between collaborators;
- Requires students and teachers to commit to specific meeting time;
- Difficult for one to many communication; and
- Problematic in large classes.

Three Types of Instructional Interaction

Interactivity is a critical component of instruction that exists between and among the instructor, the learner, and the content (Moore & Kearsley, 1996). In online education, each of these three types of interactivity (see Figure 6.2) are considered necessary to achieve success in a course or program. In designing instructional activities, faculty and students must be comfortable in interacting with each other as well as with the content. As mentioned in Chapter 3, the community of inquiry model developed by Garrison, Anderson, and Archer (2000) is based on the concept of *presence* comprising three essential components: cognitive, social, and teaching. While all three are important, social presence addresses specifically the need for interaction. Many other instructional designers have also espoused a "social presence" approach for encouraging interactivity in an online education environment (Whiteside, Dikkers, & Swan, 2017).

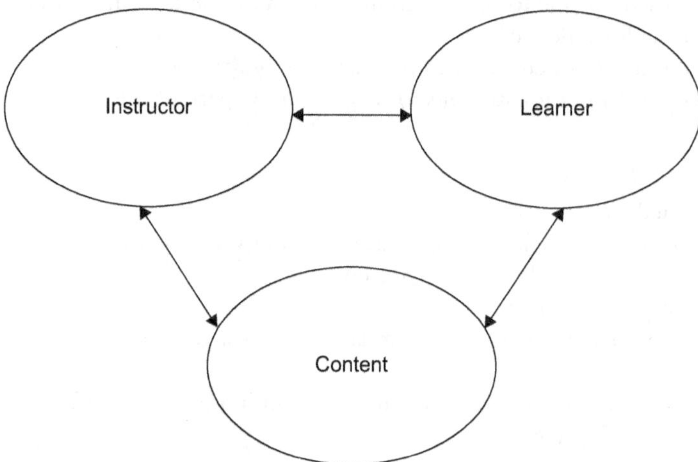

Figure 6.2 Three Types of Instructional Interaction

Designing Vibrant Online Classes—Think Social Presence!

Designers can greatly enhance the vibrancy of an online course by utilizing techniques aimed at fostering regular and student-friendly interactions. When designers enhance social presence the online learning environment provides a welcoming style and means of communication. Simple-to-use blogs and discussion boards continue to be the mainstay for many online course activities. They are easy to use and the technology does not get in the way of carrying out class discussions. Furthermore, they help organize discussions by threading topics, comments, and responses, thereby making it easier for students to review the material. Here are several practical suggestions for engaging students in online discussions:

- To take advantage of the asynchronous nature of threaded discussions, allow students sufficient time (i.e., several days) to respond to a posting;
- Use first names rather than Mr., Ms., or Dr. on postings to increase the comfort level for students;
- Compliment students regularly, both publicly on blogs and discussions boards as well in private emails;
- Make a point of referring to student postings to develop and advance an online discussion;
- Respond promptly to student questions;
- Use media (photographs, video, and audio) to add variety to text postings.

One of the most effective ways of developing social presence is to have students assume ownership of a discussion so that interaction is not just between instructor and students but students and students. Assigning students as discussion facilitators is an effective way of accomplishing more student ownership. Rotating students on a weekly basis as facilitators ensures that all students have a chance to help lead a discussion.

Develop material, especially questions for discussion, carefully. Depend on open-ended questions designed to answer the why and how rather than the who, when, or where. Also develop some questions that allow students to bring their own experiences into a discussion. Malcolm Knowles, who has been mentioned several times in this book, suggested that adult students in particular can be reached by relating material as much as possible to their own lives (Knowles, Holton, & Swanson, 1998). Start a question with: "In your experiences, have you ever . . .?"

Lastly, screen for misinformation. It is quite possible that during a discussion, a student or two will post something that is not accurate. The instructor should screen for such postings and make all students know in as friendly a way as possible about the inaccuracy. This will prevent any extensive discussion based on the misinformation.

Grading, Testing, and Assignments

Grades, tests, and student assignments are important aspects of the design of online courses. Instructors traditionally have used a variety of student evaluation methods including multiple-choice tests, essays, take-home examinations, term projects and papers, and oral reports. In online learning environments, all of the above are possible; however, depending upon the technology available, some forms of evaluation are easier to administer than others. Here are some suggestions.

First, special attention should be given to developing formative as well as summative evaluations. Formative evaluation is defined simply as enabling or assisting students to learn from the evaluation activity, while summative evaluation assesses whether students have mastered the content or skill. Self-paced instruction, common in adaptive learning software, requires students to know that they have mastered the content or skill before moving on to the next module or lesson. By the same token, if students are having difficulty, they need to know what material to review or reread. Good instructional design will provide for self-administered tests that can advance students to the next module or direct them to additional material as needed.

Second, a variety of assessment strategies should be considered. In addition to testing, instructors should consider student projects including writing essays and reports, creating media, developing portfolios, and group problem-solving activities. For online courses directed to adult students, assessments might be geared to the workplace including activities that might involve case study analysis, group exercises, and open-ended questions aimed at allowing more self-expression and reflection.

Third, the online environment provides graceful facilities for collaborative evaluation projects and activities. Group essays, reports, presentations, and other projects can be facilitated and enhanced by online technology. Blogs, wikis, group email, and video conferencing allow students to maintain easy contact with each other and to share activities with one another. A major benefit of collaborative activities is that a good deal of informal learning can occur as students explore and share ideas with one another. Having students evaluate each other's work is very easily accomplished as part of a collaborative activity.

Fourth, instructors need not compromise their methods of evaluation but should consider what the online environment can provide to support, enhance, or replace them. Many online programs and course/learning management systems maintain standard testing procedures which may be proctored either in person or electronically. A number of proctoring services are now available for testing and assessing students online. However, the online environment also facilitates on-going student evaluation and can be especially effective for documenting student interaction in online course sessions and group activities.

Multimedia

Responding to a question about a leading soprano's singing and acting talents, James Levine (1995), the artistic director of the Metropolitan Opera in New York City, commented that good music does not need words. His point was that music alone was enough to communicate emotion and beauty to those with the ability to appreciate it. However, when a Verdi melody is combined with words, the result is an aria that allows the audience to better appreciate the melody within the context of a story or event. Add actors in colorful dress, a set depicting a quaint mountain village, some graceful dancers, and the result can be an opera that appeals to and communicates with the entire world.

The expansion of a melody into an aria and an aria into an opera is an appropriate metaphor for introducing the subject of multimedia. In the case of teaching and learning, words conveyed through writing and reading alone may not be sufficient to reach all students. Combining words with images, sounds, and movement can extend the teaching/learning process and help communicate a lesson to many more students.

The term *multimedia* refers to many types of communication processes, delivery systems, and events. It is a term that is used in connection with entertainment, advertisement, museum exhibitions, theme parks, video games, and dozens of other areas of human endeavor. Multimedia adds a certain technological chic and conjures up images of color, movement, dazzling special effects, and provocative sounds. Because of the variety of ways in which the word has been used, multimedia has come to mean different things to different people.

Generically, multimedia can be defined as any combination of two or more media including sound, images, text, animation, and video. However, when used with digital technology, it also implies interactive navigational or hypermedia capabilities that can be invoked and controlled by the user. *Hypermedia* is the integration of sights, sounds, graphics, video, and other media into an associative or linked system of information storage and retrieval. In online education, students have begun to expect some media will be integrated into every course. From simple video lectures to more advanced gaming and simulation software, media is becoming commonplace in teaching and learning since it has become much easier and less costly to provide images and video material. An iPhone or other PDA device can record decent video at the touch of a button. However, since much of the media in an online course will be used over and over again, it might be beneficial to plan the production and to seek the assistance of technical staff who can best help to develop the material. In addition, there is a good deal of free (open source) or low-cost instructional material on the World Wide Web that should be considered as long as there are no copyright infringement issues. Websites such as *Finding Supplementary Material for your Online Course* provide information on a number of resources that can be accessed for educational media (www.goconqr.com/en/blog/finding-supplementary-material-for-your-online-course/).

Scripting

Scripting is a technique used to plan a class session and involves identifying key tasks that will be performed. It is very similar to lesson planning as commonly used by many teachers at all levels and is a highly recommended instructional design tool especially for those who are new to online education. Boxes 6.5a, 6.5b, and 6.5c provide scripts for three different online education sessions, all dealing with the same topic, *Brown v. Board of Education*. Box 6.5a scripts an asynchronous learning class; Box 6.5b scripts an interactive video session; and Box 6.5c scripts a blended learning class. All can work if implemented well.

Asynchronous Learning Using the Internet and World Wide Web

Box 6.5a Excerpt of a Script for an Asynchronous Online Discussion

This script could be part of a module on the United States Supreme Court's *Brown v. Board of Education* in 1954. Online discussions in this class typically last one week starting on Sunday and ending on Saturday.

Friday—Remind student facilitators (discussion leaders) for the coming week's discussion to read/view material and become familiar with key questions.

Sunday—Instructor initiates the week's activity on the course discussion blog by introducing the topic and concluding with the following, open-ended question for students to comment:

> "Why is the *Brown v. Board of Education* decision regarded as one of the most significant decisions of the U.S. Supreme Court during the 20th century?"

Refer students to the reading and viewing material to develop their responses.

Monday—Monitor student comments and questions on the discussion blog.

Tuesday—Compliment students who made exceptionally good postings on the topic. Review the wording of the *Brown* decision (Brown I) and the implementation decree (Brown II). Conclude with the open-ended questions for students to comment:

> "What was the reaction to the *Brown* decision on the part of various segments of American society?"
>
> "How did different parts of the country respond to the *Brown* decision?"

Wednesday—Monitor student comments and questions on the discussion blog.

Thursday—Compliment students who made exceptionally good postings on the topic. Review the discussion for the week and emphasize that the *Brown* decision did not just affect the states that had established de jure segregated school systems but that it affected the entire country. Provide examples in New York and Boston.

Conclude with the following question for students to comment:

> "What has been the effect of the *Brown* decision on American society in general?

Friday—Monitor student comments and questions on the discussion blog.

Saturday—Compliment students who made exceptionally good postings on the topic.

Indicate that a summary of the discussion along with other instructor notes will be available at the course website by 4:00 pm this (Saturday) evening.

Remind students that a written assignment is due this Sunday and that students should be prepared to provide a short synopsis on the discussion blog starting on Sunday evening.

Thank student facilitators for their assistance.

Box 6.5a provides the script for an asynchronous learning class using the Internet and the World Wide Web. Instructional activities described in this script rely on Internet-based facilities typically found in a course management/learning management system (CMS/LMS). Students participate from their homes, places of business, or wherever they have access to the Internet and at a time that is convenient for them. A good CMS/LMS will facilitate developing many of these materials for the Web.

In this example, the course is organized into weekly discussion topics. Each discussion commences on a Sunday evening on the course discussion blog and formally concludes on the following Saturday morning. Additional material is provided at a class Web site. Several students are selected each week to serve as facilitators and are reminded on Friday of this assignment via e-mail. Student facilitators are expected to be especially active in making comments, in responding to questions, and in moving the discussion along for the week. In asynchronous learning, open-ended questions are very effective in allowing students to express themselves and are highly recommended. In the example script, each scheduled posting by the instructor concludes with an open-ended question. In addition to the discussion blog, students are encouraged to contact the instructor directly via individual e-mail if need be throughout the session. In the absence of face-to-face contact, positive feedback and reinforcement techniques such as frequent compliments or references to students are desirable.

In this particular script, the discussion ends with the instructor providing a summary of the week's discussion and posting his or her notes on the class Web site. At the Web site, students can also find the reading and writing assignments. In this example, the reading assignment includes material provided at another site on the Web from a symposium that was held on the *Brown v. Board of Education* decision. When possible, using the information resources of the Web is highly recommended for asynchronous, Internet-based learning. Students in these classes are familiar with the Web and generally can easily access Web-based materials. Depending upon the topic and content, quality reading and other instructional materials may not always be available online. While book and journal publishers are moving toward providing access to their materials on the Web, user fees may be required. An instructor might be tempted to scan in excerpts of text or images from a particularly useful article and post it on a course Web site; however, if the material is copyrighted, permission may have to be secured. The writing assignment in this example can be submitted electronically via the CMS/LMS "digital drop box."

The Interactive Videoconference

Box 6.5b Excerpt of a Script for a Two-Way Interactive Videoconference

This excerpt could be part of the module on the *Brown v. Board of Education* decision of 1954.

1:00 p.m.—Prepare audio-visual setup for today's session.

Test interactive video connection for audio and video quality.
Test instructor and student microphones.
Discuss with teaching assistants at the remote and local sites that they have received back-up material and understand the lesson and procedures for today's session.

1:30 p.m.—Interactive video session starts.

Welcome the students at both sites and verify that they can see and hear you.
Take attendance.

1:40 p.m.—Begin the lesson.

Orally present the synopsis of the U.S. Supreme Court's *Brown v. Board of Education* decision from prepared notes.

2:00 p.m.—Ask for questions from each of the sites. Cite key questions.
2:10 p.m.—Orally present background of major personalities involved with the decision from prepared notes.
2:30 p.m.—Ask for questions from each of the sites. Cite key questions.
2:40 p.m.—Break
2:50 p.m.—Welcome the students back.

Provide a brief summary of the material/discussion during the first half of this session.

3:00 p.m.—Show a series of video clips from the award-winning documentary Blackside/PBS.

Video *Eyes on the Prize.* These clips will include the following:

Additional background on the *Brown* decision;
Footage of the integration of Central High School in Little Rock, Arkansas, in the 1950s;
Footage of the school decentralization movement in New York City in the 1960s;
Footage of the school busing issue in Boston in the 1970s.

3:40 p.m.—Highlight pertinent comments/scenes made in the video clips.
4:00 p.m.—Ask for questions from both of the sites. Cite key questions.
4:15 p.m.—Distribute/announce/refer students to the reading and writing assignments.
4:20 p.m.—Ask if there are any questions with the assignment.
4:30 p.m.—Interactive video session ends.

Box 6.5b provides an excerpt from a script for a 3-hour interactive videoconference in which an instructor teaches to both a local and a distant student audience. Scripting is highly recommended in developing any type of conference (audio, video, one-way, two-way, multipoint). The conference should be carefully organized according to a time schedule provided to the parties at all sites to ensure a clear understanding of the sequence of a lesson's activities. In addition to helping an instructor organize his or her lesson, the script is used extensively by site facilitators to prepare for and assist in the delivery of the conference.

For the oral delivery in an interactive videoconference, an instructor can adapt much of his or her own traditional teaching style to the lesson. However, encouraging the students to ask questions, particularly at the remote site(s), is critical. A major advantage of interactive videoconferencing is its inherent interactivity, and instructors should plan their lessons accordingly. Study and observation of videoconferences indicate that the students at the local sites are frequently able to read the body language and energy of the instructor better than those at the remote sites, especially at the beginning of a course. It is not unusual to see students at a local site asking more questions than students at the remote sites. A good script will identify specific periods for questions from all sites. Instructors should also be comfortable with camera angles and positioning, and to the extent possible look into the camera. Another advantage of interactive videoconferencing is the ability to incorporate media such as videos, slides, and document cameras. Where appropriate, instructors are encouraged to use media to enhance their basic oral delivery.

The script excerpted in Box 6.b starts with a testing of all technology, especially audio and video connections. Site facilitators or teaching assistants should be familiar with the session's activities. A backup plan is highly recommended in case a connection is lost or some other technical difficulty occurs. The session starts promptly at 1:30 p.m. with a welcome, another brief test of audio and video quality, and the taking of attendance. The instructor proceeds to introduce the topic orally, just as he or she would in a traditional class. The script allocates frequent and specific time periods for questions to ensure that the students at the remote site(s) are encouraged to interact. In a videoconference of two or more hours, at least one break is recommended. The example script also makes use of video material to illustrate and support the oral presentation. PBS markets the highly acclaimed *Eyes on the Prize* documentary series on the civil rights movement in the United States in several video formats. In this particular situation, where several video clips are being used, DVD with its direct accessing capability is the recommended choice.

Distributing prepared notes on the topic is generally the prerogative of the instructor. Some instructors in traditional classes make their notes available; others do not. The same is true in online lessons. Minimally, teaching assistants and site facilitators should receive a copy of the instructor's notes. The reading assignments are generally provided as part of the entire schedule of assignments in the course syllabus. It may be helpful for students to have writing assignments scheduled in advance, but some instructors prefer to distribute writing assignments as needed.

Blended Learning Course

Box 6.5c Excerpt of a Script for a Blended Learning Class

This excerpt could be part of the module on the *Brown v. Board of Education* decision in 1954. This class would normally meet face-to-face on Monday, Tuesday, and Friday. However, the instructor has decided to replace the Tuesday class activities with online activities so that the class now meets face-to-face only two days per week (Monday and Friday).

Friday—Remind student facilitators via e-mail for the coming week's discussion that they should have read all the material and are familiar with key questions.

Monday—In Class Session:
Initiate week's discussion in class by introducing the topic and concluding with the following open-ended question:

> "Why is the *Brown v. Board of Education* decision regarded as one of the most significant decisions of the U.S. Supreme Court in the 20th century?"

Show two video clips from the award-winning documentary Blackside/PBS Video *Eyes on the Prize*. These clips will include the following:

> Additional background on the *Brown* decision;
> Footage of the integration of Central High School in Little Rock, Arkansas, in the 1950s.

Ask students to discuss this topic on the course discussion blog.

Each student is to make at least two postings between now and Friday.

Refer students to a synopsis and major personalities of the case that is available at the class Web site.

Tuesday—Monitor student comments and questions on the discussion blog.

Wednesday—Compliment students who made exceptionally good postings to the discussion blog over the past 48 hours.

Review the wording of the Brown I and Brown II Decisions.

Conclude with the following open-ended question:

"What was the reaction to the *Brown* decision on the part of various segments of American society?"

"How did different parts of the country respond to the *Brown* decision?"

Ask students to continue their discussion on the discussion blog.

Thursday—Monitor student comments and questions on the discussion blog.

Friday—In-Class Session

Compliment students who made exceptionally good postings to the discussion blog over the past three days.

Briefly review the online discussion.

Emphasize that the *Brown* decision did not just affect the states that had established de jure segregated public school systems.

Show two video clips from the Blackside/PBS Video *Eyes on the Prize.* These clips will include the following:

Footage of the school decentralization movement in New York City in the 1960s;
Footage of the school busing issue in Boston in the 1970s.

Conclude with an open-ended question:

"What has been the effect of the *Brown* decision on American society in general?"

Ask students to post a brief reflective essay by Sunday summarizing this question on the discussion blog.

Sunday—Read, grade, and comment on student reflective essays.

Monday—Compliment the students who wrote exceptionally good essays.

Start next lesson on the *Brown v. Board of Education* module.

Box 6.5c provides the script for a blended learning course that meets face-to-face and online. The traditional face-to-face course would meet three days per week (e.g., Monday, Tuesday, and Friday), however, the instructor with approval from his department chairperson has developed a blended learning version of this course that meets face-to-face two days per week (Monday and Friday) and meets online during the week instead of attending a Tuesday class session. Several students are selected each week to serve as facilitators of instruction especially for the online portion of the course and are reminded on Friday of this assignment. Student facilitators are expected to be especially active in making comments, in responding to questions, and in moving the discussion along for the week.

In this particular script, the class covers a week's worth of instruction and ends with the instructor providing a summary of the week's discussion. At the course Web site, students can also find the reading and writing assignments. In this example, the reading assignment includes material provided at another site on the Web from a symposium that was held on the *Brown v. Board of Education* decision. The instructor also makes use of video clips for the face-to-face sessions on Monday and Friday. The blog is used so that the student entries can be shared with others and possibly serve as discussion points for a future class.

Summary

This chapter focused on the design of instruction for online education. It referred to some of the ideas and material presented in Chapter 3 on learning theory. The chapter applied theory to the real world of instructional design as appropriate for online education. The generic ADDIE Model (analyze, design, develop, implement, evaluate) originally developed by the U.S. Armed Services in the 1970s was used as a design framework. The principles outlined in this chapter can refer to entire academic programs, courses, or course modules. The chapter concluded with scripts for several different models of online education courses.

As a conclusion to this chapter, readers might want to look at the Online Learning Consortium's evaluation criteria for online course design. These can be found in Appendix D.

Further Reading/Case Studies

Readers may wish to refer to the Appendix A—Case Studies in Online Education specifically to:

Athabasca University
Florida Virtual School
University of Illinois Chicago
Western Governors University

References

Bloom, B. S. (1956). *Taxonomy of educational objectives handbook: Cognitive domains.* New York, NY: David McKay.

Dick, W., Carey, L., & Carey, J. O. (2014). *Systematic design of instruction.* Boston, MA: Pearson.

Gagné, R. M. (1977). *The conditions of learning.* New York, NY: Holt, Rinehart & Winston.

Garrison, D. R., Anderson, T., & Archer, W. (2000). Critical inquiry in a text-based environment: Computer conferencing in higher education model. *The Internet and Higher Education, 2*(2–3), 87–105.

The Glossary of Education Reform Website. (2016). *21st century skills.* Retrieved July 4, 2017 from http://edglossary.org/21st-century-skills/

Kemp, J. E., & Smellie, D. C. (1989). *Planning, producing, and using instructional media* (6th ed.). New York: Harper & Row

Knowles, M. S., Holton, E. F., & Swanson, R. A. (1998). *The adult learner* (5th ed.). Houston, TX: Butteworth-Heineman Publishers.

Levine, J. (1995, September 26). Interview with Charlie Rose, on *Charlie Rose* [Television Broadcast]. New York: Public Broadcasting Service.

Moore, M., & Kearsley, G. (1996). *Distance education: A systems view.* Belmont, CA: Wadsworth Publishing Co.

Picciano, A. G. (2002). Beyond student perceptions: Issues of interaction, presence, and performance in an online course. *Journal of Asynchronous Learning Networks, 6*(1), 21–40.

Tynan, B., Ryan, Y., Hinton, L., & Mills, A. L. (2012). *Out of hours: Final report of the project e-teaching leadership: Planning and implementing a benefits-oriented costs model for technology enhanced learning.* Australian Learning and Teaching Council.

Wagner, T. (2008). *Even our 'best' schools are failing to prepare students for 21st-century careers and citizenship.* Tony Wagner Transforming Education Website. Retrieved July 4, 2017 from www.tonywagner.com/244

Whiteside, A. L., Dikkers, A. G., & Swan, K. (Eds.). (2017). *Social presence in online learning: Multiple perspectives on practice and research.* Sterling, VA: Stylus Publishing.

Zeffirelli, F. (1998, November 9). *Lecture at Lincoln Center.* New York City.

Chapter 7

Academic, Administrative, and Student Support Structures

Libraries, in concert with centers for learning, have existed for thousands of years. In the Middle East, the earliest libraries began as repositories of clay tablets. Ramses II formed one of the first Egyptian libraries with 20,000 papyrus scrolls in 1250 BC. The Moors, using Chinese methods of papermaking, established a library of more than 400,000 volumes in the 10th century in Cordoba, Spain. The Bibliotheque Nationale de France in Paris traces its origins to King Charles IV in the 14th century and now houses more than 10 million books. In 1638, John Harvard bequeathed 300 books to start the library at the university in Cambridge, Massachusetts that now bears his name.

For centuries, scholars traveled from places around the world to these libraries to explore the knowledge that existed on their shelves. Today in every college and school library, students can be found studying, writing, and researching information. Teachers and students need the place we call the library. Indeed, the success of any academic program depends upon a library as well as science laboratories, media centers, and other support facilities and services. Happily, we have reached a point in digital technology where all of these necessities can exist in the virtual world and be at the fingertips of students 24 hours a day and 7 days a week. Increasingly, as online education continues to evolve, faculty and students expect that instructional resources will be available to them in any place and at any time.

Successful online education initiatives require leadership and the support from all parts of an organization. Dependable technology infrastructure and support services frequently can "make or break" academic programs, especially those that are serving fully online distance students. Administrative leadership that works well with various constituents including faculty, administrative, and support staffs can go a long way in bringing an institution together to move forward with online initiatives that are at times viewed with skepticism. This chapter will also review several policy issues that have arisen as colleges and schools move to more online instruction. Readers may wish to review the material in Chapter 5 that provides an overall planning model for online education.

Support Starts With Leadership

While teaching and learning are the mainstays and the core of an education enterprise, the overall success of instructional programs depends upon a number of other services such as advisement, counseling, library, and professional development. For fully online programs, every service that a college or school provides must be duplicated electronically. To provide these services sound leadership from the top of the organization is required. College presidents, superintendents, and principals need to be clear as they lead their schools in mounting and providing online education services. The creation of successful online programs will test the skills of most leaders because they have to rely on the knowledge and experience of others. Increasingly, they have to consider contracting for part or all of their technology infrastructure to outside vendors. Those colleges and schools that have already built a sound technology infrastructure for other purposes are better positioned to move forward with online education initiatives. Those that have not must decide whether to start from the ground up or to contract with vendors to provide services. Regardless of how the infrastructure is provided, leaders need to demonstrate to their constituents that they are committed to providing the necessary support resources.

The development of substantive technology projects usually involves change and therefore adjustment in an organization. Some observers such as Clayton Christensen would suggest that it may "disrupt" the organization. This does not have to be the case. With careful planning as presented in Chapter 5, and sound leadership major change can occur without disruption that can lead to internal strife and dissonance. Assuming that the college or school is not in dire fiscal straits, major technology infrastructure projects can evolve deliberately and carefully. The organizational leadership must exercise the patience and understanding needed to accomplish this well.

As noted in Chapter 5, one of the most important decisions with regard to infrastructure and support for online education initiatives is the placement of the administration of the program within in the organization. For fully online programs, the choices usually come down to:

1. Centralizing online education in one specific department that takes on responsibility for the development of programs, providing support services, contracting with faculty, recruitment, admissions, and registration across academic departments; or
2. Integrating online education into existing academic department structures with coordination and oversight provided by an administrative officer.

For blended online education, it is more likely that much of the development, design, and implementation emanates in existing academic departments. It is becoming commonplace for individual faculty to decide how to blend online and face-to-face instruction in ways that make the most pedagogical sense. This is especially the case for individual courses.

Regardless of organizational location, the coordination of the development of online academic programs is a critical undertaking. Determining program development costs, professional development needs, and market feasibility are integral to good academic planning and generally occur at college and universities in the chief academic or provost's office. In most institutions of higher education, there is shared governance, so faculty need to be consulted and involved with decision making involving the development of academic programs whether online or not.

In addition to academic program coordination, planning must take place at the institutional level to ensure that the proper infrastructure and support services are available. For instance, a common course/learning management system (CMS/LMS) is highly desirable for facilitating faculty development as well as for ease of student access. Selecting, implementing and maintaining a (CMS/LMS) requires technology expertise usually provided by a chief information officer's staff. Integrating the student and course databases with the CMS/LMS will require chief information officer expertise as well. While there are a number of variations, in recent years, the chief information officer responsible for administrative and academic technology services at a school or college frequently reports directly to a president, chancellor or school district superintendent. In addition to hardware and software decisions, consideration has to be given to the possible expansion of academic and student support services to include fully online access. Increasingly, schools and colleges are moving many of these services to online modes, even for traditional students who enroll in on-ground programs. Many colleges and universities now provide facilities for students to apply, register, and pay their tuition fees entirely online. For fully online students, moving these services online becomes an absolute necessity.

Major Components of the Infrastructure Needed for Online Education

The major components for the infrastructure needed to support online education are illustrated in Figure 7.1.

MIS, CMS/LMS, and Library and Digital Resources

The center column of Figure 7.1 contains the management information system (MIS), the course/learning management system (CMS/LMS), and the Library and Digital Resources. The five major databases that constitute a MIS for most education organizations are as follows:

1. Student database (demographic, transcript, academic progress, special needs);
2. Personnel database (demographic, history, salary, assignments);
3. Course database (course offerings, history, pre/co-requisites);
4. Financial database (budget, accounting, purchasing, bursar);
5. Facilities database (room inventory, equipment, maintenance).

These five databases should be integrated to the extent possible. Integration is important for data flows among the various databases and for accessing critical management information. In recent years, the integration of these databases and the development of accurate and timely data flow has been referred to as an "enterprise system." For online education applications, it is critical that the student and course databases are fully integrated and compatible with one another. In most online instructional applications, student and course data generally move back and forth regularly between these two databases. In addition to these five, other important

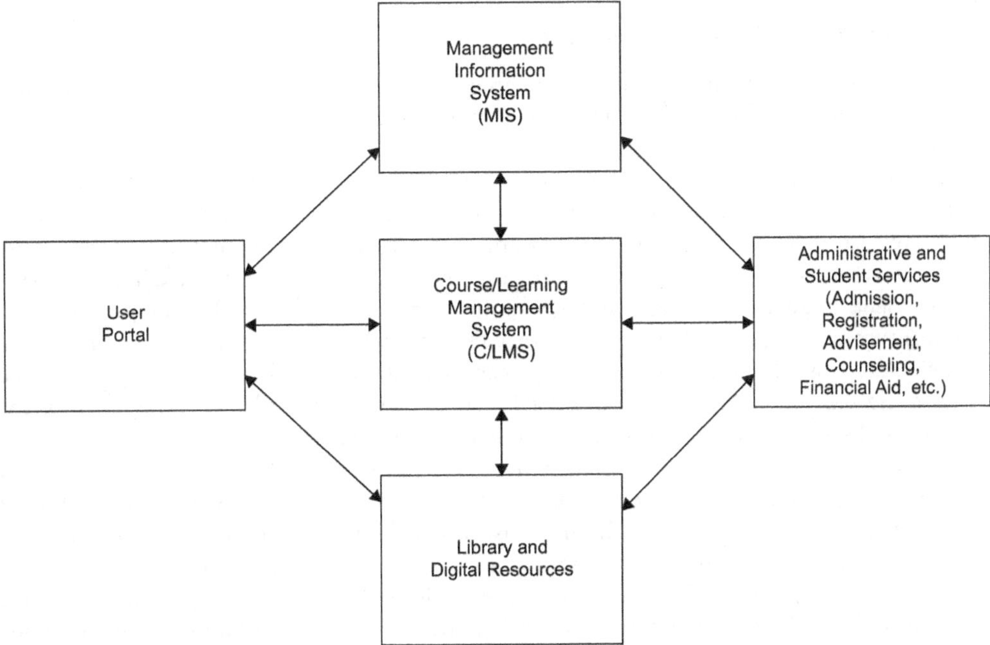

Figure 7.1 Major Components of Online Education Infrastructure

databases might be developed for areas such as alumni and marketing that become increasingly important in the competitive world of online education.

The CMS/LMS is usually a commercially provided software system such as Blackboard or Canvas that is purchased or leased. The CMS/LMS provides the platform for faculty and instructional designers to build courses and instructional modules. Very large university systems and school districts sometime consider building their own CMS/LMS platform, but most colleges and schools will purchase or lease. Increasingly, CMS/LMSs are being provided via cloud services.

The library and digital resources provide depositories of materials (books, video, audio) that are available to faculty and students for teaching and learning. These resources contain local files or links to files at other schools or organizations. Since the advent of the Internet in the 1990s, librarians and instructional designers have developed expertise in locating instructional materials on the Internet and do not necessarily have to store these on local college or school servers.

User Portal

The user portal is the critically-important entry point through which students, faculty, and support staff gain access to files, courses, and information related to the education enterprise. By virtue of its design, this portal needs to provide easy access to relevant information. Prospective students, especially, will be greatly influenced by the portal in deciding whether or not they will enroll in an academic program. Gone are the days when a school's website consisted of several pages of text and some photographs of the campus. Today's portals not only provide information but are designed to guide students through various processes. They also make available 24/7 access to individuals who might be of assistance in answering questions and providing guidance. Increasingly, they also provide students with easy access to services such as email, social networking, and other activities.

Administrative and Student Services

Administrative and student services are the applications that are made available to students, faculty, and other administrators for a host of activities related to library, advisement, counseling, and other support services. Online students expect to be able to conduct all basic services such as admissions, registration, financial aid, and bursar operations via a college website. A friendly, well-designed student interface to these services has become critical for marketing to, attracting, and keeping students enrolled in online programs. Faculty, teaching assistants, and tutors also use these services for advisement, for monitoring student progress, and to participate in professional development. Increasingly colleges and schools have provided a good deal of their professional training through Web-based applications that faculty and others can use with convenience in their offices and homes. Adjunct faculty, who generally teach a large percentage of online courses and may be geographically dispersed, may depend extensively on access to all of the facilities and services that are normally available to on-site faculty.

A number of colleges such as Western Governors University have moved to attach student advisement and counseling to every course, so that in addition to an instructor each student has someone who can assist with the non-instructional aspects of their education. In some institutions, this student adviser is assigned to a student for his or her entire academic career. In this age of big data and learning analytics, schools and colleges are beginning to provide access to online advisement systems that track student progress. In addition to overall grade and other performance indicators, alert systems have been developed. For example, Rio Salado Community College implemented the Progress and Course Engagement (PACE) system for automated tracking of student progress. Michael Cottam, associate dean for instructional design at Rio Salado, described the development of PACE:

> we crunched data from tens of thousands of students, we found that there are three main predictors of success: the frequency of a student logging into a course; site engagement—whether they read or engage with the course materials online and do practice exercises and so forth; and how many points they are getting on their assignments. All that may *sound* simple, but the statistics we encounter are anything but simple. And we've found that, overwhelmingly, these three factors do act as predictors of success . . .
>
> The reports we generate show green, yellow, and red flags—like a traffic light—so that instructors can easily see who is at risk. We can predict, after the first week of a course, with 70 percent accuracy, whether any given student will complete the course successfully (with a grade of "C" or better). That's our "eighth day" at risk model. A second model includes weekly updates using similar predictive factors.
>
> (Crush, 2011)

Rio Salado instructors can review student engagement at any time throughout the course and data in PACE is maintained on a real-time basis. Several other colleges such as Northern Arizona University and Purdue University have developed similar applications. Northern Arizona University's early warning alert and retention system is called *Grade Performance System (GPS)*. Purdue University's *Course Signals System* is designed to increase student success in the classroom. Both *GPS* and *Course Signals* detect early warning signs and provide interventions that might help students do better in their courses. For further information, readers may wish to refer to the websites of professional organizations for administrative and student support services such as:

- American Association of Collegiate Registrars and Admissions Officers (AACRAO) www.aacrao.org/
- American Counseling Association (ACA) www.counseling.org/
- American College Counseling Association (ACCA) www.collegecounseling.org/
- American College Personnel Association (ACPA) www.myacpa.org/
- Association of College Administration Professionals (ACAP) http://acap.webstarts.com/
- National Academic Advising Association (NACADA) www.nacada.ksu.edu/
- National Association of College and University Business Officers (NACUBO) www.nacubo.org/
- National Association of Student Financial Aid Administrators (NASFAA) www.theacademicportal.com/Pages/AidProfessionals.aspx
- National Association of Student Affairs Professionals (NASAP) www.naspa.org/
- University Professional and Continuing Education Association (UPCEA) http://upcea.edu/

Library and Digital Resources

As mentioned in the introduction to this chapter, libraries have provided a critical support function for millennia. In recent years the nature of this support has changed radically. Books on shelves have given way to digital repositories and virtual information centers that make the world's knowledge only keystrokes away on a laptop or mobile device. Possibly no other academic support function has been more affected by online technology than the library. With the advent of the Internet, libraries around the world have retooled to digitize their collections and to provide a host of media materials including text, photographs, maps, oral histories, and multimedia. All of these can be accessed easily online with a little assistance from an online help service. This retooling has been such that some libraries no longer call themselves libraries and instead use names such as DSpace (Massachusetts Institute of Technology), The Loop (Blackpool and Fylde College), or The Learning Grid (University of Warwick) for part or all of their facilities and services (TeachThought Staff, 2017). The University of Wisconsin at Madison announced plans in 2017 to close 22 of its libraries and create six "hubs" designed to facilitate the work of today's students and scholars. Its plan follows a study that found its professors and students use more research material online and work more frequently in groups. That pattern, the university argues, makes hubs—with better technology and flexible space—a good approach. It is hoped that the change will allow library staff to focus less on space management and more on assisting students and researchers.

Libraries are also digitizing the most popular books in their collections and making them available as e-books. Stanford University's Library makes more than 1.5 million e-books available to students who no longer have to wait for a book to be returned in order to borrow it. In addition to e-books, the periodicals sections of libraries have given way to electronic journal collections. Access to massive databases with millions of records are now routinely provided at most research universities. Instructional software for doing statistical analysis, for simulating lab experiments, or for designing spaces is made available online. The services of reference librarians are supplemented by electronic assistants. Furthermore, all of these repositories and services are increasingly being made available 24 hours a day, 365 days a year for access from student and faculty homes, offices, and mobile devices. It should also be noted that these services, while vital for students enrolled in online education, are being used extensively by students in traditional on ground courses.

Digital resources for teaching and learning pertinent to online education have been established in libraries or other academic service centers. These resources may be stored locally or are made available on the World Wide Web. The job of cataloguing and providing access to these educational resources is critical and when done well provides a treasure trove of educational material. These resources include e-books, case studies, simulations, games, tests, quizzes, assessment tools, presentations (e.g., PowerPoint), and multimedia. While many of these resources exist in local school and college repositories, they also may be uploaded to larger open education resources (OER) that include organizations such as Merlot, MIT's OpenCourseWare Project, and the Creative Commons. With the popularity of flipped classrooms, the posting of lectures and class presentations has become commonplace using college and school repositories, Youtube, podcasting, and other free media websites. Libraries or other academic service centers can provide the facilities and assistance to students and faculty who need to locate these materials. For example, a Youtube search for "analysis of variance" or ANOVA will result in hundreds of videos by faculty and others explaining the intricacies of this statistical procedure. One or more of these can be of great assistance to faculty and instructional designers who no longer need to develop all aspects of a statistics course. This is part of a continuing trend as more faculty integrate freely available content into their courses. And outside of formal course assignments, students are seeking out these materials to help them understand a topic or practice a skill.

For additional information regarding library services and digital resources, readers may wish to examine material available from professional librarian associations such as:

- ALA: American Library Association

  "The American Library Association (ALA) is the oldest and largest library association in the world, providing association information, news, events, and advocacy resources for members, librarians, and library users. Founded on October 6, 1876 during the Centennial Exposition in Philadelphia, the mission of ALA is to provide leadership for the development, promotion, and improvement of library and information services and the profession of librarianship in order to enhance learning and ensure access to information for all." See: www.ala.org/

- AASL: American Association of School Librarians

  The American Association of School Librarians (AASL), a division of the American Library Association, "is the only national professional membership organization focused on the needs of school librarians and the school library community. We serve the needs of more than 7,000 school librarians in the United States, Canada, and around the world." See: www.ala.org/aasl/

- ACRL: Association of College & Research Libraries

  The Association of College and Research Libraries (ACRL) is a division of the American Library Association. ACRL "is a professional association of academic librarians and other interested individuals. It is dedicated to enhancing the ability of academic library and information professionals to serve the information needs of the higher education community and to improve learning, teaching, and research. ACRL is the largest division of the American Library Association (ALA). ACRL currently has a membership of more than 12,000 members, accounting for nearly 20% of the total ALA membership." See: www.ala.org/acrl/

  (USC Libraries Research Guides, 2017)

Policies and Practices for Serving Students With Disabilities

With respect to policy issues associated with online education, most schools and colleges will review bylaws, governance documents, and collective bargaining contracts to insure that no infringements exist when mounting an online education initiative. Policies related to curriculum approval, workload, intellectual property, accreditation compliance, faculty observations, and evaluation generally are reviewed by legal counsel and human resources personnel. If a college or school district has developed a substantial online program, any policy issues should have been reviewed and addressed. If not, they should be.

One of the great benefits of online education is that it has made learning available and accessible to students who because of geography or time commitments were not able to attend traditional schools. In the present day, disabilities are preventing some students from attending online courses as well. In New York State eight lawsuits were filed in federal court in 2017 charging that college websites were inaccessible to blind students and were in violation of the Americans with Disabilities Act (ADA). The lawsuits were part of a growing number of actions involving accessibility and the Internet. Federal law requires that public accommodations be accessible to those with disabilities, and legal battles have long revolved around physical spaces and physical solutions, such as elevators or wheelchair ramps. The plaintiffs in the New York cases claimed that websites are also public spaces and need to be accessible, with things like captions or audio descriptions. Since January 2015, at least 751 lawsuits have been filed over the issue. Thirty-seven colleges have been the subject of federal investigations and have been accused of noncompliance with disability law (Wang, 2017). Advocates for the deaf sued Harvard and MIT in 2015 for failing to caption online lectures, courses, and other educational materials. In 2016, the Department of Justice's civil rights division found that the University of California, Berkeley had violated the ADA by not providing the appropriate accommodations for deaf students for its video lectures and podcasts. The Association of Governing Boards of Colleges and Universities warned in 2011 that many colleges and universities were relegating compliance with ADA mandates to the faculty members who develop online courses. It warned that "erratic and inconsistent compliance may leave many institutions vulnerable to formal complaints or legal action" (Green and Wagner, 2011). At the time of this writing, the cases in New York were still being heard. Whether the plaintiffs will prevail or not is unclear since the Americans with Disabilities Act, written in 1990, makes no mention of the Internet. The lesson here is that whatever online content, and especially course material, is made available, accommodations will likely have to be considered for students with disabilities. Furthermore, it behooves administrators to address this situation positively and consistently to ensure that policies and practices are in place to serve this student population. Box 7.1 provides 20 tips for designing online course materials to comply with ADA requirements.

Box 7.1 20 Tips for Teaching an Accessible Online Course

For course Web Pages, Documents, Images, and Videos

1. Use clear, consistent layouts and organization schemes for presenting content;
2. Structure headings (using style features built into the learning management system, Word, PowerPoint, PDFs, etc.) and use built-in designs/layouts (e.g., for PPT slides);
3. Use descriptive wording for hyperlink text (e.g., "DO-IT Knowledge Base" rather than "click here");
4. Minimize the use of PDFs, especially when presented as an image; make sure the text is accessible by testing to see if you can copy and paste it. Always offer a text-based alternative as well;
5. Provide concise alternative-text descriptions of content presented within images;
6. Use large, bold fonts on uncluttered pages with plain backgrounds;
7. Use color combinations that are high contrast and can be read by those who are colorblind;
8. Make sure all content and navigation is accessible using the keyboard alone;
9. Caption or transcribe video and audio content.

With Respect to Instructional Methods

10. Assume students have a wide range of technology skills and provide options for gaining the technology skills needed for course participation;
11. Present content in multiple ways (e.g., in a combination of text, video, audio, and/or image format);
12. Address a wide range of language skills as you write content (e.g., spell out terms rather than relying on acronyms alone, define terms, avoid or define jargon);
13. Make instructions and expectations clear for activities, projects, and assigned reading;
14. Make examples and assignments relevant to learners with a wide variety of interests and backgrounds;
15. Offer outlines and other scaffolding tools to help students learn;
16. Provide adequate opportunities for practice;
17. Allow adequate time for activities, projects, and tests (e.g., give details of project assignments in the syllabus so that students can start working on them early);
18. Provide feedback on project parts and offer corrective opportunities;
19. Provide options for communicating and collaborating that are accessible to individuals with a variety of disabilities;
20. Provide options for demonstrating learning (e.g., different types of test items, portfolios, presentations, discussions).

Source: Burgstahler, S (2017). ADA compliance for online course design. *EDUCAUSE Review*. Retrieved October 13, 2017 from https://er.educause.edu/articles/2017/1/ada-compliance-for-online-course-design. The text of this article is licensed through the Creative Commons (NC-ND 4.0) and allows others to copy and redistribute the material in any medium or format.

Proctoring in Online Education Environments

As schools and colleges have expanded their online education activities, there have been growing concerns about academic integrity with regard to test taking and other types of assessments. The Higher Education Opportunity Act of 2008 states that an institution offering "distance education" needs to have processes in place for verifying student identity to ensure that the student who registers for a class is the same student who participates in the class, completes assignments, and receives the academic credit. The various regional accreditation agencies have also established guidelines for assuring academic integrity, most of which echo the Higher Education Opportunity Act. To address this concern, online education programs have developed a number of approaches including:

1. Requiring students to come to the school or college to take an examination in person;
2. Requiring students to take an examination under the supervision of a proctor at some location that is convenient;
3. Using video cameras to observe/monitor students taking an examination.

A number of companies specialize in providing proctoring services for online education programs. One of the more successful companies, ProctorU, uses a multi-step step process to establish a student's identity:

1. A live proctor sees the student via a webcam, checks the student's ID and takes a photo to verify the student's identity;
2. Techniques based on fraud protection and banking standards are employed to ask the student a series of questions;
3. Keystroke analysis software creates a profile for the student.

(ProctorU, 2017)

Schools and colleges have always established policies related to academic integrity. The online education environment provides unique challenges in this regard and these should be addressed accordingly.

Policies for Contracting Out Academic and Student Services

Schools and colleges are showing increased interest in contracting out academic and student services to third party providers generally referred to as online program managers (OPMs) or online program providers. As mentioned in Chapter 5, these arrangements can be very beneficial especially for institutions that need to get a jump-start on an online education program. However, such arrangements should be entered into carefully and with the full involvement of all stakeholders, especially faculty. There have been several instances such as one at Eastern Michigan University where faculty have objected to supporting courses and programs developed by OPMs (Supiano, 2017). A report by The Century Foundation identified three specific cautions related to OPMs: sharing student data with private marketers; honesty in advertisement in terms of who developed and may be teaching the courses; and the for-profit mindset of OPMs. A major conclusion of this report was:

> the involvement of a third-party—particularly a profit-seeking entity—in providing services so intertwined with the actual teaching and learning . . . presents potential risks to quality and value in the education.
>
> (The Century Foundation, 2017)

Policies and guidelines should be in place that specify scope, deliverables, costs, and evaluations of OPM arrangements. Institutional governing bodies including college or faculty councils should be involved in developing these policies and in the procurement process.

There are a number of other policies mentioned earlier that need to be considered. Trustees and senior administrators need to make sure that a review of these policies is undertaken before moving forward with any online education initiatives. Readers wanting to take a more in depth look at how policies involving online education have developed might consider *Online Education Policy and Practice* (2017) authored by Anthony G. Picciano, and published by Routledge/Taylor & Francis.

Summary

This chapter examined academic, administrative, and student support services for online education. It expanded on the ideas and material presented in Chapter 5 on planning for online education and emphasized that implementation of online education starts with good leadership. A model for developing the proper infrastructure was also provided and served as a thread for the remainder of the chapter. Critical components of the model included:

- Management information system;
- Course/learning management system;
- User portal;
- Library and digital resources;
- Academic, administrative, and student services.

The chapter looked at policy issues related to online learning and specifically at issues related to students with disabilities.

Further Reading/Case Studies

Readers may wish to refer to the Appendix A—Case Studies in Online Education specifically to:

Embry-Riddle Aeronautical University
Rio Salado Community College
University of Wisconsin Milwaukee
Virtual High School Global Consortium
Western Governors University

References

The Century Foundation. (2017). *The private side of public education.* Retrieved November 18, 2017 from https://tcf.org/content/report/private-side-public-higher-education/

Crush, M. (2011, December 14). Monitoring the PACE of student learning: Analytics at Rio Salado Community College. *Campus Technology.* Retrieved November 1, 2017 from http://campustechnology.com/Articles/2011/12/14/Monitoring-the-PACE-of-Student-Learning-Analytics-at-Rio-Salado-College.aspx?Page=1

Green, K. C., & Wagner, E. (2011, January/February). *Online education: Where is it going? What should boards know?* Association of Governing Boards of Colleges and Univeristies Website. Retrieved October 13, 2017 from www.agb.org/trusteeship/2011/januaryfebruary/online-education-where-is-it-going-what-should-boards-know

ProctorU. (2017). *Simple testing solutions for institutions.* Retrieved November 18, 2017 from www.proctoru.com/institutions/

Supiano, B. (2017, November 15). Faculty members at one more university push back at online programs. *The Chronicle of Higher Education*. Retrieved November 18, 2017 from www.chronicle.com/article/Faculty-Members-at-One-More/241788

TeachThought Staff. (2017). The library of the future will probably look something like this. *TeachThought Website*. Retrieved October 12, 2017 from www.teachthought.com/literacy/the-library-of-the-future-will-probably-look-something-like-this/

USC Libraries Research Guides. (2017). *Library and information science professional associations*. University of Southern California Website. Retrieved October 12, 2017 from http://libguides.usc.edu/libsci/associations

Wang, V. (2017, October 11). College websites must accommodate disabled students, lawsuit says. *New York Times*. Retrieved October 13, 2017 from www.nytimes.com/2017/10/11/nyregion/college-websites-disabled.html

Chapter 8

Navigating the Current Landscape—Blending It All Together!

The Minerva Project, based in San Francisco, was established in 2012 to provide a liberal arts and sciences education to motivated students. The project admitted its first class in Fall 2014. Minerva, perhaps the first of its kind, was founded by entrepreneur Ben Nelson, whose aim was to provide an alternative to the traditional liberal arts college. Its teaching model is based largely on seven guiding principles as follows:

- Being Unconventional
- Being Human
- Being Confident
- Being Thoughtful
- Being Selective
- Being Authentic
- Being Driven

(Minerva, 2017a)

Minerva has a highly selective admissions process that includes assessments, interviews, and writing samples. It is a for-profit entity and has received private funding to build its programs and foregoes any form of federal financial aid or assistance. Minerva raised an initial $25 million from investors such as the venture capital firm, Benchmark. Tuition, housing, and student fees total approximately $30,000 per year (Minerva, 2017b).

Minerva employs a blended learning model combining face-to-face and online activities. The model is based on a proprietary Active Learning Forum platform designed especially for Minerva that has a number of customized, built-in pedagogical features. Professors conduct sessions via live video, and use interactive learning features such as collaborative breakout clusters, debates, quizzes, polls, dynamic document creation, and real-time simulations. The model uses freely available content from such entities such as Khan Academy. All courses are taught as intimate seminars with classes maximized at 19 students.

An important feature of the Minerva model is that there are no academic departments and the curriculum focuses on interdisciplinary study and global cultural experiences. For the first two semesters, students meet as a group and take courses at the main campus in San Francisco. Each of the succeeding six semesters students attend classes at campuses in different cities such as Hong Kong, New York, Berlin, and Buenos Aires. At the time of this writing it was too early to evaluate the experiences of Minerva's first cohort of students, but the program appears to be a well-thought out alternative to a traditional liberal arts education. Online technology is the integral facilitator of its pedagogical approaches, its curriculum, and its global context.

Minerva is an appropriate introduction to this chapter because it was conceived as a very different education model focusing on active student learning and built on blending several of the most current online technologies into an integrated whole to provide a unique instructional experience. This chapter picks up where Chapter 2 left off and examines the Fourth Wave of Online Education. This chapter looks at the current landscape of online education and focuses on the merging of blended learning with MOOC technology as well as a number of other approaches that enhance instruction such as:

- big data and learning analytics;
- adaptive or differentiated learning;
- expansion of competency-based instruction;
- open educational resources (OER);
- interactive media (simulations, multiuser virtual environments, and games);
- mobile technology.

All of these technologies have been evolving over a number of years and have begun to gain acceptance as important additions to the online education milieu.

When the Fourth Wave of Online Education began in 2014, MOOC courses were growing at a significant rate. The total number of MOOCs grew 201% in 2014, and were forecasted to grow at a compound annual growth rate of 56.61% by 2018. In 2017, the five major MOOC providers based on registered users were:

Coursera (U.S)	27	million	registered	users
edX (U.S.)	11	million	registered	users
XuetangX (China)	7	million	registered	users
FutureLearn (U.K.)	6.3	million	registered	users
Udacity (U.S.)	6	million	registered	users

(Class Central, 2017a)

It should be noted that the vast majority of MOOC courses were and still are not taken for college credit. In fact, in an article published in 2017 by Class Central, a website that follows MOOC development, the announcement was made that two universities (MIT and Georgia Tech) would begin accepting MOOC credits for coursework. At the time of this writing, both universities were limiting this policy to two specific courses. A total of 27 students completed the MIT course, with 4 students dropping out very early in the course. At Georgia Tech, 54 out of 59 students completed the online course (Class Central, 2017b). Blended courses for credit have become quite common at all levels of education and increasingly are the instructional modalities of choice among faculty and instructional designers. The futures of both blended learning and MOOC technologies are bright but will be brighter still as they merge. As mentioned in Chapter 2, Daphne Koller, one of the founders of the MOOC company, Coursera, in commenting on the future of her company, stated that it would not restrict itself to being a provider of entire courses but would become as well a provider of pedagogically sophisticated instructional materials that could be used in blended online formats. Her hope was that Coursera and other MOOC providers might rebrand themselves as producers of high-quality content giving faculty options in using the materials (Chafkin, 2013).

The Fourth Wave of online education technologies has a good deal of appeal to administrators, faculty, and instructional designers because it allows flexibility in their decision making about the use of technology in their academic programs. Pat James, Executive Director of the multimillion dollar California Community College Online Education Initiative, in discussing the future of online education and MOOC technology, commented:

> the opportunity we have now is one that can put everything that we know works into one solution. This project will have all of the pieces funded—a great common course

> management system, instructional design support, 24/7 help desk support, orientation for students, professional development for faculty, standards for design, and standards for qualifications, mentors, coaches and student services. Everything we have fought for, piece by piece, can happen here in one grand plan . . . My recent foray into the MOOCs showed me what our university colleagues don't know. I think our work will help them, too. All of the students of California stand to gain. It's always been about access and now it can be about success, too.
>
> (James, 2014)

While many colleges, especially those in the for-profit sector, will continue to provide fully online courses and programs, most colleges are looking to add or blend online and rich-MOOC style content into a variety of new formats at the program and/or course level. Many different models are evolving that are specific to the level of instruction, the discipline, the preferences of faculty and instructional designers, and the nature of the student body. The emphasis, particularly in the United States, is on pedagogical value as well as cost benefits. In other countries, especially those where there are not enough colleges and universities to serve growing populations, cost efficiencies as provided by the pure MOOC model are and will continue to be significant drivers of academic and course development. As a result of this next step in online education, MOOC providers are seeing competition grow intense as new companies come on the scene and as some colleges use their own resources to develop MOOC materials. In 2013, there were a handful of companies providing MOOC services; today there are over seven thousand (Shah, 2017).

Big Data and Learning Analytics

Big data and learning analytics comprise the next generation of decision making applications and software that has been evolving for the past 30 or more years as part of database management systems. The decision-support software of the 1980s coupled with the concept of data-driven decision making popularized in the 1990s has evolved into big data systems that rely on software approaches referred to as analytics. Big data is a generic term that assumes that the information or database system(s) used as a main storage facility is capable of storing large quantities of data longitudinally and down to very specific transactions. For example, college student record keeping systems have always maintained outcomes information such as students' grades in each course. This information has been used by institutional researchers to study patterns of student performance over time, usually from one semester to another or one year to another. In a big data scenario, data would be collected for each student transaction in a course, especially if the course is delivered electronically online. Every student entry on a course assessment, discussion board entry, blog entry, or wiki activity could be recorded, generating thousands of transactions per student per course. Furthermore, this data would be collected in real or near real time, as it is transacted, and then analyzed to suggest courses of action. Analytics software is the class of software applications that assist in this analysis.

The generic definition of analytics is similar to data-driven decision making. It is the science of examining data to draw conclusions and, when used in decision making, to present paths or courses of action. In recent years, however, the definition of analytics has been refined to incorporate elements of operations research such as decision trees and strategy maps to establish predictive models and to determine probabilities for certain courses of action. It uses data mining software to establish decision processes that convert data into actionable insight, uncover patterns, alert and respond to issues and concerns, and plan for the future. This might seem to be an overly complicated definition, but the term "analytics" has been used in many different ways in recent years and has become part of the buzzword jargon that sometimes emanates from new technology applications and products. Alias (2011) defined four different types of analytics that could apply to instruction including web analytics, learning analytics, academic analytics, and action analytics. The trade journal, *Infoworld*, referred to analytics as:

> One of the buzzwords around business intelligence software [that] . . . has been through the linguistic grinder, with vendors and customers using it to describe very different functions.
>
> The term can cause confusion for enterprises, especially as they consider products from vendors who use analytics to mean different things.
>
> (Kirk, 2006)

Goldstein and Katz (2005) in a study of academic analytics admitted that they struggled with coming up with a name and definition that was appropriate for their work. They stated that they adopted the term "academic analytics" for their study but that it was an "imperfect label."

What is critical to the definition of analytics is the use of data to determine courses of action and potentially to substitute software findings for human judgment and experience, especially in applications with a high volume of transactions (Ford, 2015). Common examples of analytics applications are e-commerce companies such as amazon.com or Netflix examining Web site traffic, purchases, or navigation patterns to determine which customers are more or less likely to buy particular products (e.g., books, movies). Using these patterns, companies send notifications to customers of new products as they become available.

Big data concepts and analytics can be applied to a variety of higher education administrative and instructional applications including recruitment and admissions processing, financial planning, donor tracking, and student performance monitoring. The remainder of this section will focus on teaching and learning, and hence will specifically examine *learning* analytics.

To take advantage of big data and learning analytics, it is most desirable that transaction processing be electronic rather than manual. Traditional face-to-face instruction can support traditional data-driven decision-making processes; however, to move into the more extensive and time-sensitive learning analytics applications, it is important that instructional transactions are collected as they occur. This would be possible within a course management/learning management system (CMS/LMS). Most CMS/LMSs provide constant monitoring of student activity whether they are responses, postings on a discussion board, accesses of reading material, completions of quizzes, or some other assessment. Using the full capabilities of a basic CMS/LMS, a robust 15-week online course would generate thousands of transactions per student. Real-time recording and analysis of these transactions could then be used to feed a learning analytics application. Not waiting for the end of a marking period or semester to record performance measures is critical to this type of application. Monitoring student transactions on a real-time basis allows for real-time decisions. Instructors may take actions or intervene in time to alert or assist students. A CMS/LMS or a similar software platform therefore becomes critical for collecting and feeding this data into a "big" database for processing by a learning analytics software application. These instructional transactions should also be integrated with other resources such as student, course, and faculty data from the college information systems. Analytics software can then be used to distinguish patterns that are used to develop guidelines and rules for subsequent courses of action (see Figure 8.1). It should be emphasized that the accuracy and timeliness of data are required for the success of the learning analytics application. Examples of how learning analytics are being used to address student performance, outcomes, and persistence include:

1. Monitoring individual student performance;
2. Disaggregating student performance by selected characteristics such as major, year of study, ethnicity, etc.;

3. Preventing attrition from a course or program;
4. Analyzing the effectiveness of standard assessment techniques and instruments such as quizzes and exams.

As mentioned in Chapter 7, several early adopters of learning analytics systems have received a lot of favorable attention. Rio Salado Community College, Northern Arizona University, and Purdue University have developed applications that use learning analytics to provide early warning systems and recommend interventions that might help students do better in their courses. However, it is likely that learning analytics may have more appeal and be more widely adopted in the K–12 environment where there is much more emphasis on assessment and student outcomes. Furthermore, there is a lot more curriculum uniformity across K–12 school districts than in higher education, making commercial development of analytics software easier and more financially viable. Ananda Gunawardena (2017), in a review of learning analytics, cites several case studies in K–12 schools districts using Edmodo, a K–12 social learning network that connects learners, teachers, and parents with educational resources across the world. In one case study, the Chula Vista Elementary School District (CVESD) used Edmodo

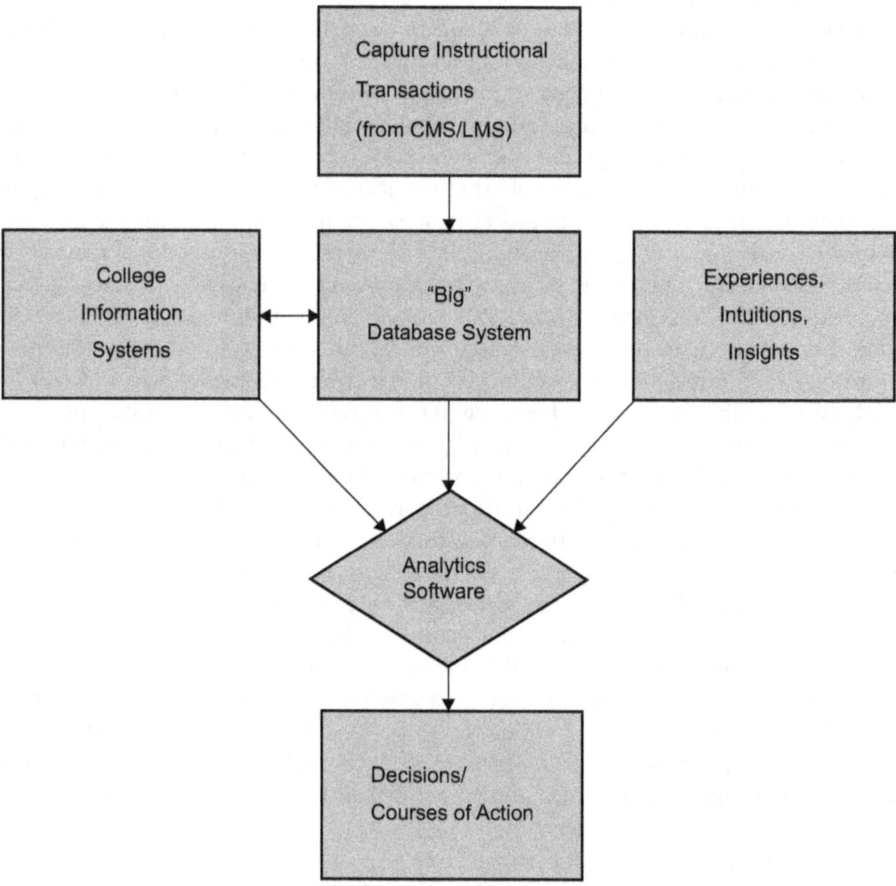

Figure 8.1 Learning Analytics Flow Model

to develop a program to help improve learning and engagement for English language learners (ELLs). As reported:

> The program served 29,000 students, 1500 teachers, and 47 schools. Administrators and teachers used data visualization on CVESD network activities and on the Edmodo teacher connection. This resulted in a well-supported, yet grassroots adoption of Edmodo district wide. Teachers, students, and parents quickly adopted the platform and within 12 months 100% of teachers and 75% of students in the district were registered users. Using Edmodo as their social learning platform, CVESD was able to focus on closing the learning gap with ELLs by providing personalized support using data analytics, as ELL students often require individual attention from a teacher to increase the chance of success.
>
> (Gunawardena, 2017)

In another case study, Edmodo helped the Chesterfield County Public Schools (CCPS) district in Virginia to support a strategic plan to scale blended learning. In 2012, CCPS identified a need for a teaching and learning platform that could meet a variety of communication and instructional needs. CCPS chose Edmodo as its learning platform for a number of reasons including its learning analytics capabilities. As reported:

> The project involved 58,800 students, 4200 teachers, and 42 schools. With Edmodo's free platform, CCPS now has a successfully executed blended learning strategy with increased student engagement and near-district-wide adoption. Building on this momentum, CCPS has scaled its blended learning efforts in the 2013–2014 school year through an expanded digital ecosystem in which Edmodo serves as the hub. The use of Edmodo data was instrumental to the success of this effort.
>
> (Gunawardena, 2017)

These cases are not isolated or unique examples but are indicative of a trend that is moving quickly in K–12 schools. The Edmodo website claims more than 85 million users around the world as members of its services (Edmodo, 2017). Granted, many—perhaps a large majority of these members—may just be curiosity seekers. Nevertheless, the large number of people interested in Edmodo services is to be noted.

There are a number of concerns with the development of big data/learning analytics applications for education. First, in order for big data and learning analytics applications to function well, data need to be accurate and timely. As a result, their benefits are maximized in fully online courses rather than in blended or traditional, face-to face courses.

Second, there are not enough individuals trained in the use of big data and analytics so schools, colleges, and universities seeking to develop big data/learning analytics applications have found it difficult to locate experienced personnel. Because of the dearth of expertise, there is a tendency to use instructional templates that are integrated into course/learning management systems. These, although convenient, may be overly simplistic. It is likely that many schools and colleges will opt to contract with commercial vendors for these services.

Third, and perhaps the most serious concern is that since learning analytics requires massive amounts of data collected on students and integrated with other databases, educators need to be careful about privacy, data profiling, and the rights of students when recording their individual behaviors. While most school and college classes have always evaluated student performance and academic behavior, learning analytics takes the recording of behavior to another level and scope. As well-intentioned as learning analytics might be in terms of helping students succeed, this "big data" approach may also be seen as "big brother is watching" and as an invasion of privacy that some students would rather not have imposed upon them. Precautions need to be taken to ensure that the extensive data collections of student instructional transactions are not abused in ways that potentially hurt individuals. Readers may wish to review the material on privacy issues presented in Chapter 5 and Appendix E.

Regardless of these concerns, learning analytics is beginning to play an increasingly important role in teaching and learning at all levels of instruction.

Adaptive Learning

The work of Patrick Suppes and Richard Atkinson during the 1960s and 1970s at The Institute for Mathematical Studies in the Social Sciences at Stanford University was introduced in Chapter 2 of this book. Their work in developing computer-assisted instruction (CAI) was a major breakthrough in the use of computers in education. Computer software programs were developed that could teach and maintain records of student progress. Although this early programmed instruction was developed in the drill and practice style, Suppes and Atkinson set the stage for the future of computerized instructional systems. By the 1990s, the successors to programs they developed mostly for K–12 were being referred to as intelligent learning systems (ILS) and were far more sophisticated than the earlier CAI models. ILS took advantage of digital hardware advances that made greater use of graphics and media to provide more stimulating instruction activities. They also operated within database software systems that facilitated the maintenance of more detailed student performance indicators. ILSs continued to evolve into what are now termed adaptive, differentiated, or personalized learning. These systems take advantage of learning analytics and artificial intelligence software to monitor student progress and performance very closely and are able to provide timely adjustments to the presentation of instructional material. Adaptive learning systems can be customized to the personal needs of each individual student and are frequently referred to as personalized learning systems. As described by one adaptive learning software provider:

> [Adaptive learning] . . . monitors how the student interacts with the system and learns, leveraging the enormous quantities of data generated by a student's online interactions with ordinary (textbook-like) and extraordinary (game- and social-media-like) content, with teachers and peers, and with the system itself. It assesses not only what a student knows now, but also determines what activities and interactions, developed by which providers, delivered in what sequence and medium, most greatly increase the possibility of that student's academic success.
>
> (Kuntz, 2010)

Like learning analytics, adaptive learning systems are finding a growing market in K–12 education. They are particularly popular in "credit-recovery" programs where high school students make up courses that they failed to complete and need for graduation. Adaptive learning systems also are growing in popularity in higher education. These systems can be used as stand-alone applications, with a teacher minimally involved, in a blended learning environment where students spend some time in a traditional class, or as a tutorial supplement to a course. They are also being integrated into textbook materials and course and learning management systems such as Blackboard and Desire2Learn. Adaptive learning approaches are enjoying a degree of success in subject areas such as mathematics that require a good deal of scaffolding or building upon previous skills and knowledge in order to advance to a next level of understanding and mastery. MOOC providers increasingly are using adaptive learning as part of their course materials as well.

A number of colleges, universities, school districts, textbook publishers, and large education software companies such as Pearson, McGraw-Hill, and Blackboard have agreements with adaptive learning providers. CCKF, Inc. (Dublin, Ireland) has contracts for its Realize^{it} adaptive software with colleges and universities in the United States including the University of Central Florida, the University of Texas, and Indiana University. Its largest contract is with the for-profit Career Education Corporation where Realize^{it} is being used in 300 sections of courses in English, mathematics, and business management (Riddell, 2013).

Knowillage Systems (Vancouver), the creators of the adaptive learning engine LeaP, was acquired by the CMS/LMS provider Desire2Learn. LeaP enables teachers to personalize learning paths and specializes in using natural language processing techniques and analytics to assist students struggling with course material.

The publishing company Macmillan entered into a partnership with the adaptive learning companies Knewton and PrepU. The latter focuses on college level biology, nursing, chemistry, and psychology courses.

John Wiley & Sons, Inc. and Snapwiz, a Fremont California-based company that specializes in adaptive and personalized learning solutions, announced the launch of WileyPLUS with ORION, the initial offering to come out of their partnership. Aimed at giving students highly personalized experiences that improve learning outcomes, the solution goes further in creating adaptive, collaborative, and interactive learning spaces than anything currently on the market. WileyPLUS with ORION will be included at no extra cost to students using WileyPLUS across some of Wiley's leading titles in subjects such as Introduction to Business, Introduction to Psychology, Financial Accounting, and Anatomy and Physiology.

As noted in Chapter 4, the research on adaptive learning is expanding and early results in terms of student achievement are positive (Dziuban, Moskal, Cassisi, & Fawcett, 2016; Bowen, Chingos, Lack, & Nygren, 2012). A recent study by Dziuban, Moskal, Jonson, and Evans (2017) examined the issue of student time to completion of a course. Adaptive systems by their nature generally allow students to proceed at their own pace. They can speed up or slow down the pace of instruction as they proceed through the adaptive system course or module. These researchers collected data from the University of Central Florida and Colorado Technical College. Their conclusion was that:

> Adaptive learning is an alternative that has the potential to provide some learning latitude for students living in poverty, but also for those who face the pressures of the contemporary world of work and family responsibility. Adaptive learning also provides an alternative that takes into account and can incorporate the knowledge that adult students have from attendance in previous institutions, workplace training and development, and military training. The curriculum is altered into modular structures so that students can navigate a course according to the demands of their educational needs and lifestyles. Adaptive design provides to students who fall behind multiple options for getting back on track. In fact, within certain constraints, there is much less chance of falling behind in adaptive learning. Although there are many confounding factors for students living in scarcity, the big one is time to accomplish the work. Fundamentally, adaptive learning is about time (Adam, 2004; Norberg, Dziuban, & Moskal, 2011). Time to reach competency. Time to reflect. Time to assess. Time to practice and revise. Time to complete.
>
> (Dziuban et al., 2017)

Given the major concerns in higher education about student attrition/persistence, time to degree, and costs, adaptive learning is an approach that may be appropriate for addressing these issues.

In K–12, an interesting project is underway at the University of Florida using adaptive learning software. *Algebra Nation* is an online resource that helps students master Algebra 1—a gateway math course in middle school, high school, and college. *Algebra Nation* provides 24-hour access to high-quality instructional videos, workbooks, collaborative learning tools, and adaptive assessments and support. *Algebra Nation* also completely customizes its content to the academic standards of each of its partner states and works with local universities to validate their alignment for each state (Algebra Nation, 2017). Currently *Algebra Nation* provides custom-built resources in a number of states including Florida, Mississippi, Michigan, Alabama and New York. Researchers at the University of Florida's Virtual Learning Lab are presently conducting a three-year study of *Algebra Nation* software being used by more than 3,000 teachers and 200,000 math students from all 67 Florida school districts; the students are mostly ninth graders gearing up for the mandatory end-of-course exam in Algebra 1. At the time of this writing, the study was ongoing, but early results were indicating positive student outcomes (Beal, 2017).

Adaptive learning has definitely found its place as an enhancement to existing course modalities (fully online, face-to-face, blended), although its greatest popularity at the time of this writing is probably in blended learning environments. In all likelihood, its popularity will continue in various modes for the next decade and beyond.

Competency-Based Online Education

Competency-based education requires a student to demonstrate competency(ies) in a subject area in order to receive credit for a course rather than simply attending or participating in formal class (online or face-to-face) activities. Competencies can be demonstrated by performing successfully on pre-established assessments that include testing, essay writing, and other activities.

The Western Governors University (WGU) was conceived in 1995, chartered in 1996 as a private nonprofit university in 1997, and began accepting students in 1999. It has evolved into a national university, serving more than 86,000 online students from all 50 states. In addition, a number of other states including Indiana, Texas, Missouri, Tennessee, and Washington have created state-affiliated WGUs that offer similar programs and curricula. The most interesting copy of WGU is probably Southern New Hampshire University (SNHU). In 2009, SNHU was a small New England university with 2,000 residential students when a new president initiated a competency-based online program and enrollments grew to almost 40,000 in five years (Kahn, 2014). While WGU and SNHU have received much of the attention, other colleges and universities such as the University of Wisconsin, Northern Arizona University, the University of Texas, and Capella have also launched competency-based programs. Whether competency-based online education is an important model that will flourish in the years to come or is a modest alternative that will have a limited student market is difficult to determine at this time.

While schools have been delivering competency-based education offline for decades, the online model developed by WGU provides a convenience that has a lot of appeal to adult learners (Wiese, 2014). Many of these adult learners work full-time and their goals for higher education are primarily career-oriented. Others are college stopouts who already have some college credits and who see a competency-based online program as a way to finish a degree. International students who live in countries with limited access to higher education are attracted to competency-based online programs as well, especially when offered by an accredited American institution.

On the other hand, competency-based programs have been criticized for giving credit for what students already know (Neem, 2011). In addition, low graduation rates (O'Shaughnessy, 2012) and very high student to faculty ratios (Career Index, 2015) at schools like WGU are reasons for concern. However, the impressive enrollment growths at WGU and SNHU cannot be ignored. Whether such programs will expand extensively throughout higher education in the foreseeable future is questionable. It is quite possible that a number of competency-based providers will partner with corporate, public, and private entities to develop customized programs that align competencies with industry needs. In all likelihood competency-based online programs will grow for a limited market of working adults and international students.

At the time of this writing, the U.S. Department of Education's Office of Inspector General had released the results of an audit of Western Governors University, with negative findings that could threaten the University and its financial aid eligibility. Citing concerns about an inadequate faculty role—which the university contests—the Inspector General called for the U.S. Department of Education to make WGU pay back at least $713 million in federal financial aid. The final audit report also stated that the nonprofit university should be ineligible to receive any more federal aid payments. In 2017, Western Governors University was appealing the Office of Inspector General's findings.

Open Educational Resources

The open source movement is one of the most interesting aspects of the Internet. As more and more people use the Internet, software and applications are being made available and shared freely among online communities. The Internet is such a convenient and user-friendly medium that many people give away freely much of what they produce on it. In the early days of computer programming (the 1950s and early 1960s) a culture of sharing existed among coders and other technical people. One of the early programming languages, FORTRAN (short for *Formula Translation*) was built on the idea of storing and using subroutines that could be utilized across many programs. Developed by a team of engineers at IBM led by John Backus, FORTRAN was one of the first compiler languages and perhaps the most popular of its time because of the efficiency with which code in the form of subroutines could be exchanged. FORTRAN programmers typically made a copy of a subroutine on a magnetic disk, tape or a deck of Hollerith cards, and gave it away to others with similar applications. While many of these subroutines were small helpful applications, perhaps to improve the speed of sorting a file or to connect more efficiently one computing device to another, there was also some large-scale "freeware" available. It is only natural that in the present day, the ubiquity of the Internet has spurred a movement toward open source software such as Linux, Adobe Reader, Google products, Moodle, and iPad apps. The same has happened for software designed for online instruction.

Open educational resources (OER) are electronic resources available for free or for reduced costs for use in teaching and learning. A series of surveys by the Babson College Survey Research Group concluded that OER are slowly growing in popularity but that faculty need assistance and support in locating appropriate material (Seaman & Seaman, 2017). OER include a wide array of materials such as textbooks, reading material (e.g., case studies), simulations, games, tests, quizzes, assessment tools, presentations (e.g., PowerPoint), and multimedia. OER materials are provided by faculty, instructional designers, and non-profit and commercial entities that are willing to share their work and intellectual property with others. Many faculty put their lectures on Youtube for free access by other faculty and students. For example, a Youtube search for "quantum mechanics" will result in thousands of videos of lectures and entire courses by faculty explaining this complex topic. With the recent advent of flipped classrooms, the posting of lectures and class presentations using Youtube, podcasting, and other free media websites has become commonplace. Websites such as MERLOT provide large repositories of materials that faculty, students, and instructional designers can access freely. The MERLOT project (www.merlot.org) began in 1997, when the California State University Center for Distributed Learning (CSU-CDL at www.cdl.edu) decided to provide a vehicle that allowed faculty to share course materials. The MERLOT collection consists of tens of thousands of discipline-specific learning materials, learning exercises, and content webpages together with associated comments, and bookmark collections, all intended to enhance the teaching experience. All materials added to MERLOT go through a peer-review screening process to ensure a degree of quality. All of these items have been contributed by the MERLOT community members, who have either authored the materials themselves or who have discovered the materials, found them useful, and wished to share their enthusiasm for the materials with others in the teaching and learning community (MERLOT, 2017).

OpenStax, a non-profit OER publisher based out at Rice University, makes available electronic textbooks for courses at significantly reduced prices. OpenStax started operations in 2012 and has produced 20 electronic textbooks for college and Advanced Placement (AP) courses.

Course developers such as Khan Academy are also making much of their content available online for free. Khan Academy was founded by Salmon Khan in 2005 and offers entire courses as well as practice exercises, instructional videos, and other materials that enable learners to study at their own pace in and outside of the classroom. Khan videos especially are very well done and are used by educators at all levels from K–12 through graduate school. Its development partners include NASA, the California Academy of Sciences, the Museum of Modern Art, and MIT (Khan Academy, 2017).

As a result of OER facilities such as those just mentioned, faculty and instructional designers no longer need to develop all aspects of a course, but can instead search for appropriate course content and integrate it as needed. There is every indication that this trend will continue and accelerate as more faculty integrate freely available content into their courses. The OER movement will serve to spur the development of online education especially blended learning.

It should be mentioned that while most textbook authors still work with traditional publishing companies and receive royalties, there are a growing number who make their books available as free resources on the Internet. Perhaps one of the most critical questions related to the OER movement is: how do the traditional textbook publishers adjust or compete with the OER movement? In many cases, they are trying to integrate their content with some limited OER. While publishing companies are still profitable and authors still receive royalties, but traditional printed books are giving way to e-books that can be purchased or rented at much less expense. The purchase or rental of an eBook can include access to other free, Web-based materials and media. These "accompanying" websites enhance the textbook so that it resembles an online course with each chapter equivalent to a weekly class session or module. PowerPoint presentations, video lectures, and assessments are now routinely found on the websites of major college textbooks. This will suffice for the near future, but further down the road textbook publishers will have to rethink their traditional book model. Simply transferring the content to electronic form will likely not suffice. Faculty and instructional designers will look to assemble course materials from the best possible and freely available OERs.

Interactive Media: Simulations, Multiuser Virtual Environments, and Educational Games

Interactive media refer to any media-based learning activity that allows students to engage with the material (i.e., manipulate, make decisions, alter outcomes) as opposed to passive media such as video or film that only allow watching and listening. In this section, the term interactive media will refer to the trio of simulations, multiuser virtual environments (MUVE), and games, all of which hold great promise for online education. Before continuing, defining these three terms is in order.

Simulations attempt to copy real life processes, environments, or procedures in a virtual form that allows students to manipulate them and see the results of their actions. Scientific experiments, ecological systems, and historical or current events can be duplicated by using computer simulation models to represent the real-life situations. For instance, a simulation at McGill University called *The Open Orchestra* gives music students the feel of playing with a full orchestra in order to familiarize them with being surrounded by the sounds of different musical instruments. In chemistry classes, reactions can be simulated so that students can immediately and safely see the result of adding a chemical or changing its amount or potency. In fact, a good deal of science research today in areas such as astronomy depends extensively upon simulated processes and environments. As a result, the move to simulations in science courses is generally accepted and even encouraged.

Multiuser virtual environments or MUVEs provide virtual environments in which students can participate in a variety of activities with other students. A generic MUVE such as *Second Life* provides the user with tools for developing and manipulating avatars in virtual environments. It leaves the nature of the interactions and activities to the imaginations of the participants. A teacher, for example, might assign a group project activity utilizing a *Second Life* experience. Project themes related to identity, gender, and race can take on interesting meanings in a MUVE. Proponents argue that the freedom to develop and manipulate avatars in a virtual environment unleashes a plethora of creativity on the part of the users that can be beneficial within a wide range of educational activities.

Educational games use the challenge of a competitive digital environment to teach content and/or skills. Games, as entertainment for the general populace, have become incredibly popular. According to the Entertainment Software Association (2017), 2.6 billon people worldwide play electronic games. Sixty-five percent of U.S households are home to at least one person who plays three or more hours of video games a week, and Americans spent $30.4 billion on video games, hardware, and accessories in 2016. It is only natural that game technology found its way into instruction. Clark Aldrich, founder of Clark Aldrich Designs, a company that builds simulations and games, estimates that every medical student is likely to encounter a game or simulation in the classroom, as well as about 80% of M.B.A. students, 40% of undergraduates, and 20% of high school students (Wecker, 2012). Educational games are particularly useful in presenting problem-solving scenarios that require critical-thinking where students use cognitive, analytical, and reflective process skills. Material is presented in game format so that students compete with one another or with the computer. A classic example of an educational game that has been popular in economics and business programs for many years is to have students compete with one another as traders in the stock market over some period of months to see who can maximize an initial investment of "play money." Today, in the immediacy of the online environment, this game takes on whole new dimensions as trading activity can be monitored on a minute by minute basis, across time zones, and across stock markets. Similar games representing real-life situations or case studies are also becoming popular in a number of other professional programs such as health (e.g., dealing with an emergency situation) and education (e.g., developing a school district budget with competing constituents). Gaming has been integrated into K–12 education for many decades, however, the Internet provides a whole new vehicle for their use by teachers and students. *Tech & Learning* (see Box 8.1) regularly lists gaming websites for K–12 education. Ariel D. Anbar, professor in the School of Earth and Space and Exploration at Arizona State University, together with Lev Horodyski, an instructional designer, have developed a very

Box 8.1 Popular Educational Games for K–12 Students

Funbrain—One of the most popular educational gaming sites for K–8 students; covers a variety of subjects. www.funbrain.com/

Game Classroom—Excellent, safe, teacher-approved, state-standard-aligned games for grades K–6. Also, lots of teacher resources, including videos, lesson plans, worksheets, and more. www.gameclassroom.com/

Minecraft—For K–12 students and based on the popular Lego products. https://minecraft.net/en-us/

Gameaquarium—Great site for games for kids K–6 in all types of subjects. Videos, eBooks, and teacher resources can be found here as well. www.gamequarium.com/

Braineos—Site where games are based on flash cards. A registered user can include their own study lists and flash cards in the games. www.braineos.com/

Tucoola—Wonderful site for skill-building games for younger kids where parents can track their progress. www.tucoola.com/en

iCivics—Games designed to engage high school students in critical thinking. www.icivics.org/games?gclid=EAIaIQobChMImbnmvZiJ1wIVjFmGCh0Dxw-wEAMYASAAEgJYm_D_BwE

What2Learn—Excellent site for educational games where a teacher can track students' progress through a paid account. Users can create custom-made games as well. www.what2learn.com/

Abcya—Great site for elementary students that covers a wide variety of subjects. Also has educational apps for mobile devices. www.abcya.com/

Source: Several of the above were provided by *Tech & Learning*. www.techlearning.com/default.aspx?tabid=100&entryid=3268

well-done game, called *HabWorlds* which stands for Habitable Worlds. As described in a recent *Chronicle of Higher Education* article:

> *HabWorlds* introduces astronomy, biology, chemistry, geology and physics to nonscience majors as they explore the search for life beyond Earth. They must find and describe hypothetical habitable planets through interactive tutorials in which they test ideas in a simulator, which tells them whether they're right or not. For example, after watching a short video on types of stars, students are asked to hypothesize which ones live the longest. Then they run a test and are told whether their answer is correct.
>
> (McMurtrie, 2017)

It should also be mentioned that the design and development of an instructional game can require significant resources and effort. Dr. Anbar in describing the game commented that he had support from the National Science Foundation, NASA, and Smart Sparrow, a company that makes adaptive, interactive instructional software.

James Gee (2007), a theoretical linguist, is an often-quoted proponent of gaming. In an interview, he summed up his views of the benefits of games as:

> Video games are like an external version of the mind. When we understand things and plan actions we run game-like role-playing simulations in our heads. In a sense, our mind is a game engine. We can combine elements from disparate experiences and create fantasies and think through complex problems.
>
> System thinking involves being able to think in terms of complex interacting variables that make a system more than the sum of its parts. We most certainly want to see much of the social and natural world in these terms, . . .
>
> Video games are complex systems composed of rules that interact. Gamers must think like a designer and form hypotheses about how the rules interact so they can accomplish goals and even bring about emergent results. Thinking like a designer in order to understand systems is a core 21st Century skill . . .
>
> Understanding oral and written language involves essentially running video-game like simulations in our heads. We run problem-based simulations where we try out various actions in our heads (as ourselves or someone else) and gauge their possible consequences.
>
> (Shapiro, 2014)

Gee is not alone in his views about the benefits of interactive media. Joichi Ito, the director of the MIT Media Lab, supports much of what Gee says and adds:

> I don't think education is about centralized instruction anymore; rather, it is the process establishing oneself as a node in a broad network of distributed creativity . . .
>
> Neoteny, one of my favorite words, means the retention of childlike attributes in adulthood: idealism, experimentation and wonder.
>
> (Ito, 2011)

Jane McGonigal (2011), the former director of Games Research and Development at the Institute for the Future, sees games as transforming real life and able to be used to increase students' resilience and well-being. Bryan Alexander (2014), Senior Fellow, National Institute for Technology in Liberal Education, sees interactive media especially their role-playing features as "the future of higher education." With so many respected thinkers supporting interactive media, and gaming in particular, it is likely that their future in education and especially online education is secure but there are issues that need to be considered.

First, it takes time and skill to develop interactive media applications, and the skills necessary are typically beyond the technological knowledge of most faculty and instructional designers. Second, while it is possible to purchase an existing instructional game or access it through a website (the organization Online Colleges maintains a website; see www.onlinecolleges.net/about/) containing dozens of education games, many of which can be tested for little or no fee) many pedagogues prefer to customize instructional materials and do not like to lack control over some critical part of their class. In addition, some media available at proprietors' websites charge fees on a per user basis and this can become expensive. Third, instructional media can require a good deal of class time forcing the instructor to choose a game, simulation, or MUVE over some other course activity(ies).

Despite these issues, interactive media have a future in online education, especially simulations which already are catching on rapidly in science courses. Gaming and MUVEs will progress more slowly but will nonetheless continue to appear in online education.

Mobile Technology

Mobile technology is another important element of the Fourth Wave of online education. Like other familiar technologies, it did not suddenly appear on the scene but evolved from the microcomputers of the 1980s, to the laptops of the late 1990s and early 2000s, to the tablets and smart phones of the present day. As each of these devices appeared, instructional technology changed. Today, laptops or tablets are the primary devices of choice among students even though they may also have smart phones that can access much of the course material. While phones keep students connected to course material and allow them to respond and contribute to specific questions, for deep reading and careful analysis, it appears that laptops, tablets, or e-readers are preferred. The EDUCAUSE Center for Analysis and Research study of undergraduates found that of all students saying they used these devices for class-related purposes:

70%	used	laptops
59%	used	smartphones
35%	used	tablets

Among students who owned their own devices:

74%	used	laptops
66%	used	smartphones
62%	used	tablets

(Dahlstrom & Bichsel, 2014, p. 14)

In this same study, of the 99% of the students who owned mobile devices, 8% owned just one device; 92% owned at least two devices; and 59% owned three or more devices.

The work of the EDUCAUSE ECAR Center is well-respected, and the data support the notion that students are using their mobile devices extensively but they are picking and choosing which devices to use depending upon the nature of their interactions. It is likely that short, concise messages are fine on smartphones but reading substantive articles and other text might be best accomplished on a laptop or tablet. While this report did not study the use of books and other paper-based text, it can be assumed that a good deal of reading is done using these "mobile devices" also.

The Pew Research Center—Internet, Science, and Technology (2014) conducted a survey of American reading habits. The findings indicated that:

> As of January 2014, some 76% of American adults ages 18 and older said that they read at least one book in the past year. Almost seven in ten adults (69%) read a book in print in the past 12 months, while 28% read an e-book, and 14% listened to an audiobook.
>
> (Zickuhr & Rainie, 2014)

For printed book lovers, this might sound like positive news, but the breakdown by age of the survey population shows significant differences. For example, in examining different age groups that used an e-book for their reading in 2014, here are the percentages:

Age Group	18–29	30–49	50–64	Older than 65
Percentage	47%	42%	35%	17%

The trend for younger people is definitely on the upswing, and especially notable when comparing the results for three years 2012, 2013, and 2014, the percentage of 18–29 year olds using e-books increases from 25% to 35% to 47% respectively (Zickuhr & Rainie, 2014).

For faculty and instructional designers of online education, these data provide important information on mobile technology use among the population and especially students. The implications are that students are likely to use a mix of devices to access course material; that formatting of course material should be friendly to mobile technologies; and that students can be expected to keep up to date with online discussion activities. Also, while it is convenient to upload reading material to a course website so that students can easily download it onto their devices, faculty should not compromise their standards by failing to assign a substantive book(s) if it is not available in electronic form. The use of mobile technology also has implications related to cloud computing, popular social media websites (i.e., Facebook, Twitter, and LinkedIn), and data security, all of which take on new dimensions in a hand-held world. With the proliferation and widespread use of mobile devices, online education has been integrated into the daily lives of students and is no longer something apart.

Summary

This chapter examined the current landscape of online education, including a variety of pedagogical approaches using multiple formats and instructional tools. Social- and multimedia use has expanded significantly throughout society as well as in education. Mobile devices (laptops, tablets, PDAs) for accessing and participating in course activities are forcing even experienced online education providers to upgrade their course and program delivery. In addition, a number of new facilities and approaches are expanding significantly. These include:

1. learning analytics;
2. adaptive or differentiated learning;
3. expansion of competency-based instruction;
4. open resources including material meant to replace traditional textbooks;
5. gaming and multiuser virtual environments (MUVE);
6. mobile technology.

All of these approaches, as well as traditional lectures, class discussions, laboratory work, and internships typical of face-to-face classes, are at the disposal of faculty and instructional designers. How to harness all of these facilities is the challenge facing many educators today and for the next several years.

Further Reading/Case Studies

Readers may wish to refer to the Appendix A—Case Studies in Online Education specifically to:

Babson College
Kaplan University
California Community Colleges
Western Governors University

References

Adam, B. (2004). *Time.* Cambridge, UK: Polity.

Alexander, B. (2014). Gaming the future of higher education. *Blog posting: The Academic Commons for a liberal education.* Retrieved June 17, 2015 from www.academiccommons.org/2014/07/24/gaming-the-future-of-higher-education/

Algebra Nation. (2017). *About us.* Retrieved October 21, 2017 from www.algebranation.com

Alias, T. (2011). *Learning analytics: Definitions, processes, and potential.* Unpublished paper. Retrieved October 15, 2017 from http://learninganalytics.net/LearningAnalyticsDefinitionsProcessesPotential.pdf

Beal, C. (2017, October 20). *Minutes of the meeting of the Advisory Committee for the Virtual Learning Lab Project evaluating Algebra Nation.*

Bowen, W. G., Chingos, M. M., Lack, K. A., & Nygren, T. I. (2012). *Interactive learning online at public universities.* New York: ITHAKA.

Career Index. (2015). Western Governors University. *Career Index.* Retrieved October 10, 2017 from www.educationnews.org/career-index/western-governors-university/

Chafkin, M. (2013, December). Udacity's Sebastian Thrun: Godfather of free online education, changes course. *Fast Company.* Retrieved October 15, 2017 from www.fastcompany.com/3021473/udacity-sebastian-thrun-uphill-climb

Class Central. (2017a). By the numbers. *Class Central.* Retrieved October 20, 2017 from www.class-central.com/report/mooc-stats-2017/

Class Central. (2017b). At MIT and Georgia Tech, MOOCs are showing up on campus: For the first time, on campus students can earn credit from a MOOC. *Class Central.* Retrieved October 20, 2017 from www.class-central.com/report/mit-georgia-tech-moocs-show-up-on-campus/

Dahlstrom, E., & Bichsel, J. (2014, October). *ECAR study of undergraduate students and information technology, 2014.* Research Report. Louisville, CO: ECAR. Retrieved October 16, 2017 from https://net.educause.edu/ir/library/pdf/ss14/ERS1406.pdf

Dziuban, C., Moskal, P., Cassisi, J., & Fawcett, A. (2016). Adaptive learning in psychology: Wayfinding in the digital age. *Online Learning, 20*(3). Retrieved June 8, 2017 from https://olj.onlinelearningconsortium.org/index.php/olj/article/view/972/223

Dziuban, C., Moskal, P., Johnson, C., & Evans, D. (2017). Adaptive learning: A tale of two contexts. *Current Issues in Emerging eLearning, 4*(1). Retrieved October 21, 2017 from http://scholarworks.umb.edu/ciee/vol4/iss1/3

Edmodo. (2017). *About us.* Retrieved October 21, 2017 from www.edmodo.com/about#story

Entertainment Software Association. (2017). *Facts about the computer and video game industry.* Retrieved October 16, 2017 from www.theesa.com/

Ford, M. (2015). *Rise of the robots.* New York, NY: Basic Books.

Gee, J. P. (2007). *What video games have to teach us about learning and literacy* (2nd ed.). New York, NY: Palgrave Macmillan Trade.

Goldstein, P. J., & Katz, R. N. (2005). *Academic analytics: The uses of management information and technology in higher education.* Boulder, CO: EDUCAUSE Center for Applied Research.

Gunawardena, A. (2017, January 1). A brief survey of analytics in K12 and higher education. *International Journal of Innovations in Education, 1*(1). Retrieved October 21, 2017 from http://onlineinnovationsjournal.com/streams/analytics/07ea372322ccb0f5.html

Ito, J. (2011, December 5). In an open-source society, innovating by the seat of our pants. *New York Times.* Retrieved June 17, 2015 from www.nytimes.com/2011/12/06/science/joichi-ito-innovating-by-the-seat-of-our-pants.html?_r=2

James, P. (2014, May 13). The CCC Online Education Initiative vision: How did we get here? *TechEdge.* Retrieved October 16, 2017 from http://ccctechedge.org/opinion/miscellaneous/428-the-ccc-Online-education-initiative-vision-how-did-we-get-here

Kahn, G. (January 2, 2014). How tiny, struggling Southern New Hampshire University has become the Amazon of Higher Education. *Slate.* Retrieved April 27, 2018 from www.slate.com/articles/life/education/2014/01/southern_new_hampshire_university_how_paul_leblanc_s_tiny_school_has_become.html?via=recirc_recent

Khan Academy. (2017). *About us.* Retrieved October 23, 2017 from www.khanacademy.org/about

Kirk, J. (2006, February 7). 'Analytics' buzzword needs careful definition. *Infoworld.* Retrieved October 7, 2017 from www.infoworld.com/t/data-management/analytics-buzzword-needs-careful-definition-567

Kuntz, D. (2010). The Knewton blog: What is adaptive learning? *Knewton.* Retrieved June 11, 2015 from www.knewton.com/blog/adaptive-learning/what-is-adaptive-learning/

McGonigal, J. (2011). *Reality is broken: Why games make us better and how they can change the world.* New York, NY: Penguin Press.

McMurtrie, B. (2017, October 27). Designing an online science course with video-game appeal. *The Chronicle of Higher Education*. Retrieved October 25, 2017 from www.chronicle.com/article/Ariel-Anbar-Designs-Online/241480

MERLOT. (2017). *Who we are?* Retrieved October 22, 2017 from http://info.merlot.org/merlothelp/index.htm#who_we_are.htm

Minerva. (2017a). *Minerva: Seven guiding principles*. Retrieved October 18, 2017 from www.minerva.kgi.edu/about/guiding-principles/

Minerva. (2017b). *Minerva: Admissions, tuition and fees*. Retrieved October 18, 2017 from www.minerva.kgi.edu/admissions/tuition_fees

Neem, J. (2011, April 1). Online university doesn't offer 'real college education'. *Seattle Times*. Retrieved April 18, 2015 from www.seattletimes.com/opinion/online-university-doesnt-offer-real-college-education/

Norberg, A., Dziuban, C., & Moskal, P. (2011). A time-based blended learning model. *On the Horizon, 19*(3), 207–216.

O'Shaughnessy, L. (2012). Fifty colleges with the best and worst graduation rates. *CBS Money Watch*. Retrieved October 15, 2017 from www.cbsnews.com/news/50-private-colleges-with-best-worst-grad-rates/

Riddell, R. (2013). Adaptive learning: The best approaches we've seen so far. *Education Dive*. Retrieved June 12, 2015 from www.educationdive.com/news/adaptive-learning-the-best-approaches-weve-seen-so-far/187875/

Seaman, J., & Seaman, J. (2017). *Opening the textbook: Educational resources in U.S. higher education, 2017*. Needham, MA: Babson College Survey Research Group. Retrieved December 18, 2017 from www.onlinelearningsurvey.com/oer.html

Shah, D. (2017). *Massive list of MOOC providers around the world. Where to find MOOCs: The definitive guide to MOOC providers*. Retrieved October 20, 2017 from www.class-central.com/report/mooc-providers-list/

Shapiro, J. (2014). Games can advance education: A conversation with James Paul Gee. *Mindshift*. Retrieved June 17, 2015 from http://ww2.kqed.org/mindshift/2014/07/03/games-can-advance-education-a-conversation-with-james-paul-gee/

Wecker, M. (2012, April 9). College students find 'serious' video games educational, fun. *U.S. News and World Report*. Retrieved October 23, 2017 from www.usnews.com/education/best-colleges/articles/2012/04/09/college-students-find-serious-video-games-educational-fun

Wiese, M. (2014, October 17). The real revolution in online education isn't MOOCs. *Harvard Business Review*. Retrieved October 10, 2017 from https://hbr.org/2014/10/the-real-revolution-in-online-education-isnt-moocs/

Zickuhr, K., & Rainie, L. (2014). A snapshot of reading in America in 2013. *Pew Center for Research—Internet, Science, & Technology*. Retrieved October 16, 2017 from www.pewinternet.org/2014/01/16/a-snapshot-of-reading-in-america-in-2013/

Chapter 9

The 2020s, 2030s, and Beyond!

As noted Chapter 5, Joseph E. Aoun is the president of Northeastern University and author of *Robot Proof, Higher Education in the Age of Artificial Intelligence*. In looking at the future of higher education and the changes that will occur as a result of technology, he acknowledged American colleges and universities as among the fullest expressions of human culture that ever flowered. He further commented that they are perhaps the most effective institutions for intellectual advancement ever developed. However, he cautioned that if they fail to respond creatively and deliberately to the technological challenges that they face, "they will wither into irrelevance" (Aoun, 2017, p. 12). In considering a future dominated by advanced technologies, educators should seek to integrate technology into a comprehensive plan that addresses other major issues that they will be facing in the not too distant future.

Drew Faust, the president of Harvard University, in a message to the World Economic Forum in 2015, described three major forces that will shape the future of higher education:

1. the influence of technology;
2. the changing shape of knowledge;
3. the attempt to define the value of education.

She went on to extol the facilities that digital technology and communications will provide for teaching, learning, and research. She foresees great benefits in technology's ability to reach masses of students around the globe and to easily quantify large databases for scaling up and assessment purposes. On the other hand, she made it clear that "residential education cannot be replicated online" and stressed the importance of physical interaction and shared experiences.

On the nature of knowledge, she stated that the common organization of universities by academic departments may disappear because "the most significant and consequential challenges humanity faces" require investigations and solutions that are flexible and not necessarily discipline specific. Doctors, chemists, social scientists, and engineers will work together to solve humankind's problems.

On defining value, she accepts that quantitative metrics are now evolving that can assess the importance of meaningful employment. She also believes that higher education provides something very valuable: it gives people "a perspective on the meaning and purpose of their lives." Furthermore, it is not possible to quantify this type of student outcome. She concluded that:

> So much of what humanity has achieved has been sparked and sustained by the research and teaching that take place every day at colleges and universities, sites of curiosity and creativity that nurture some of the finest aspirations of individuals and, in turn, improve their lives—and their livelihoods. As the landscape continues to change, we must be careful

> to protect the ideals at the heart of higher education, ideals that serve us all well as we work together to improve the world.
>
> (Faust, 2015)

While Faust presented three key elements in higher education's future, it is the interplay of these elements that will become most crucial in predicting its future. Will technology drive the shape of knowledge and the definition of value or will it be the other way around? Techno-centrists see technology as the driver while others who look at higher education holistically see technology as a tool serving the needs of the other elements.

Predicting the Future

Any attempt at predicting the future is based on calculated speculation. "What" is difficult enough, but the "when" is even more difficult. Niels Bohr, the Danish physicist, was fond of saying that "prediction is very difficult, especially if it's about the future." While he did not originate this quote, he fervently believed it. Levitt and Dubner (2014), the authors of the best-seller *Freakonomics*, tell the following story of Nobel laureate, Thomas Sargent, during an interview:

> **Moderator:** "Tonight, our guest: Thomas Sargent, Nobel laureate in economics and one of the most-cited economists in the world. Professor Sargent, can you tell us what CD rates will be in two years?"
>
> **Sargent:** "No."
>
> (Levitt & Dubner, 2014, p. 27)

Levitt and Dubner go on to reference Paul Krugman, another Nobel Laureate in economics, who said that too many economists' predictions fail because they overestimate the impact of future technologies. They also point out that Krugman made erroneous predictions about the growth of the Internet. Levitt and Dubner's comments illustrate the difficulty of prediction and are pertinent to our discussion of online technology and the future of higher education as well. Every attempt will be made not to overestimate the impact of technology and to take a measured and informed view of its potential in effecting education's future. To start, let's take a look at what others have said about the future of higher education.

Technology and Education's Future—The 2020s

Clayton Christensen, in his 1997 book, *The Innovator's Dilemma*, laid out his theory of "disruptive innovation" that posits that corporations need to quickly and abruptly adjust to new technologies in order to survive. Christensen has applied the same theory to other organizations including colleges and universities. Christensen, Horn, and Johnson (2008) predicted that K–12 education in the 2020s would be mostly delivered via online technology. In 2013, Christensen and Horn (2013) predicted that in the 2020s, the "bottom 25% in every tier" of higher education will close or merge if they do not adapt to online education. These views are being considered seriously by education policymakers and other leaders in private and public enterprises, but they should be taken with some caution.

A good example of this thinking appeared in an editorial in *The Economist* (June 28, 2014) titled "Creative destruction: A cost crisis, changing labor markets and new technology will turn an old institution on its head." The editorial stated that "the Internet, which has turned businesses from newspapers through music to book retailing upside down, will upend higher education." The editorial continued on to promote MOOC technology, the establishment of common standards, and national testing for all of higher education. An alternate view of MOOC technology recognized its place in higher education as well as its need for significant maturation and modification before being widely adopted. As for a common set of standards and assessments, this idea has been tried in K–12 education beginning with the adoption of the federal government's *No Child Left Behind* (NCLB) education policy in 2001. NCLB has been less than successful since most states sought and were granted waivers from its testing and assessment requirements. The reauthorization by the U.S. Congress of NCLB in December 2015, significantly reduced standardized assessments/testing and Common Core requirements for K–12 education.

There has been no shortage of books and articles that support Christensen's view that education needs "disruptive" change in light of online technology. Examples include:

The New Education: How to Revolutionize the University to Prepare Students for a World In Flux, Davidson (2017);
Change We Must: Deciding the Future of Higher Education, Goldstein and Otte (2016);
The End of College: Creating the Future of Learning and The University of Everywhere, Carey (2015);
College Disrupted: The Great Unbundling of Higher Education, Craig (2015);
The Idea of the Digital University: Ancient Traditions, Disruptive Technologies and the Battle for the Soul of Higher Education, McCluskey and Winter (2012);
College UnBound: The Future of Higher Education and What It Means for Students, Selingo (2013).

While all of those listed see education as changing and moving toward combinations of traditional face-to-face, online, and blended courses to meet the needs of students and to contain costs, there is no reason why the coming decade has to be characterized as one of disruption for education. However, adaptive learning, open education resources, data analytics, and mobile technology in support of online education will become common over the next decade.

In Chapter 5, Michael Crow and William Dabars were mentioned regarding their work at Arizona State University (ASU) on institutional planning for technology. Their book, *Designing the New American University*, published in 2015, provides readers with a model based on the practices, approaches, and policies that have moved ASU to serve over 98,000 students (2016 enrollment figure) and to become the largest research university in the country (Arizona State University, 2017). Many think that the ASU model portends the future of the American university. In Crow and Dabars' approach, technology is not the driver of change but the enabler. While they use a good deal of technology, theirs is not a technocentric view of the future of higher education, but a holistic one. Nor does it provide a quick fix. They state that it takes time to plan and as much as "a decade to operationalize" (Crow & Dabars, 2015, p. 17). In sum, they advise that colleges and universities must first understand what they are, what their missions are, who their faculty and students are and then use the appropriate technology to meet these needs.

Technologies for the 2020s

Figure 9.1 provides an overview of the major man-machine digital technologies that are presently in various stages of development and evolution. It shows nanotechnology and quantum computing as forming the base for the development of man-machine interfaces such as artificial intelligence, bio-sensing devices, robotics, and super cloud computing.

In the 2020s, these technologies will be more visible, however, it is in the 2030s and beyond that they will begin to mature, integrate, and have their greatest impact. The remainder of this chapter will speculate on how these technologies will develop in the coming decades.

As several of the authors previously mentioned predicted, most educational institutions will be using some aspect of online education to serve their students through the 2020s. However, there is little to indicate that there will be a mass disruption of schools and colleges. The vast majority of the institutions that exist today will exist through the 2020s. Because the demand for education is strong, higher education will continue to attract students who see the value of a college education. The concept of lifelong learning has rapidly gained ground and indicates students will seek to continue their educations well into their mature years. Large public and private universities will offer a wide variety of academic programs geared increasingly to careers and employment. Students will have options for fully online programs, face-to-face programs, and especially blended programs. Every program and course will likely have an online component. New institutional models comparable to Western Governors University and the Minerva Project will add to the mix of already existing institutions but will not replace them. In K–12 education, a movement exists in many school districts to provide all students with laptop computers fully equipped with appropriate instructional software. This movement will continue for the next decade and will be commonplace in the 2020s.

If there were to be a major national or international development such as an economic depression, or a natural or manmade catastrophe, education would be affected as would all other elements of the world order. However, in the absence of any major world calamity it is likely that there will be new technological developments that will have significant ramifications. The technologies selected to be discussed in this section are already in evidence but have not had a major impact on education at the time of this writing. It is likely that their impact will be felt in the 2020s, 2030s, and beyond.

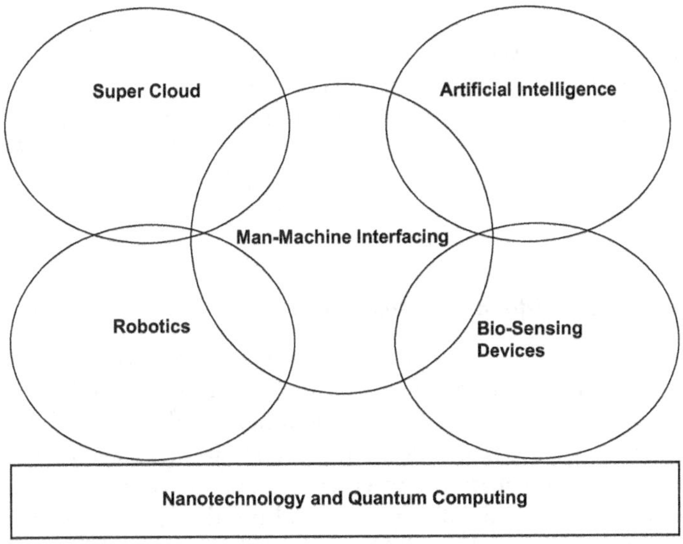

Figure 9.1 Technologies Shaping the Future of Man–Machine Interfacing

Nanotechnology and Quantum Computing

The simplest definition of nanotechnology is technology that functions at the atomic level. "Nano" refers to a billionth of a meter or the width of five carbon atoms. Governments around the world have been investing billions of dollars to develop applications using nanotechnology. These applications for the most part have focused on areas such as medicine, energy, materials fabrication, and consumer products. However, companies such as Intel and IBM have been developing nanochip technology, which has the potential to change the scope of all computing and communications equipment. IBM, for instance, announced in July 2015 a prototype chip with transistors that are just 7 nanometers wide, or about 1/10,000th the width of a human hair (Neuman, 2015). As this nanochip technology develops into commercial production, the whole concept of a digital computer may give way at some point to a quantum computer that operates entirely on the scale the size of atoms and smaller. As of this writing, quantum computers are in their infancy but prototypes are exceeding the speed of conventional computers by 3,600 times or at the speed of today's supercomputers (Dodson, 2013). Another decade of research and development on quantum computers may find their speed thousands of times faster than the speed of today's supercomputers. The storage capacity of such equipment will replace the gigabyte (10^9) and terabyte (10^{12}) world of today with zettabyte (10^{21}) and yottabyte (10^{24}) devices. Large-scale digitization of all the world's data will occur with access available on mobile devices. And all of this technology and computing power will be less expensive than it is now and will be available to everyone. Nanotechnology and quantum computing will provide the underlying base for the development of a host of new applications including those used in education. Such a development will have as great if not a greater impact on humankind as the Internet and World Wide Web. The first generation of quantum computers will likely be available via the cloud and geared to specific applications related to large-scale, complex research in areas such as neuroscience, NASA projects, DNA, climate simulations, and machine learning. To be fair, not everybody believes that quantum computing will be a game-changer in the world of computer science. Gil Kalai, a mathematician at Hebrew University in Jerusalem, is one of a number of mathematicians, physicists, and computer scientists who argue that quantum computing will not be able deliver on its promises and that

> —the "qubits"—will never be able to consistently perform the complex choreography asked of them. Others say that the machines will never work in practice, or that if they are built, their advantages won't be great enough to make up for the expense.
>
> (Moskvitch, 2018)

Time will tell.

Cloud Computing and Education Resources

In his 1994 book, this author described a place called Futuretown where in the year 2025, people would be served by an all-inclusive Communications and Computer Services Utility (CCSU) (Picciano, 1994). This digital utility would provide all services related to computer, television, communications, and transaction processing and it would be a one-stop utility for all information and entertainment services. Government, corporate America, hospitals, schools, and colleges would all use this utility for their operations. In 1994, the Internet and World Wide Web were in their nascent stages of development. There were few applications available other than file transfer (ftp), email, and electronic messaging. Home access was non-existent in most parts of the country and where it was available, users relied on slow-speed dial-up modems. While there were some limited facilities for uploading and downloading images, video was impossible due to these slow-speed connections. This began to change as higher-speed connectivity became available via cable modems, fiber optics, and digital subscriber lines (DSL) in the early 2000s. With the improvement in the speed and quality of connectivity, cloud computing or simply "the cloud" evolved wherein users no longer relied on their personal computers for storing files and running programs. Cloud computing services became available through major companies such as Google, Amazon, and Microsoft. Best-selling author, Nicholas Carr describes cloud providers as having turned data processing into utility operations that "allow vast amounts of information to be collected and processed at centralized plants" and fed into applications running on smartphones and tablets (Carr, 2014, p. 194). Essentially cloud services can take responsibility for all file handling and storage as well as applications such as email, text messaging, and social networking. It is likely that a cloud-based database establishing a national registry of all citizens will be created similar to ones in Sweden and several other European countries. A Swedish citizen's complete medical and education information, for instance, is maintained on the national registry database. All Swedish citizens also are assigned a personal identification number (PIN) which is keyed to the national registry database. The PIN is then used for a host of services in medicine, banking, purchasing, and education.

On the education front, cloud computing is just beginning to make inroads. While there has been some movement to low-cloud applications such as personal email and middle-cloud applications such as course and learning management systems, mission-critical applications such as student or financial database systems are still mostly maintained locally by colleges or school districts (Green, 2015). A survey of college information technology officers in 2015 found:

> 12 percent of the survey participants report that their campus has moved or is converting to cloud computing for ERP (administrative) services, . . . And less than a fifth of institutions expect to be running mission-critical finance and student information systems on the cloud by Fall 2020.
>
> (Green, 2015)

Public school districts, on the other hand, especially those with limited technical staff have already begun to move to cloud-based services for both administrative and instructional applications.

By the mid-2020s, it is likely that the cloud will be providing many, if not most digital services to all of education. By then, there will be little need for schools and colleges to maintain their own administrative databases or course/learning management systems, and the implications of cloud computing will be significant especially for instructional course development. First, instructors will be able to access large numbers of courses and course materials developed by other faculty or commercial developers. We are beginning to see this now in the open education resources (OER) movement, but an efficient and all-inclusive file sharing system does not presently exist. While some websites and services assist with this, the vast majority of all course materials still reside on school or campus-based computer systems with restricted access. Furthermore, since many faculty customize their materials to their own courses, they are not thinking about the convenience that sharing with others would provide. Second, the MOOC movement allows for high investment in course development. A single course might cost $1 million or more to develop and make available to a customer base. At most schools and colleges, this type of funding and investment in course development is a rarity but is beginning to catch on, usually in partnership with private enterprise and corporate partners. Some of the materials, especially media files, are very well done and are attracting faculty who use them for their own non-MOOC courses. These courses also integrate state of the art features such as learning analytics, adaptive/personalized learning, and micro assessments. Third, MOOC materials are setting a standard for high quality course content development and may in fact be leading to course standardization. This is especially true for introductory and gateway required courses that make up large portions of the curriculum. If all of this course development is moved away from MOOC and other private developers and onto computer facilities in the cloud, the ease with which faculty and students can access course material will increase tremendously and be most attractive. It is not unfathomable to think that there will be great pressure both inside and outside education to make use of these course materials as well as entire courses. Policy makers who seek standards and promote common assessments will have readily accessible material available to them in the cloud. Perhaps most importantly, students also will have access to these courses and materials and will be able to develop their own programs of study with the guidance of faculty mentors and advisers.

Artificial Intelligence and Learning Analytics Software

Learning analytics software is still in its developmental stages but is gaining traction as an important facility for teaching and learning. This software increasingly depends upon artificial intelligence (AI) techniques that use sophisticated algorithms to understand instructional processes. The software also relies on large amounts of "big" data to build a series of decision processes. Significant increases in the speed and storage capabilities of computing devices that will be possible through nanotechnology will also increase the capabilities and accuracy of AI-driven learning analytics software. What is presently known as big data will be small in comparison to the "superbig" data that will be available with nano-based computer systems.

AI allows learning analytics to expand in real time to support adaptive and personalized learning applications. For these applications to be successful, data must be collected for each instructional transaction that occurs in an online learning environment. Every question asked, every student response, every answer to every question on a test or other assessment is recorded and analyzed and stored for future reference. A complete evaluation of students as individuals as well as entire classes is becoming more common. Alerts and recommendations can be made as the instructional process proceeds within a lesson, from lesson to lesson, and throughout a course. Students can receive prompts to assist in their learning and faculty can receive prompts to assist in their teaching. The more data available, the more accurate will be the prompts. By significantly increasing the speed and amount of data to be analyzed through nanotechnology, the accuracy and speed of adaptive or personalized programs will be improved. Faculty will make inquiries about individual students to understand particular strengths and needs. They will be able to use an "electronic teaching assistant" to determine how instruction is proceeding for individual students and the class as a whole. They will be able to receive suggestions about improving instructional activities. Several colleges and universities such as Georgia Tech and Penn State are already experimenting with AI applications for teaching and advisement of students. In 2016, students in Georgia Tech's Online Master's Program in Computer Science nominated Jill Watson as teaching assistant of the year. The students did not know that Jill was an AI application running on IBM's Watson supercomputer (Popenici & Kerr, 2017). While presently in their beginning stages, these types of AI applications will become more prevalent in the 2020s. Most AI in use today, and for the near future, are narrow in their application and focus on a specific activity. In the years to come, general purpose AI will have much broader capabilities and will be applied to a variety of activities.

Low Cost/High Quality Media

Every year the quality of digital media improves. Much of this improvement has occurred because of the increased speed and storage capacity of computer equipment. Digitally developed animation has come a long way since the early days of games like *Pacman*, *Pong*, and *Space Invaders*. Major motion picture companies now produce feature-length films with special effects that blur the distinction between real-life action and animation. Eventually digital animations will be indistinguishable from real-life filming. The film *Avatar* set an entirely new standard of sophistication in digital animation. In 2009, at a cost of $500 million, *Avatar* dazzled audiences with its special effects in the fictional world of Pandora. In 2016, the Star Wars sequel, *Rogue I*, had the actor Peter Cushing reprising his role as Grand Moff Tarkin. Nothing too unusual about this except that Cushing died in 1994. Lucasfilms had used digital imaging and holography superimposed on a human face to represent Cushing as if he were still acting in the flesh. The advances in media technology are finding their way into education applications as well with games, simulations and multi-user virtual environments. The first educational applications in augmented reality, using special interfaces to see, hear, and interact with virtual environments, are becoming available. In the 2020s, these applications will be far more sophisticated and will grow in popularity, especially for courses that already use gaming and simulations. Popular lectures delivered by a talking head star teacher will be incredibly enhanced for students who will use devices that allow their senses to feel subject matter in virtual learning and augmented reality learning environments. Furthermore, these educational applications will be relatively inexpensive to produce as the cost of computing in general continues to decline.

The 2030s and Beyond

In January 1956, Herbert Simon, Nobel Laureate in economics (1978), told his students that over the Christmas break he and his colleague Al Newell had developed a computer program that could do simple logic problems on what he termed "a thinking machine" (Brynjolfsson & McAffee, 2014). He spent the next several years developing computer programs that could solve more sophisticated problems and play games. In 1958, he predicted that a digital computer would be the world chess champion by 1968 (Crevier, 1993). Simon was right about the computer chess champion although he was off by about 30 years; in 1997, an IBM computer named Deep Blue beat the world chess champion, Gary Kasparov. Ten years later, chess programs comparable to Deep Blue's were running on ordinary personal computers and laptops. By 2017 the big news in computer game playing was that Google's AlphaGo, designed to play Go (a game far more complex than chess) beat the Chinese Go master, Ke Jie. AlphaGo is a sophisticated artificial intelligence software program that not only plays the Go game but learns from competition including competition with itself. As reported by the *New York Times:*

> It isn't looking good for humanity.
>
> The world's best player of what might be humankind's most complicated board game was defeated on Tuesday by a Google computer program. Adding insult to potentially deep existential injury, he was defeated at Go—a game that claims centuries of play by humans—in China, where the game was invented.
>
> The human contender, a 19-year-old Chinese national named Ke Jie, and the computer are only a third of the way through their three-game match this week. And the contest does little to prove that software can mollify an angry co-worker, write a decent poem, raise a well-adjusted child or perform any number of distinctly human tasks.
>
> But the victory by software called AlphaGo showed yet another way that computers could be developed to perform better than humans in highly complex tasks, and it offered

> a glimpse of the promise of new technologies that mimic the way the brain functions. AlphaGo's success comes at a time when researchers are exploring the potential of artificial intelligence to do everything from drive cars to draft legal documents—a trend that has some serious thinkers pondering what to do when computers routinely replace humans in the workplace.
>
> (Mozur, 2017)

These vignettes illustrate the difficulty of predicting the future, especially in the dynamic and fluid field of digital technology. They also point to the fact that in the not too distant future artificial intelligence will make significant inroads into our lives and especially our work. In this section, possible new technologies that will have major impacts (as opposed to incremental changes) on education, will be explored. The educational innovations foreseen here will impact many other human endeavors as well, much like the Internet did in the 1990s.

Best-selling author Steven Johnson in *How We Got to Now: Six Innovations that Made the Modern World*, observes that technological innovations "have set in motion a much wider array of changes in society than you might reasonably expect" (Johnson, 2014, p. 2). He goes on to describe innovations to prove his point. For instance, Johannes Gutenberg's printing press created a surge in demand for eyeglasses because the "new" or expanded practice of reading made many Europeans realize that they were far-sighted. Or more recently when Google launched its search software in 1999 it was a breakthrough improvement far beyond any previous search mechanisms for exploring the World Wide Web's trove of information. The entire World Wide Web became more useful and functional. However, several years later when Google started selling advertisements tied to search requests, the nature of advertising changed unexpectedly. Advertisement agencies and their company clients flocked to Google and other Web-based services to promote products. Johnson goes on to comment that a case can be made that Google's revolution in advertising "hollowed out the advertising base of local newspapers" thereby having serious consequences for newspaper journalism in general as previous lucrative advertising contracts declined (Johnson, 2014, p. 7). The same will likely be true for instruction; a major new technology will evolve that will have significant repercussions on many human endeavors including education. For example, NASA announced a project to send humans to the planet Mars by 2030. The next Mars Rover, designed to gather information, will be launched in 2020 and will include computing equipment using large-scale miniaturized technology (NASA Jet Propulsion Laboratory, 2015). In the past, major federally-funded programs such as NASA's 1960s space program fueled a number of breakthroughs in digital technology in the following decades especially with regard to microcomputing technology. At that time, computer memory and central processing unit components in particular changed radically from expensive metallic magnetic core storage to relatively cheap semiconductor silicon chips. It is quite possible that new NASA projects such as the Mars Rover and subsequent landings will also result in major advances in digital technology. It will be interesting to see how NASA will make greater use of nanotechnology and quantum systems in its probes, rovers, and other space exploration equipment.

As events continue to unfold, another area of significant research and technological investment is neuroscience. Many well-established teams of individuals are focusing on mapping brain functions. Mapping involves developing an understanding of how certain thought functions occur and how the brain processes information from our senses. Experiments using digital technology are now duplicating certain brain functions. While this work is rudimentary at present, it is very possible that some brain functions will be improved using digital technology in the next two decades. At some point, the combined digital and biological research and development will yield breakthroughs that will have ramifications for all humankind and especially for education.

The Computer, the Mind, and Bio-Sensing

Ray Kurzweil, one of the world's best known futurists, has spent his lifetime studying man-machine interfaces. Trained as a computer scientist at MIT, Kurzweil was appointed Director of Engineering at Google in 2012 where he directs a team developing machine intelligence and natural language understanding. He has been described as "the restless genius" by *The Wall Street Journal* and "the ultimate thinking machine" and the "rightful heir to Thomas Edison" by *Forbes*. PBS selected Kurzweil as one of 16 "revolutionaries who made America" over the past two centuries.

Kurzweil (2013, 2006, 2000, 1992) has published several best-sellers on man-machine interfaces and bio-sensing. He predicts that sometime in the late 2030s or 2040s, a singularity will occur in which computers are developed that take over certain brain functions (Kurzweil, 2006). A central idea of his prediction rests on what he calls *the law of accelerating returns* or LOAR:

> an evolutionary process inherently accelerates and that its products grow exponentially in complexity and capability . . . it pertains to both biological and technological evolution.
>
> (Kurzweil, 2013, p. 4)

The key to Kurzweil's prediction is exponential growth especially when applied to the capacity, capability, and speed of computer chip technology and central processing units (CPUs). CPUs provide basic control/communication, memory, and arithmetic/logic functions on all digital computing devices, whether supercomputers or the microchip in a microwave oven. As discussed earlier, nanotechnology and quantum computing are evolving so that in another decade or so, quantum computers will have speeds and storage capacities well beyond today's supercomputers. Kurzweil envisions this technology developing computer-brain interfaces that will significantly expand the ability to think, to reason, and to create knowledge. Eventually, this technology will mature to the point where its capacity and speed will exceed that of the human brain. When this happens, the aforementioned singularity will occur that begins the transfer of human mental capacities to mind or "thinking" machines. He posits that these machines will be capable of improving and recreating themselves while significantly expanding and improving their mental capacities. Kurzweil (2013) credits John von Neumann with first using the word "singularity" in 1958 in the context of human technological history. He also establishes that while he understands that a computer is not a brain, it can "become a brain if it is running brain software" based on algorithms that simulate brain activity (Kurzweil, 2013, p. 181). Kurzweil describes a host of possibilities that include integrating and enhancing the senses, especially seeing and hearing, with neural implants that are designed to expand mental and memory capacities in the neocortex, the part of the brain where the most complex human mental activities take place. He also predicts that intelligent self-generating nanobots will be infused into our bloodstreams to keep our bodies healthy at the cellular and molecular levels.

> They [nanobots] will go into our brains noninvasively through the capillaries and interact with our biological neurons, directly extending our intelligence.
>
> (Kurzweil, 2013, p. 279)

Kurzweil goes on to say that while intelligent nanobots might seem overly futuristic and may not be available for three decades, cell-sized devices have already been developed that detect and destroy cancer cells in the bloodstream.

Kurzweil is a computer scientist and has great faith in the benefits and the potential of technology. However, his predictions are not without critics. In fact, a number of prominent computer scientists, neuroscientists, and biopsychologists such as Daniel Dennett, Rodney Brooks, David Gelernter, and Paul Allen question Kurzweil especially regarding the algorithmic comparisons of computers and the brain. New York University psychology professor Gary Marcus wrote a highly-critical review in *The New Yorker* of Kurzweil's *How To Create A Mind* stating that:

> Kurzweil's pointers to neuroanatomy serve more as razzle-dazzle than real evidence for his Theory . . . what I find is that it's a very bizarre mixture of ideas that are solid and good with ideas that are crazy.
>
> (Marcus, 2012)

Miguel Nicolelis, a research neuroscientist at Duke University, dismissed Kurzweil's coming singularity as "a bunch of hot air," and went on further to declare that:

> the brain is not computable and no engineering can reproduce it. You could have all the computer chips ever in the world and you won't create a consciousness.
>
> (Murray, 2013)

However, Nicolelis does not dismiss the idea that human intelligence will be augmented by digital technology in the 2030s or beyond. He himself has developed and conducted experiments on monkeys using what he terms *neuroprosthesis* devices. While rudimentary at present, neuro-prostheses are not that far afield from Kurzweil's neural implants.

Just as provocative as neural implants are brain-machine interfaces that allow multiple physical brains to work together (i.e., teacher and student brains) in a common digital environment. Nicolelis and his colleagues at Duke University astonished neuroscientists in 2015 by reporting on what is generally believed to be the first experiment using brain networks or brainets in monkeys to collaboratively solve a problem. The results of their experiment were reported in *Nature* as follows:

> Traditionally, brain-machine interfaces (BMIs) extract motor commands from a single brain to control the movements of artificial devices. Here, we introduce a Brainet that utilizes very-large-scale brain activity (VLSBA) from two (B2) or three (B3) nonhuman primates to engage in a common motor behavior. A B2 generated 2D movements of an avatar arm where each monkey contributed equally to X and Y coordinates; or one monkey fully controlled the X-coordinate and the other controlled the Y-coordinate. A B3 produced arm movements in 3D space, while each monkey generated movements in 2D subspaces (X-Y, Y-Z, or X-Z). With long-term training we observed increased coordination of behavior, increased correlations in neuronal activity between different brains, and modifications to neuronal representation of the motor plan. Overall, performance of the Brainet improved owing to collective monkey behavior. These results suggest that primate brains can be integrated into a Brainet, which self-adapts to achieve a common motor goal.
>
> (Ramakrishnan, A. et al., 2015, p. 1)

As one editorial noted:

> the idea of interconnected brains sounds a bit terrifying, especially since the Duke University team behind this study argues that it's also possible with people and plans to try and create human brain-to-brain networks.

> . . . there are a lot of perks to going the extra mile and creating human brain-to-brain networks. For instance, brainets could help with the rehabilitation of individuals with limited mobility and sensitivity by allowing them to tap into and mimic the neuronal activity of healthy volunteers.
>
> . . . experiments like the ones carried out by scientist Miguel Nicolelis and his colleagues are bound to pave the way for the development of so-called organic computers, i.e. brains linked together and able to synchronize to solve more or less complex problems.
>
> (Softpedia Editorial, 2015)

Neural implants, nanobots, and brainets may seem like science fiction and doubts rightfully exist regarding their realization over the next several decades. At the same time, well-respected scientists who themselves express concerns and misgivings, are devoting time, energy, and resources to developing man-machine interfaces that minimally augment brain function if not radically change the way humans use their brains and intelligences. In 2016, The Defense Advanced Research Projects Agency (DARPA), a branch of the US Department of Defense, announced a new initiative to implant neural devices into the brains of soldiers to facilitate digital interfacing. DARPA is the same agency that initiated the development of the Internet in 1960s. As stated on its website,

> A new DARPA program aims to develop an implantable neural interface able to provide unprecedented signal resolution and data-transfer bandwidth between the human brain and the digital world. The interface would serve as a translator, converting between the electrochemical language used by neurons in the brain and the ones and zeros that constitute the language of information technology.
>
> (Defense Advanced Research Projects Agency, 2016)

In 2015, a team of scientists at Ohio State University announced that they had "grown" the first human brain in a laboratory. The brain, engineered from adult human skin cells and grown in a dish for 15 weeks, is about the size of a pencil eraser, according to the university. It has the maturity of a 5-week-old fetal brain, and contains 99% of the genes in a fully developed human fetal brain (Caldwell, 2015). The implications of all of this brain function research for intelligence and knowledge development are extensive including the potential to significantly alter how education and instruction are delivered. If brain functions can be augmented by any of the technologies mentioned previously, the nature of our instructional paradigms will need to change dramatically.

If all of this sounds much too futuristic, Elon Musk, the founder and CEO of Tesla (electric cars, energy, solar panels) and SpaceX (space transportation) has stated that advanced technologies such as bio-sensors have the potential of turning human beings into tame "housecats" and has promoted the idea of developing a digital layer of intelligence he called a "neural lace" for the human brain.

> I think one of the solutions that seems maybe the best is to add an artificial intelligence layer . . . A third, digital layer that could work well and symbiotically with the rest of your body . . . this wouldn't have to be something inserted by "chopping your skull off," but that the technology could be inserted through the jugular vein . . . If we can create a high-bandwidth neural interface with your digital self, then you're no longer a house cat.
>
> (D'Onfro, 2016)

In 2017, Musk launched Neuralink, a medical research firm in California, to develop neural lace that involves implanting electrodes into the brain in order to create a wireless brain-computer interface capable of augmenting natural intelligence by downloading or uploading thoughts to or from a computer. Prototypes of this technology have already been developed by nanotechnologists such as Charles Lieber at Harvard University. He has demonstrated a way to implant via injection a flexible mesh circuit into mice that can insinuate itself into living neurons and in a sense "eavesdrop" on their chatter (Powell, 2015).

The New Supercloud and Robotics

Discussions of future digital technology frequently lead to speculation about robotics focusing on manufacturing, assembly lines, and other tasks that can most easily be subjected to specific algorithmic sequences or programs. Martin Ford (2015) reviews various possibilities in *The Rise of the Robots: Technology and the Threat of a Jobless Future*, and makes several predictions. He does not see a world controlled by *Terminator* or *Starwars* androids, but allows that digital technology will surely lead to more robotic applications in certain industries. These applications will be enhanced by artificial intelligence software that will be far more advanced than the present day versions. Artificial intelligence software will be expanded with man-machine interfaces to take advantage of breakthroughs in neuroscience. For the next ten years or so, Ford sees current online learning, augmented by artificial intelligence software, evolving into more seamless and more widely accepted adaptive or personalized instructional applications similar to those discussed earlier. But what about beyond the 2020s? Adaptive or personalized learning applications will grow and become more sophisticated over the next decade, but will not evolve into full acceptance until the 2030s or beyond. The true teaching machine will become common in the post-2030 period. Instruction will be delivered on a personal laptop or mobile digital device that will access a "supercloud" network computer for instruction.

The term supercloud is used to distinguish existing cloud computing, already generally available from Google, Microsoft, Amazon, and other companies. Current cloud facilities and their evolution over the next decade will essentially consist of digital utility systems that provide access to generic applications in communications, entertainment, and information retrieval. They will become as routine as electric, cable TV, and telephone utilities are today. Several prototypes exist at MIT, in Europe, and in China of "supercloud" networks that essentially provide access to a host of applications similar to the cloud services of today albeit with far more capacity and capability.

In the 2030s, however, a new type of supercloud computer service will evolve that will go beyond utility functions. It will be more personalized and more integrated into people's daily lives. In Stanley Kubrick's *2001: A Space Odyssey*, HAL, the computer that controlled all the functions of the spacecraft, is an illustration of a supercloud computer that will provide services geared to our everyday existence. It can wake us up, make our breakfast, set the day's schedule, start the car (giving us the option of driving ourselves or using a self-drive feature), handle many of our work activities, and entertain us in the evening with movies, culture, games, and sports. This supercloud computer of the future will also provide a host of important services such as medical diagnoses, legal consultations, advice on financial investments, and education. It will have access to the world's knowledge including books, reports, digital copies of art and architecture, video archives of speeches, music and dance productions, medical databases, legal databases, and secondary and postsecondary education courses. It will also have a friendly interface so that requests will be handled via spoken natural language. Doctors will be required by their HMOs to do all of their diagnoses using this HAL-type supercloud computer. Scientists will see much of their laboratory work conducted through simulations on a supercloud computer. Judicial systems will rely extensively on the supercloud to arrive at judgements.

All education will be integrated within the supercloud. It is likely that colleges and school districts will merge and/or consolidate during the 2030s or beyond. Large public university systems will likely utilize one central administration center that provides the full gamut of support services presently provided by individual colleges. State education departments will more directly be involved with operational aspects of K–12 education. Teachers and faculty will be knowledge managers and tutors who produce, disseminate, and help students to acquire and gain understanding of humankind's nature, existence, and future. Teachers and faculty will also be required to use a supercloud computer to prepare programs of instruction personalized to each of their students and to assess progress according to national standards. Many class or student group activities will be optional and will occur synchronously or asynchronously on the supercloud computer network. This supercloud network computer will be a game-changer for education and for every other profession and occupation. Big brother will have arrived.

Artificial Intelligence and the End of Humanity

Will artificial intelligence be the end of humanity? The technologies described previously generate mixed reactions among people. On one hand, there are many great benefits to be derived from intelligent man-machine systems. They can provide valuable assistance in endeavors such as health, medicine, and education, as well as the overall advancement of the human society. Sundar Pichai, CEO of Google, was quoted as saying that artificial intelligence is going to have a bigger impact on the world than some of the most ubiquitous innovations in history.

> "AI is one of the most important things humanity is working on. It is more profound than. . . . electricity or fire" said Pichai, speaking at a town hall event in San Francisco.
>
> (Clifford, 2018)

On the other hand, there are concerns about the dangers related to the loss of control over our lives, our existence, and our future. These issues go well beyond education, colleges, and universities. As was noted previously, critical to the development and advancement of intelligent machines is artificial intelligence software. Stephen Hawking, one of the preeminent physicists of the 20th and 21st centuries, created headlines when he stated in a 2014 interview that:

> I think the development of full artificial intelligence could spell the end of the human race. Once humans develop artificial intelligence, it will take off on its own and design itself at an ever-increasing rate.
>
> (Holley, 2014)

Hawking, because of amyotrophic lateral sclerosis (ALS), had been confined to a wheelchair for most of his adult life and was dependent on a number of digital technologies for his mobility and communication with others. His speech was only possible because of artificial intelligence technology that assisted him in forming words and sentences that reflected his thoughts. This technology used an infrared switch to detect the motions in his left cheek muscle which he used to select individual characters and build sentences. A cursor scrolled across the keyboard on Hawking's wheelchair-mounted tablet. When the cursor reached the letter Hawking wanted, he moved his cheek and an infrared switch picked up the motion. In this way he was able to build words and sentences which were sent to his voice synthesizer (Hawking, 2015).

Even though Hawking benefitted extensively from current artificial intelligence technology, he issued his grave warning that unchecked it threatens humankind's very existence.

Hawking was not alone in his concerns. In 2014, Stanford University invited leading thinkers from several institutions to begin a 100-year effort to study and anticipate how artificial intelligence will affect every aspect of people's lives. This project, called the *One Hundred Year Study on Artificial Intelligence* or *AI100*, was the idea of computer scientist and Stanford alumnus Eric Horvitz, a Distinguished Scientist and Director of the Microsoft Research Main Laboratory in Redmond, Washington. He is also a former president of the Association for the Advancement of Artificial Intelligence (AAAI). It was in his capacity as President of AAAI that Horvitz convened a conference in 2009 at which top researchers considered advances in artificial intelligence and its influences on people and society, a discussion that illuminated the need for continuing study of AI's long-term implications. Horvitz and Russ Altman, a professor of bioengineering and computer science at Stanford, have formed a committee that will select a panel to begin a series of periodic studies on AI's effect on automation, national security, psychology, ethics, law, privacy, democracy, and other issues. At a conference convened by Horvitz and Altman, Stanford President John Hennessy stated:

> Artificial intelligence is one of the most profound undertakings in science, and one that will affect every aspect of human life . . . Given Stanford's pioneering role in AI and our interdisciplinary mindset, we feel obliged and qualified to host a conversation about how artificial intelligence will affect our children and our children's children.
>
> (Cesare, 2014)

In a white paper describing the need and purpose of the *One Hundred-Year Study . . .*, Horvitz outlined several areas for the study. While praising the possibilities inherent in artificial intelligence and the rich opportunity for "better understanding the impressive capabilities of the brain via computational models, methods, metaphors, and results," he stated that the field also faces:

> potential challenges to privacy that might come to the fore with advances in AI research and development, including efforts in machine learning, pattern recognition, inference, and prediction? What are the implications for privacy of systems that can make inferences about the goals, intentions, identity, location, health, beliefs, preferences, habits, weaknesses, and future actions and activities of people? What are the preferences and levels of comfort of people about machines performing such inferences? How might people be protected from unwanted inferences or uses of such inferences? Are there opportunities for innovation with new forms of insightful (yet lightweight?) regulatory guidance, policies, or laws?
>
> (Horvitz, 2014)

The challenges are formidable, and while Horvitz convenes the world's most accomplished researchers and scientists in the field to study artificial intelligence, there are few if any restrictions on unscrupulous individuals and entrepreneurs with respect to weapons development, the breaching of national security systems, and profiteering from advanced artificial intelligence technology. Joseph Aoun, the president of Northeastern University, commented:

> If technology can replace human beings on the job, it will. Preventing business owners from adopting a labor-saving technology would require modifying the basic incentives built into the market economy.
>
> (Aoun, 2017, p. 46)

The Future of Life Institute (2015) initiated an open letter titled *Research Priorities for Robust and Beneficial Artificial Intelligence* that expressed the same concerns about artificial intelligence development as described by Horvitz and Aoun. The open letter is signed by Stephen Hawking, Elon Musk (founder of SpaceX and Tesla Motors), Steve Wozniak (co-founder of Apple), and many of the world's top computer scientists. Their concerns reflect the concerns of humanity over our ability to control the advancements of artificial intelligence in what Ray Kurzweil called the coming *singularity*.

Summary

This chapter speculated on online education in the 2020s, 2030s, and beyond. In the 2020s, online education will have matured and Internet technology will have been integrated into the vast majority of all education through a wide variety of delivery designs. Online education will be viewed as routine and students will have come to expect that every course will have online components. The effects of new technological breakthroughs such as widespread use of nanotechnology and quantum computing in the design of computer chips and the implications for cloud computing, artificial intelligence, and media production were also considered.

The chapter also examined digital technologies that will have major impacts on most human endeavors including higher education in the year 2030 and beyond. Predicting what will happen in the future is difficult; the timing of predictions in particular is very speculative. The work of futurist Ray Kurzweil was featured, especially with regard to the singularity, when man-machine technology will begin to outperform human brain functions and will begin to repair and replicate itself. It is likely that technology to augment the human brain such as neural implants, intelligent, self-generating nanobots, and brainets will evolve in the post-2030 timeframe. Many of these technologies will communicate with and rely on super cloud computer networks that will be far more advanced than the cloud computing of the present day. Artificial intelligence will dominate much of the man-machine interface technologies, and concerns are rightfully considered about the loss of control over humanity's future to technology. Major thinkers including Stephen Hawking have issued warnings to this effect.

References

Aoun, R. E. (2017). *Robot proof: Higher education in the age of artificial intelligence.* Cambridge, MA: The MIT Press.

Arizona State University. (2017). *About Arizona State University.* Retrieved November 2, 2017 from https://about.asu.edu/

Brynjolfsson, E., & McAffee, A. (2014). *The second machine age: Work, progress and prosperity in a time of brilliant technologies.* New York, NY: W.W. Norton and Company.

Caldwell, E. (2015). Scientist: Most complete human brain model to date is a 'brain changer'. *Posting on Ohio State University.* Retrieved August 19, 2016 from https://news.osu.edu/news/2015/08/18/human-brain-model/

Carey, K. (2015). *The end of college: Creating the future of learning and The University of Everywhere.* New York, NY: Riverhead Books.

Carr, N. (2014). *The glass cage: Automation and us.* New York, NY: W.W. Norton and Company.

Cesare, C. (2014). Stanford to host 100-year study on artificial intelligence. *Stanford News.* Retrieved August 17, 2015 from http://news.stanford.edu/news/2014/december/ai-century-study-121614.html

Christensen, C. M. (1997). *The innovator's dilemma: When new technologies cause great firms to fail.* Boston, MA: Harvard Business Review Press.

Christensen, C. M., & Horn, M. B. (2013, November 1). Innovation imperative: Change everything: Online education as an agent of transformation. *New York Times.* Retrieved July 23, 2015 from www.nytimes.com/2013/11/03/education/edlife/online-education-as-an-agent-of-transformation.html

Christensen, C. M., Horn, M. B., & Johnson, C. W. (2008). *Disrupting class: How disruptive innovation will change the way the world learns.* New York, NY: McGaw-Hill.

Clifford, C. (2018, February 1). Google CEO: A.I. is more important than fire or electricity. *CNBC Making it.* Retrieved February 5, 2018 from www.cnbc.com/2018/02/01/google-ceo-sundar-pichai-ai-is-more-important-than-fire-electricity.html

Craig, R. (2015). *College disrupted: The great unbundling of higher education.* New York, NY: Palgreave/Macmillan.

Crevier, D. (1993). *AI: The tumultuous history of the search for artificial intelligence.* New York, NY: Basic Books.

Crow, M. M., & Dabars, W. B. (2015). *Designing the New American University.* Baltimore, MD: Johns Hopkins Press.

Davidson, C. (2017). *The new education: How to revolutionize the university to prepare students for a world in flux.* New York, NY: Basic Books.

Defense Advanced Research Projects Agency. (2016). *Bridging the bio-electronic divide: New effort aims for fully implantable devices able to connect with up to one million neurons.* Retrieved January 25, 2016 from www.darpa.mil/news-events/2015-01-19

Dodson, B. (2013, May 13). D-Wave quantum computer matches the tenth ranked supercomputer for speed. *Gizmag.* Retrieved July 18, 2015 from www.gizmag.com/d-wave-quantum-computer-supercomputer-ranking/27476/

D'Onfro, J. (2016, June 2). Elon Musk thinks we need brain-computers to avoid becoming 'house cats' to artificial intelligence. *Business Insider.* Retrieved November 3, 2016 from www.businessinsider.com/elon-musk-on-neural-lace-2016-6

The Economist. (2014, June 28). Editorial. Creative destruction: A cost crisis, changing labour markets and new technology will turn an old institution on its head. Retrieved July 10, 2015 from www.economist.com/news/leaders/21605906-cost-crisis-changing-labour-markets-and-new-technology-will-turn-old-institution-its

Faust, D. (2015). Three forces shaping the university of the future. *World Economic Forum.* Retrieved July 9, 2015 from https://agenda.weforum.org/2015/01/three-forces-shaping-the-university-of-the-future/

Ford, M. (2015). *The rise of the robots: Technology and the threat of a jobless future.* New York, NY: Basic Books.

Future of Life Institute. (2015). *Research priorities for robust and beneficial artificial intelligence: An open letter.* Retrieved August 17, 2015 from http://futureoflife.org/AI/open_letter

Goldstein, M., & Otte, G. (2016). *Change we must: Deciding the future of higher education.* New York, NY: Rosetta Books.

Green, K. (2015). *The 2015 campus computing survey.* Encino, CA: The Campus Computing Project. Retrieved November 23, 2015 from www.campuscomputing.net/item/2015-campus-computing-survey-0

Hawking, S. (2015). The computer. *Posting on Stephen Hawking website.* Retrieved November 3, 2017 from www.hawking.org.uk/the-computer.html

Holley, P. (2014, December 2). Stephen Hawking just got an artificial intelligence upgrade, but still thinks AI could bring an end to mankind. *The Washington Post.* Retrieved August 17, 2017 from www.washingtonpost.com/news/speaking-of-science/wp/2014/12/02/stephen-hawking-just-got-an-artificial-intelligence-upgrade-but-still-thinks-it-could-bring-an-end-to-mankind/

Horvitz, E. (2014). *One-hundred year study of artificial intelligence: Reflections and framing.* Unpublished White Paper. Stanford University. Retrieved August 17, 2017 from https://stanford.app.box.com/s/266hrhww2l3gjoy9euar

Johnson, S. (2014). *How we got to now: Six innovations that made the modern world.* New York, NY: Riverhead Books.

Kurzweil, R. (1992). *The age of intelligent machines.* Boston, MA: MIT Press.

Kurzweil, R. (2000). *The age of spiritual machines: When computers exceed human intelligence.* New York, NY: Penguin Books.

Kurzweil, R. (2006). *The singularity is near: When humans transcend biology.* New York, NY: Penguin Books.

Kurzweil, R. (2013). *How to create a mind: The secret of human thought revealed.* New York, NY: Penguin Books.

Levitt, S. D., & Dubner, S. J. (2014). *Think like a freak: The authors of Freakonomics offer to retrain your brain.* New York, NY: William Morrow/ HarperCollins Publishers.

Marcus, G. (2012, November 15). Ray Kurzweil's dubious new theory of mind. *The New Yorker.* Retrieved August 12, 2015 from www.newyorker.com/books/page-turner/ray-kurzweils-dubious-new-theory-of-mind

McCluskey, F. B., & Winter, M. L. (2012). *The idea of the digital university: Ancient traditions, disruptive technologies and the battle for the soul of higher education.* Washington, DC: Westphalia Press.

Moskvitch, K. (2018, February 7). The argument against quantum computers. *Quanta Magazine.* Retrieved February 8, 2018 from www.quantamagazine.org/gil-kalais-argument-against-quantum-computers-20180207/

Mozur, P. (2017, May 23). Google's AlphaGo defeats Chinese Go master in win for A.I. *New York Times.* Retrieved November 12, 2017 from www.nytimes.com/2017/05/23/business/google-deepmind-alphago-go-champion-defeat.html?ref=oembed

Murray, P. (2013). Leading neuroscientist says Kurzweil singularity prediction a 'bunch of hot air'. *SingularityHub.* Retrieved August 12, 2015 from http://singularityhub.com/2013/03/10/leading-neuroscientist-says-kurzweil-singularity-prediction-a-bunch-of-hot-air/

NASA Jet Propulsion Laboratory. (2015). Mars future rover plans: Launch 2020. *NASA Website.* Retrieved July 30, 2015 from http://mars.nasa.gov/mars2020/mission/rover/

Neuman, S. (2015, July 9). *IBM announces breakthrough in chip technology. The two way: Breaking news from NPR.* Retrieved July 17, 2015 from www.npr.org/sections/thetwo-way/2015/07/09/421477061/ibm-announces-breakthrough-in-chip-technology

Picciano, A. G. (1994). *Computers in the schools: A guide to planning and administration.* New York, NY: Merril/Macmillan.

Popenici, S. A., & Kerr, S. (2017). Exploring the impact of artificial intelligence on teaching and learning in higher education. *Research and Practice in Technology Enhanced Learning, 12*(22). Retrieved November 27, 2017 from https://telrp.springeropen.com/track/pdf/10.1186/s41039-017-0062-8

Powell, D. (2015, June 8). A flexible circuit has been injected into living brains. *Smithsonian.com.* Retrieved November 3, 2017 from www.smithsonianmag.com/science-nature/flexible-circuit-has-been-injected-living-brains-180955525/?no-ist

Ramakrishnan, A., Ifft, P.J., Pais-Vieira, M., Byun, Y.W., Zhuang, K.Z., Lebedev, M.A., & Nicolelis, M.A.L. Computing arm movements with a monkey brainet. *Nature Scientific Reports, 5,* 10767; doi:10.1038/srep10767n. Retrieved August 14, 2017 from www.nature.com/srep/2015/150622/srep10767/full/srep10767.html

Selingo, J. (2013). *College Unbound: The future of higher education and what it means for students.* Boston, MA: New Harvest/Houghton Mifflin Harcourt.

Softpedia Editorial. (2015). Brainets: A higher form of communication or downright terrifying? *Softpedia Website.* Retrieved August 14, 2017 from http://news.softpedia.com/news/brainets-a-higher-form-of-communication-or-downright-terrifying-486662.shtml

Warner, J. (2015, January 25). ASU is the 'New American University'—It's terrifying. *Inside Higher Education: Blog Posting.* Retrieved July 13, 2016 from www.insidehighered.com/blogs/just-visiting/asu-new-american-university-its-terrifying

Appendix A

Case Studies in Online Education

Appendix A offers examples of colleges and schools that have developed extensive online education programs and have provided important insights into our understanding of the field. The institutions found here do not represent a national selection of "the best" online education programs but are mini case studies of colleges and schools that have added some distinct aspects to the study of online education. Many of the entries in this appendix have already been introduced in the main body of text in this book.

Index to Appendix A

Institution

American Public University System (For-Profit College/University)
Apex Learning Virtual School (K–12 Distance Education Provider)
Athabasca University—Canada (Postsecondary Distance Education Provider)
Babson College (College With a Unique Mission)
California Community Colleges (Community College)
Embry-Riddle Aeronautical University (College With a Unique Mission)
Florida Virtual School (K–12 Distance Education Provider)
Kaplan University (For-Profit College/University)
Northern Virginia Community College (Community College)
Penn State (Postsecondary Distance Education Provider)
Rio Salado Community College (Community College)
University of Central Florida (Online Program in Large Urban Area)
University of Illinois-Chicago (Online Program in Large Urban Area)
University of Maryland-University College (Postsecondary Distance Education Provider)
University of Phoenix (For-Profit College/University)
University of Wisconsin-Milwaukee (Online Program in Large Urban Area)
Virtual High School Global Consortium (K–12 Distance Education Provider)
Western Governors University (College With a Unique Mission)

Postsecondary Distance Education Providers

A number of colleges have become leaders in providing well-developed online programs aimed at a distance education student population. There are many such institutions in the United States and worldwide that have focused on students who do not come to a physical campus and instead take all or most of their coursework online. Some of these institutions such as the Pennsylvania State University, Athabasca University (Canada), and the University of Maryland

University College have a long history of providing distance education via other, pre-Internet technologies such as television, radio, and programmed instruction course packs.

Penn State

The Pennsylvania State University is one of the early pioneers of distance education in the United States. It offered its first correspondence program in 1892 and has been expanding ever since using a variety of communications technologies to provide education opportunities for students who cannot come to a physical campus. Penn State, as early as the 1920s, was broadcasting courses over the radio. In the 1940s, Ray Carpenter had begun to research educational uses of film. He subsequently received a Ford Foundation grant to test the use of television for high-enrolled classes at Penn State. Carpenter and others experimented with televised courses throughout the 1950s and in 1965; Penn State's WPSX-TV received its full license to broadcast as an educational television station offering services for both the K–12 and higher education student populations. With a firmly established distance education program, in 1998, Penn State launched its World Campus, which has become the "online campus" of Penn State offering 125 online undergraduate, graduate, and certificate programs including associate, baccalaureate, masters, and doctoral degree programs. The breadth of its programs is impressive and includes majors such as "Turf Grass Science and Management", "Engineering Management", and "Doctor of Nursing Science." The Penn State World Campus is the second largest campus in The Pennsylvania State University system with nearly 18,000 students.

An important aspect of the World Campus is that most of its programs have ongoing relationships with Penn State's on-campus academic units and colleges that allow involvement by Penn State full-time faculty. This assures that the quality of the online programs are the same as the "on-ground" programs. Penn State also offers several blended masters programs where residencies of a few days to a few weeks are required. The basic instructional model is based on asynchronous activities that allow students to participate anytime and anyplace that they have access to the Internet. Courses and programs also make extensive use of chat, video conferencing, phone calls, email, social media, and electronic bulletin boards to help students stay connected with fellow students and faculty.

The World Campus has also made a special commitment to military personnel and has aligned their online degree and certificate programs, student support services, and policies to address the unique needs of military and veteran students. Its website states that "no matter where you are in the world, you can advance your education and career with the help of Penn State" (Penn State World Campus, 2017).

The Penn State World Campus has had a number of leaders such as Gary Miller, Craig D. Weidemann, and Larry Ragan who have made major contributions to the development of online education. Penn State has also housed the American Center for the Study of Distance Education, which was founded by Michael G. Moore in 1986, one of the first of its kind in the United States. Moore also established the *American Journal of Distance Education* (AJDE) in 1986, a leading publication on the research and practice of distance education. Moore's own work, especially his theory of *transactional distance,* is widely recognized as a major contribution to the study of distance education.

Athabasca University—Canada

Athabasca University in Alberta, Canada, has a 50-year history of providing higher education opportunities to students. It describes itself as Canada's "open university", styled after the Open University of the United Kingdom that has been providing distance education since 1969.

Athabasca was founded in 1970 as a traditional college, but in 1972 decided to focus on distance education. Its main campus is in northern Alberta in the town of Athabasca and it has satellite facilities in Edmonton, St. Albert, and Calgary. If you visit Athabasca's main campus, you will see a number of traditional campus buildings, however, there are very few faculty and practically no students in them. Athabasca has used various technologies over the years to provide distance education and started using closed computer networks in the 1980s. As a result, it was a fairly easy progression for Athabasca to migrate to the Internet and online education in the 1990s. In 2016, it was serving more than 40,000 students worldwide in 55 undergraduate and graduate programs (Athabasca University, 2016a). In 2006, Athabasca became the first Canadian public university to receive accreditation in the United States, through the Middle States Commission on Higher Education (MSCHE), which is one of six regional organizations in the U.S. that accredit universities. It was also one of the first foreign online universities to receive accreditation from one of the six U.S. regional accreditors.

Athabasca's online education program primarily uses a programmed instruction model that allows students to progress at their own pace. Each program and course is carefully designed and tested. Athabasca makes extensive use of part-time faculty who follow the programmed coursework carefully and function more as tutors than as teachers. At the time of admission, all students are also assigned a tutor who is with them throughout their academic careers. As is typical in many online distance education programs, students have access to a course website, tutorial support, and a learning resources package that may include:

- textbooks (or e-texts);
- workbooks;
- lab kits;
- study guides;
- online resources (including audio and video resources);
- manuals;
- a recommended study schedule.

In some courses, the learning resources are available entirely online. In others, the resources may be a combination of online course materials and offline materials such as a textbook(s), CDs, and/or DVDs. Also at Athabasca, the entire learning resources package for some programs may still be print-based and are mailed (Athabasca University, 2016b).

The majority of students at Athabasca enroll in individualized study where students proceed at their own pace. Athabasca has a modified rolling admissions and registration system where individualized courses begin on the first day of each month. However, grouped study courses are also available online and on-site at selected locations across Canada. Students in grouped study courses are required to complete their work on a pre-set schedule similar to a semester system.

One of the major contributions that Athabasca has made to the field of online education is its dedication to research through its Centre for Distance Education. A number of its faculty including Terry Anderson, Randy Garrison, Walter Archer, and Marti Cleveland-Innis have done significant online education research. In 2000, Garrison, Anderson, and Archer introduced the Community of Inquiry (COI) framework that was discussed extensively in Chapter 3 of this book. The original framework identified the education experience as occurring at the convergence of three presences: cognitive, teaching, and social presence. Presence was defined as a state of alert awareness, receptivity, and connectedness to the social, cognitive, emotional, and physical workings of both the individual and the group in the context of their learning environments. The Community of Inquiry (CoI) is based on the work of John Dewey and constructivist views of experiential learning. Terry Anderson (2011) has also done extensive research work in attempting to develop an overall model for online education.

Athabasca has maintained a commitment to serving diverse worldwide student populations through its Centre for World Indigenous Knowledge and Research and collaborates with a number of colleges and universities around the world. It has been active in international distance education consortia including The University of the Arctic (UArctic) which is a cooperative network of universities, colleges, and other organizations in North America, Europe, and Asia committed to higher education and research in the northern polar areas. Its members share resources, facilities, and expertise to build post-secondary education programs geared especially for northern indigenous students.

University of Maryland-University College

The University of Maryland-University College (UMUC) has a long tradition of providing adult and continuing education going back to 1947. It was originally founded as a branch of the University of Maryland's College of Education located in College Park. It quickly expanded its mission by directing some of its resources to the development of education facilities in Europe and Asia to serve active-military personnel. In 1964, UMUC opened a five-story Center for Adult Education in College Park. In 1970, UMUC transitioned into an independent institution, and in 1978 the university established what is now the Graduate School of Management and Technology. Since then UMUC has opened a number of centers throughout the world.

The inclusion of "university" and "college" in its name has always sparked questions. The "University of Maryland" part signifies that it is part of the University System of Maryland and the "University College" is a British term that captures what it does, that is to "Take courses and programs from all academic departments and offer them outside of the university's walls and normal class times" (University of Maryland University College, 2016).

UMUC was one of the early leaders in online education and started offering courses in the mid-1990s. With headquarters in Adelphi, Maryland, and administrative offices in Asia and Europe, UMUC now offers 90+ academic programs and serves more than 80,000 students worldwide. It also maintains over 20 locations in Maryland, Washington, D.C., and Virginia and has an on-site presence in 140 worldwide locations in more than 20 countries and territories. Eighty-eight of its locations are located at or near military bases and serve large numbers of armed forces personnel.

The student population at UMUC can be characterized as mainly working adults as described in its website:

- The median age of stateside undergraduate students is 30
- More than 81 percent of undergraduate stateside students are working
- More than half of UMUC stateside students are working parents
- Approximately 75 percent of stateside undergraduate students work full-time
- 60 percent of our worldwide student population are military and affiliates
- 30 percent of stateside students are African American students
- Minority students constitute 46 percent of total enrollment.

(University of Maryland University College, 2017)

One of the major contributions that UMUC made to online education is that it realized early on that fully online courses might not be for everybody. Even though it had established successful fully online programs, it also started offering blended or hybrid programs to complement its fully online and fully face-to-face programs. It was able to do this mainly because it had established physical facilities around the world and students could attend traditional classes as need be. However, because it realized that time and traveling to a campus or center might not be convenient, it developed blended programs that allowed students to fit their education around their own personal schedules. UMUC now offers blended programs at 25 of its locations. It has found that the blended format is particularly popular with its active military students.

For-Profit Colleges/Universities

For-profit higher education has a long history in this country but it never played a major role until the end of the 20th century and the advent of online education. The majority of the institutions in this sector were not degree-granting, and instead offered certificates concentrating on career education. Students enrolling in these programs could expect a credential within several months and could apply for licenses issued by the states if applicable. The subjects of these certificate programs varied significantly from personal grooming/cosmetology to large-equipment operation. While certificate schools still dominate the postsecondary, for-profit sector, major changes occurred in the 1990s. A number of these institutions decided to expand and to offer degrees. They incorporated and became publicly held corporations gaining them substantial new financing while also making them more accountable to Wall Street investors. And, they used their new financing to expand their operations especially in the area of online education. Several for-profit colleges such as the University of Phoenix, the American Public University System, and Kaplan Higher Education expanded their operations in the 1990s and invested in online program development, resulting in significant increases in student enrollments.

University of Phoenix

The University of Phoenix (UOP) was an early leader that made important contributions to both the for-profit and non-profit higher education sectors interested in developing online programs. It has an interesting although rocky history and one that maintains a special place in the field of online education.

In 1973, John Sperling opened the Institute for Community Research and Development, specializing in adult education in Phoenix, Arizona. Shortly thereafter, it became the Institute for Professional Development (IPD) which, in 1976, established a second entity, the University of Phoenix (University of Phoenix, 2015). In 1981, Sperling created the Apollo Group which became the parent company of UOP. Under the aegis of the Apollo Group, UOP focused on creating degree-granting programs by establishing small local education centers to provide professional development opportunities for corporate clients. In 1994, the Apollo Group made a public offering and at that time enrolled 27,000 students (including about 2,000 distance education students) at 60 IPD and UOP locations. Flush with new capital from the public offering, the Apollo Group grew within ten years to over 200 locations all over the world enrolling 228,000 students, of which 100,000 were online learners. The investment in online learning, although not the only reason for its growth, certainly was a major factor.

The UOP used the asynchronous learning network (ALN) model of online education. In addition, it tightly controlled its curricula and scripted most of its courses, designed by a small cadre of full-time faculty. Their online courses had several interesting features including a small class size of no more than 13 students per section. Their courses did not follow the traditional 15-week semester calendar but instead could be completed in eight weeks. Most courses were taught by part-time faculty who were hired on a course by course basis. UOP has had one of the highest percentages (as high as 97.9%) of part-time faculty of any higher education institution (private or public, non-profit or for-profit) in the world (Kinser, 2006, p. 91). The use of part-time faculty combined with the online delivery mode significantly reduced its instructional costs and combined with increased student enrollments, its profits soared. By the early 2000s, UOP became the largest private, for-profit or non-profit university in the country and became the face of large, publicly-held, for-profit higher education. However, several questions about UOP practices emerged regarding recruitment of students and federal financial aid. There were also vocal critics of the way UOP expanded. Senator Tom Harkin (Democrat, Iowa) during a series of congressional hearings held by the U.S. Senate's Health, Education, Labor and Pensions (HELP) Committee in 2012 was cited as stating:

> when the school [UOP] was founded in 1976 it had a 'pretty good model. . . . They started out as a college completion school,' says Harkin. Many of the students were successful. But then the school 'kept expanding and expanding and expanding, and so it kind of morphed into this behemoth that it is now.
>
> (Hanford, 2012)

UOP became the nation's largest private university by 2010 with an enrollment of 470,800 students, more than all the universities of the Big Ten Conference combined. But according to the HELP Committee investigation, more than 60% of the students who started degrees at the UOP in 2008–2009 ended up leaving by the middle of 2010 without a degree. The students who quit had been enrolled for a median time of four months. Harkin believes UOP went wrong in 1994 when it became a publicly traded company.

> 'I think what really turned this company is when they started going to Wall Street,' he says. '[They] started raising hedge fund money, and then they had to meet quarterly reports, and all they were interested in, basically, was "How much money ya makin?"'
>
> (Hanford, 2012)

The move to online education changed the nature of UOP as it did for a number of other for-profit institutions. It changed not only their scale but their character as well, as they sought to use the technology to aggressively compete worldwide for students.

As a result of the HELP Committee investigation and the adverse publicity from other reports, enrollments at UOP plummeted by more than 50%. In 2015, the U.S. Department of Defense put the UOP on probation and prohibited it from enrolling new students who were using the Department's Tuition Assistance Program that provides financial aid to active-duty service members. It also barred UOP officials from recruiting at military facilities. In 2016, with its stock value plummeting, the Apollo Group including the UOP was bought by a private equity firm that would reorganize its entire operations outside the public domain and not subject to the scrutiny of a publicly-traded company. At the time of this writing, the UOP is operating as a privately-held company and no longer makes public disclosures of its operation.

American Public University System

The history of the American Public University System can be traced to 1991, when retired Marine Corps officer James P. Etter founded American Military University (AMU). AMU offered career-relevant distance education to active military and veterans. Over the next 10 years, a number of undergraduate and graduate programs were added to help prepare students for leadership roles both within the military and for transition into post-military careers.

In 2002, AMU was reorganized into the American Public University System (APUS), and American Public University (APU) was founded to provide quality, affordable, and flexible education to a broader audience of motivated working adults. In 2008, APUS became a publicly-traded corporation (American Public University, 2017a).

Today, APUS is one of the largest providers of online higher education offering more than 200 academic programs to over 88,000 students enrolled worldwide, the majority of whom are connected to the military (American Public University, 2017b). Its enrollment peak occurred in 2013 when 110,000 students were enrolled.

Its programs have received wide recognition from the Online Learning Consortium, "Best for Vets" distinction from the *Military Times*, and *U.S News and World Report* rankings. Unlike a number of other major for-profit private universities, APUS has never been implicated or mentioned in a negative light during federal investigations into questionable student recruitment and financial aid practices.

Through its Office of Research and Development, APUS has made significant contributions to the subject of student retention in online education (Boston, Diaz, Gibson, Ice, Richardson, & Swan, 2008; Ice, Gibson, Boston, & Becher, 2011). Phil Ice, a former vice president at APUS, with colleagues around the country, has done important groundwork on the subject especially through the Predictive Analysis Reporting (PAR) Framework that was housed at the WICHE Cooperative of Educational Technologies. The main focus of PAR was to develop and leverage common data definitions and predictive analytics in the service of student success. The PAR Framework specifically aimed to identify factors impacting loss, progression, and completion for postsecondary students. In guiding PAR research initiatives, PAR investigators combined student and course data from six institutions representing the community college, public and private four-year, and for-profit categories into one large, federated dataset. The six original founding institutions included American Public University System (APUS), Colorado Community College System, Rio Salado Community College, University of Hawaii System, University of Illinois Springfield, and the University of Phoenix. The PAR Framework members have issued several studies and reports documenting student factors for success that have added to our understanding of this aspect of student outcomes in online courses (Ice et al., 2012).

Kaplan University

Kaplan University traces it roots to the American Institute of Commerce (AIC) established in 1937, and which later changed its name to Quest College. In 1938, Stanley H. Kaplan started a small business offering tutoring services to immigrant families eager to expand their opportunities in America and improve their education. Over the decades, Kaplan, Inc. grew to become one of the major companies providing tutoring and test preparation services especially for individuals taking college entrance examinations such as the Scholastic Aptitude Test (SAT). In 1984, Kaplan was acquired by *The Washington Post* but operated as a separate entity. In November 2000, Kaplan, Inc. acquired Quest College and changed the name to Kaplan College. It started offering graduate courses in 2004 and became Kaplan University (Kaplan University, 2017). Like the University of Phoenix and several other for-profit colleges and universities, Kaplan's reputation was damaged for its recruitment and financial aid practices during the U.S. Senate's HELP Committee 2012 hearings and subsequent report. At its enrollment height, Kaplan enrolled more than 100,000 students worldwide. Today Kaplan enrolls 30,000 students in online, blended, and face-to-face courses. It operates 15 education centers around the country. Many of its programs are competency-based.

Perhaps Kaplan's most significant contribution to online education is yet to come. In April 2017, the non-profit, publically-funded Purdue University announced that it was paying $1 and 12.5% of future revenues to Graham Holdings (Kaplan's parent company) for the university. The deal would allow Purdue to create a separate, online university using all of Kaplan's academic, technical and support infrastructure. Betty Vandenbosch, the current president of Kaplan University, would be the chancellor of the new university. At the time of this writing, the Kaplan acquisition was still under review by state and federal oversight agencies including the U.S. Department of Education.

The acquisition was not without controversy both inside and outside of Purdue. From within, faculty members at Purdue University in May 2017 took a strong stance against the unorthodox acquisition of Kaplan University, passing a University Senate resolution calling the deal "a violation of common-sense educational practice and respect for Purdue faculty." The resolution called on Purdue President Mitch Daniels and the university's Board of Trustees to rescind any decisions made about the acquisition. It also called on Purdue leaders to include faculty members in all future decisions going forward about the deal. From outside Purdue, Bob Shireman, a senior fellow at the Century Foundation, and an Education Department official during the Obama administration who played a leading role in the department's crackdown on for-profits colleges stated: "There are some dangerous aspects of this agreement because of the continued involvement of a company that had recruiting issues" (Fain and Seltzer, 2017).

Kaplan University's relationship with Purdue will be very carefully followed in the coming years in that it represents a very different higher-education organizational model merging for-profit and non-profit entities.

K–12 Distance Education Providers

K–12 education has seen significant growth in online education in the past 20 years. For a while it lagged behind higher education in developing online programs but quickly caught up in the early part of the 21st century. Today, there are many virtual K–12 schools and companies that offer entire programs and courses online. In recent years, these entities have also moved to develop blended courses that teachers can integrate into regular classroom instruction.

Florida Virtual School

The Florida Virtual School (FLVS) was founded in 1997 as the first virtual high school in the country. It is considered one of the more successful of such schools. While it enrolls students from throughout the United States, FLVS is a public entity and receives funds from the state of Florida and from participating school districts. It operates on a funding model that is based on the number of students who complete courses. FLVS students do as well if not better than students in traditional K–12 schools as far as course completions are concerned. It currently offers 150 online and blended learning courses. While its yearly enrollments have fluctuated, FLVS enrolled 200,000 part-time and full-time students in 2016. The vast majority of these students are part-time and continue to enroll in traditional high schools for much if not most of their programs. Approximately 7,700 students are enrolled full-time at FLVS (Florida Virtual School, 2016).

What is very impressive about FLVS is the breadth of its program. Courses are offered on all parts of the K–12 curriculum spectrum. At the secondary level, there is a full range of core courses that meet most high school diploma requirements including a complement of languages such as Spanish, French, Chinese, and Latin; 15 advanced placement courses; and electives in art, music, photography, and driver education. It also offers credit-recovery versions of basic required courses for students who have previously failed a subject and who might need additional assistance and tutoring. At the middle school level, FLVS offers twelve courses that fulfill core curriculum requirements and nine electives. At the elementary level, FLVS utilizes a blended or flexible learning model to offer a comprehensive elementary curriculum, including Language Arts, Social Studies, Math, Science, and Technology courses and modules.

Another very important distinction of the FLVS model is that its staff and teachers are primarily full-time employees while many other virtual and fully online programs at the K–12 or college level hire very large numbers of part-time teachers and staff to save on full-time salaries and fringe benefit costs. In 2016, FLVS had a total staff of 1,986 employees of which 516 were support staff, 1380 were full-time teachers, and 90 were part-time teachers (Florida Virtual School, 2016). The high percentage of full-time teachers (94%) at FLVS is a rarity. A good deal of credit for the success of FLVS should go to its founding president and CEO, Julie Young, who led the school for 17 years. She took on what was a revolutionary idea in 1997 and put together a team of talented individuals to not only provide quality online education services for students but also developed a model that could be emulated throughout the country and beyond. Several other states including Texas, Michigan, and Ohio established virtual schools based on the FLVS model. Ms. Young has received a number of major awards for her contribution to the field including the Harold W. McGraw, Jr. Prize in Education.

Apex Learning Virtual School

Apex Learning Virtual School (ALVS) is a privately-held company that has been providing online education to the K–12 sector for more than 20 years. It was founded in 1997 by Paul Allen, the co-founder of Microsoft, and was one of the first such companies to focus entirely on the K–12 market. The original strength of the company was in providing online Advanced Placement (AP) courses and test preparation. ALVS developed an excellent reputation for its online AP courses and was an early leader in this niche market. High school students across the country, and internationally, has in ALVS to complete AP courses, credit-recovery, or its homeschool curriculum. It presently has over 15,000 students a year who enroll either full time or part time (Apex Learning Virtual School, 2017).

While AP remains a core part of ALVS's business, it needs to be mentioned that one of its major contributions to online secondary education was investment into quality credit-recovery programs. Having established its reputation with high-end AP courses, in the mid-2000s it turned its attention to students who needed to retake courses that they had failed. The need for credit-recovery courses varies and includes students who have not completed required coursework earlier in their high school careers due to illness, scheduling conflicts, academic failure, etc. These students make up a significant portion of the high school student population that subsequently drops out or is late in graduating. By 2009, credit recovery had evolved into one of the most popular types of online courses being offered at the secondary level. Credit recovery was of particular importance to urban high schools that historically had the lowest graduation rates of any schools in the country. In the early 2000s, many urban high schools were being forced to find solutions to their high school dropout problems through pressure from state education departments and the federal No Child Left Behind mandates to improve student outcomes. Online credit recovery emerged as one cost-effective solution to the dropout problem.

While one would think that the advance of online credit recovery was a most positive development, in its early years it was the subject of much debate and talk of questionable practices. There were concerns that some school districts were using credit-recovery, whether online or face-to-face, as a quick, convenient way to move students through to graduation. As an example, a *New York Times* article, raised concerns by teachers and others that some New York City public schools were "taking shortcuts" and "gaming the system" to move students through to graduation with questionable practices related to weak credit recovery programs (Gootmen & Coutts, 2008). As a result, the early credit-recovery programs of many providers were being questioned. It took the development of high-quality credit-recovery programs that relied on blended learning models involving teachers and tutors for credit-recovery programs to gain respectability. ALVS along with other reputable providers such as Aventa Learning and Plato Learning gave credence to these programs. Today, credit-recovery programs are seen as a benefit to students who have not passed courses delivered in a traditional mode. The credit recovery online courses developed by ALVS and others allow students to proceed at their own pace and in the comfort of their homes. Many online credit recovery programs are also individualized and/or modularized so that teachers can customize the online courses to the specific needs of students and not simply have them retake the entire course as was typically done in the face-to-face instructional model. Well-designed pedagogical approaches based on individualized instruction, modularization, multimedia infusion and ongoing assessment are proving to be beneficial. Scaffolding modular approaches to concept and skill mastery to capitalize on a student's individual learning style make it possible to differentiate learning more effectively. ALVS and others have also developed accompanying materials so that teachers can effectively use them in credit-recovery programs in blended learning formats and make them readily available to assist students as needed. The work of ALVS and other providers in this regard is to be commended.

Virtual High School Global Consortium

The Virtual High School Global Consortium (VHS) traces its roots to 1996 and a U.S. Department of Education grant to develop secondary education online course materials and to train teachers on how to use Internet for teaching. Under the leadership of Liz Pape, VHS has evolved into one of the premiere developers of online courses for middle and high school students. This modest regional operation has grown significantly into a major online content and professional development provider for school districts around the world. VHS partners can be found in most U.S. states and dozens of other countries. VHS uses primarily a blended online learning model that tries to integrate online technology and the teacher into a seamless learning experience for students. School districts are able to supplement their in-person courses with online course materials. Each of the VHS courses consists of asynchronous, project-based learning opportunities containing cohorts of students in several different countries working together. Pape described VHS's early operation:

> When VHS first began, the emphasis was on developing a professional development curriculum so that classroom teachers would be prepared to instruct online. They soon recognized that, as more technology became available and a stronger vision of global learning was established, the organization needed to not only continually update courses with new technology, but a model of ongoing teacher professional development was also essential. This evolution of the professional development model was essential for teachers to keep current with their online teaching skills and the technological components of each course. As an extension of their mission to deliver quality, cutting-edge professional development, VHS has expanded its professional development focus to include preparing online teachers to integrate Web tools in online instruction.
>
> (Pape, 2009)

Without a doubt, VHS's most significant contribution to secondary online education is its deep commitment to professional development of teachers. As technology evolved, VHS not only continually updated its online course materials but also its professional development programs to insure that teachers keep their online teaching skills current.

Liz Pape and her colleagues have received well-deserved recognition for the work VHS has done in professional development. VHS has won a number of awards for its efforts including the Stockholm Challenge Award for Global Excellence in Information Technology.

Community Colleges

Community colleges have been among the most visible providers of online education in the United States. These institutions, whether providing associate degrees or certificate programs, have embraced online education and have made significant contributions to its development.

Rio Salado Community College

Rio Salado Community College was founded in 1978 and from its beginning had a focus on distance education. It is one of ten colleges in the Maricopa County Community College District (MCCCD). Its main campus is in Tempe, Arizona and it maintains twelve other centers around the state. It enrolls nearly 55,000 students annually, more than 27,000 of whom are enrolled in online programs. As do many community colleges, Rio Salado has a diverse student population. Fifty-one percent of its students are non-white. It also offers special programs to active military and incarcerated students. Rio offers 130 programs of study to meet the needs of its diverse student body including 81 certificate programs and 28 associate degree programs, as well as baccalaureate and graduate programs leading to teacher certification. Rio Salado has a highly cost effective model for delivering instruction with more than 90% of its courses taught by adjunct faculty.

In 1996, Rio Salado first launched fully online programs. It recognized early on that in addition to courses, support services were critical in helping students to succeed. For example, Rio Salado was one of the early adopters of learning analytics and implemented the Progress and Course Engagement (PACE) system for automated tracking of student progress in 2010. The purpose of PACE was to provide a continuous evaluation of student at-risk levels on a weekly basis through an automated, systematic early-alert system that would allow instructors to launch proactive interventions at any point in the course to assist students showing signs of struggle. PACE provides students and instructors with information surrounding specific student performance data in areas that predict behaviors in log-in activity, site engagement, and pace. To develop PACE, Michael Cottam, associate dean for instructional design at Rio Salado, indicated that:

> we crunched data from tens of thousands of students, we found that there are three main predictors of success: the frequency of a student logging into a course; site engagement—whether they read or engage with the course materials online and do practice exercises and so forth; and how many points they are getting on their assignments. All that may *sound* simple, but the statistics we encounter are anything but simple. And we've found that, overwhelmingly, these three factors do act as predictors of success . . .
>
> The reports we generate show green, yellow, and red flags—like a traffic light—so that instructors can easily see who is at risk. We can predict, after the first week of a course, with 70 percent accuracy, whether any given student will complete the course successfully

(with a grade of "C" or better). That's our "eighth day" at risk model. A second model includes weekly updates using similar predictive factors.

(Crush, 2011)

Rio Salado instructors can review student engagement at any time throughout the course, and data in PACE is maintained on a real-time basis. A number of other colleges have emulated Rio Salado's PACE system.

In recognition of its contributions to online education, Rio Salado has received widespread recognition from organizations such the Alfred P. Sloan Consortium, the Bill and Melinda Gates Foundation, McKinsey and Company, and *Forbes Magazine.*

California Community Colleges

As part of an overall $197 million increased funding package in 2014, Governor Jerry Brown, the California State Legislature, and the California Community Colleges agreed to establish the California Community College Online Education Initiative (OEI). This initiative was established in part because for the five-year period 2008–2013, enrollment in the California Community Colleges had declined by 485,000 students. To re-establish California's tradition of universal access to a higher education, the OEI was conceived. The goals of OEI were:

- Increase the number of college associate degree graduates and transfers to four-year colleges
- Improve retention and success of students enrolled in Online Course Exchange courses
- Increase California Community Colleges education for the underserved and underrepresented including individuals with disabilities and those with basic skills needs
- Increase ease of use and convenience of the online experience
- Decrease the cost of student education
- Significantly increase demand for online course delivery

(California Community College Online Education Initiative Website, 2014)

Pilot courses were offered in Spring 2015 and the full launch of OEI followed in Fall 2015. It was projected that within three years (2015–2018), more than 600,000 students will take advantage of courses offered through OEI.

While a number of states have had similar initiatives, the OEI is mentioned for several reasons. First, the scale and scope of the project makes it the largest such online education undertaking in public higher education. Second, the goals of the initiative are very clear in terms of increasing access to higher education. Third, the nature of OEI courses is that they would be faculty-led and designed to improve retention and success of students.

While early results appear promising with a number of colleges and faculty willing to participate in pilot projects, a formal evaluation of the program by the RP Group of San Rafael, California had not been completed (The RP Group, 2017) at the time of this writing. Building on the work of this initiative, California Governor Jerry Brown proposed in 2018 that a fully online community college be developed in the state in the 2018–2019 fiscal year.

Northern Virginia Community College

Northern Virginia Community College traces its roots to 1964 with the establishment of Northern Virginia Technical Institute. Its name was changed in 1966 to Northern Virginia Community College (NOVA). It operates six physical campuses and enrolls almost 76,000 students in 79 two-year associate degree programs, 13 certificate programs, and 53 career studies certificate programs.

NOVA began offering distance education courses in 1975 through its Extended Learning Institute (ELI) which currently serves over 20,000 students annually, the majority of whom are non-white. ELI works with the six NOVA campuses to develop programs, and to enroll and support students. In the early 1990s, ELI began converting all of its distance education courses to online education technology and was among the first community colleges to do so. Presently, ELI offers online classes in over 50 academic disciplines, and more than 30 of NOVA's academic degree and certificate programs can be completed online (NOVA, 2017).

Because it works primarily with regular faculty at its physical campuses, ELI has invested significantly in faculty development and training. Its Virtual Professional Development Center (VPDC) is designed to assist both new and experienced faculty who teach online. The VPDC is a 24/7 operation that allows faculty to access training videos, written materials on demand, and chat areas with other faculty, librarians, and instructional designers.

ELI has also adopted a very successful Open Electronic Resources (OER) initiative to provide students access to openly-licensed educational materials and eliminate the need to purchase textbooks. NOVA received the 2014 WCET Outstanding Work (WOW) award from the WICHE Cooperative for Educational Technologies for its innovative OER-Based Associate Degree Project, which was a "comprehensive approach to addressing access, affordability, and student success through the use of open educational resources" (NOVA, 2017).

Online Programs in Large Urban Areas

A number of colleges because of their location in large urban areas made important contributions to online education by serving large commuter populations. For students in these programs, geographical distance was not as much an issue as time constraints. Many of these students carefully balance work and career and family responsibilities with their higher education goals. While some welcomed fully online programs, others preferred a blended model that allowed them to take part of a program or course online and part face-to-face.

University of Central Florida

The University of Central Florida (UCF) was founded in 1963, opened in 1968 as the Florida Technological University, and changed its name to the University of Central Florida in 1978. It has evolved into a major metropolitan research university serving over 64,000 students, making it one of the largest institutions of higher education in the country. The unduplicated student credit hour (SCH) production by modality for the 2016–2017 academic year was:

Fully online courses	381,628 SCH	23.93% of total
Blended learning courses	154,169 SCH	9.67% of total
Lecture capture courses	136,631 SCH	8.49% of total
Face-to-face courses	922,306 SCH	57.83% of total

(Hartman, 2017)

It is estimated that were it not for online education opportunities, enrollment would have been limited to approximately 40,000 students (Cavanagh, 2017). UCF maintains eleven regional campuses throughout the state of Florida where students can enroll in over 93 bachelors, 86 masters, 27 research doctorates, 3 professional doctorates, and 3 specialist degree programs (University of Central Florida, 2017).

UCF has made significant contributions to the study of online education especially with regard to student outcomes and the scholarship of teaching and learning (SoTL). For example, UCF's Research Initiative for Teaching Effectiveness (RITE) has conducted a yearly longitudinal impact evaluation of online learning which has found that fully online courses result in student success rates (A, B, or C grade) that are comparable to face-to-face sections with 88–91% succeeding overall. Blended learning courses tend to have slightly higher success ranging from 91–95% (Moskal, 2015; Moskal, Dziuban, & Hartman, 2013). Among other reasons, UCF's annual student evaluation of course modalities has received a good deal of attention because its sample sizes reflect tens of thousands of students.

UCF has also been a lead institution in a Next Generation Learning Challenges (NGLC) grant program, funded by the Bill and Melinda Gates Foundation and the William and Flora Hewlett Foundation. NGLC is a collaborative, multi-year initiative created to address the barriers to educational innovation and tap the potential of technology to improve college readiness and completion in the United States. UCF in partnership with the American Association of State Colleges and Universities (AASCU) expanded the adoption of UCF's successful blended initiative to 20 participating AASCU member institutions by developing and disseminating a "Blended Learning Toolkit" based upon proven best practices that had been successfully implemented at UCF. Included in this Toolkit were strategies for blended course design and delivery, OER blended course models in English Composition and Algebra, assessment and data collection protocols, and "train-the-trainer" materials and workshops. AASCU recruited the 20 collaborating institutions and leveraged their networks and conferences to work with these institutions on blended learning implementation, while at the same time making the Toolkit and course models widely available to its entire 420 member institutions and systems. Each of the 20 partner institutions deployed one or more courses, either directly using the English Composition and Algebra templates or building other high-need courses by using the strategies and resources contained in the Toolkit (Moskal & Cavanagh, 2014).

UCF and several of its faculty and administrators Charles Dziuban, Patsy Moskal, Tom Cavanagh, and Joel Hartman have received numerous awards for their work in online education and specifically for their research efforts in student outcomes, faculty development, and the scholarship of teaching and learning.

University of Wisconsin—Milwaukee

The University of Wisconsin—Milwaukee (UWM) is an urban, research university primarily serving students in the greater Milwaukee metropolitan area. The University of Wisconsin-Milwaukee officially opened its doors and welcomed its first class of students on Sept. 25, 1956, with the merger of two Milwaukee institutions of higher learning: Wisconsin State College, Milwaukee and the local campus of University of Wisconsin-Extension. However, UWM's roots extend much deeper to the Wisconsin State Normal School founded in 1885. UWM today enrolls over 26,000 students in 92 bachelors, 63 masters, and 36 doctoral degree programs. In terms of online education, over 2,000 students are enrolled in UWM's 9 fully online bachelor's degrees and 12 graduate degrees. Over 9,000 enroll in blended (online and face-to-face) courses (University of Wisconsin—Milwaukee, 2017).

UWM was one of the early leaders in emphasizing the importance of faculty development to quality online and blended programs and courses. UWM focused especially on the need for faculty to rethink blended courses and not simply add online components to existing face-to-face courses. Under the direction of Bob Kaleta, the UWM Technology Learning Center conducted research specifically focused on faculty who opted to develop blended courses

(Garnham & Kaleta, 2002). In subsequent studies, the UWM Technology Learning Center developed recommendations for faculty and instructional designers interested in developing blended courses as follows:

1. Begin the course redesign process by re-examining course goals and objectives and by considering how they can best be achieved in the hybrid environment.
2. Develop new learning activities that capitalize on the strengths of the online and face-to-face learning environments.
3. Integrate face-to-face and online learning activities to avoid teaching two parallel and unconnected courses.
4. Learn to make the transition from a lecture-centered teaching approach to a more learner-centered teaching focus.
5. Avoid the common tendency to cover too much material and include too many activities in the redesigned course that result in a "course and a half."
6. Acquire and practice the skills needed to effectively manage and facilitate online discussion and interaction.
7. Learn to create an online community of learners by providing an inclusive, positive, and friendly learning environment where students feel safe sharing ideas.
8. Keep technology use simple in order to avoid turning the course into a support nightmare and gradually add more advanced technology.
9. Develop a plan for conducting course activities when technology fails.
10. Manage student expectations regarding the hybrid format and course workload.
11. Identify and develop plans, materials, and activities to help students with the technology and time management challenges many encounter.
12. Use the tools in the course management system to get organized and stay organized when teaching hybrid courses.

(Kaleta, Skibba, & Joosten, 2007)

These recommendations are well-understood today but it was the work done by Kaleta and colleagues at UWM that helped organize and clarify these approaches to faculty development for blended courses earlier on. The work on faculty development and blended course design continues at UWM under the leadership of Tanya Joosten, who is Director of eLearning Research and Development and is Co-Director National Research Center for Distance Education and Technological Advancements (DETA) which coordinates cross-institutional data collection for online education practices and instructional technology.

University of Illinois-Chicago

The University of Illinois-Chicago (UIC) can trace its beginnings to several private health colleges that were founded in Chicago in the 1800s. In the 20th century, new campuses were built in Chicago and later joined together to form a comprehensive university. The present UIC was born in 1982, when two campuses (Circle and Medical Center) consolidated to form a comprehensive university campus with six health science colleges and an academic medical center (University of Illinois—Chicago, 2017). UIC is now rated as a Carnegie "Research I" institution. UIC enrolls over 29,000 students in 86 undergraduate, 94 masters, and 62 doctoral degree programs (UIC Today, 2016). UIC also operates an Extended Campus that has been offering fully online programs since the 1990s, however, it was in the early 2000s that UIC launched a blended learning initiative that has proven to be quite successful for both on-campus and commuter students.

UIC's most significant contribution to blended learning came in 2004 when it hosted an invitation-only blended learning workshop. Funded by the Alfred P. Sloan Foundation and directed by Mary Niemiec of UIC, this gathering attracted about 30 individuals who were curious and interested in the new concept of blending online and face-to-face instruction into a new instructional modality. The workshop was repeated for ten more years at UIC enrolling hundreds of individuals paying to participate in its activities and added immensely to the research base and best practices that that have been applied to blended learning. Its scholarly production included a plethora of important studies and resources on what is known about blended learning. For example, the workshop has produced:

- a comprehensive look at a definition of the term "blended learning";
- the first book dedicated entirely to the research on blended learning (Picciano & Dziuban 2007); and
- an extensive review of blended learning instructional models (Picciano, 2011).

In 2016, the Blended Learning Workshop evolved into a major international conference (INNOVATE) hosted by the Online Learning Consortium that attracts several thousand on-site and on-line participants per year. The contribution that UIC made to the field of blended learning, which today in all of its ramifications such as hybrid, flipped, and web-enhanced courses is the dominant learning modality in education, cannot be overstated.

Colleges With Unique Missions

There are a number of colleges with very specific missions that have used online education as a major vehicle for instruction. Some of these institutions such Western Governors University and Minerva are new and have integrated online education into a critical aspect of their academic programs. Other colleges with a long history in providing programs for a narrow area of study, such as Embry-Riddle Aeronautical University, see great benefit in providing online education opportunities for students who live and work around the world.

Embry-Riddle Aeronautical University

Embry-Riddle Aeronautical University (ERAU) traces its history to 1925, when T. Higbee Embry and John Paul Riddle launched the Embry-Riddle Company to provide air cargo services. By 1929, it had added a flying school, one of only five certified by the federal government. By 1939, the company had evolved into the Embry Riddle School of Aviation and opened its headquarters in South Florida. In the early 1950s, ERAU re-organized as a private, non-profit entity and was renamed as Embry Riddle Aeronautical Institute and received full accreditation in 1968. In 1970, the name was changed to Embry-Riddle Aeronautical University (Embry-Riddle Aeronautical University, 2017a). Today, ERAU enrolls 31,000 students annually in 80 associates, bachelors, masters, and doctoral degrees. It operates three campuses in Florida, Arizona, and Singapore. It also maintains 125 centers throughout the country, a number of which are on military bases.

In the 1970s, ERAU started offering distance education programs using television and other pre-Internet technology. In the 1990s, it began converting its distance education programs for online delivery. ERAU has been considered a major innovator in the use of digital technology. For example, its award-winning EagleVision Classroom is a live virtual platform that can connect classrooms and instructors from virtually anywhere in the world. It allows students to connect with virtual classes and each other from their homes in an asynchronous online learning environment or in a blended program (Online Schools Center, 2017). In May 2014, Embry-Riddle Worldwide launched its Virtual Crash Lab to enhance online students' experiences. Within this environment, students are able to examine an aircraft accident scene, document evidence, and even interview survivors. During the exercise, students gather and submit data that satisfy certain accident investigation criteria: survival factors, human factors, aircraft structures, and aircraft systems operations and maintenance. Faculty can then assess student knowledge and comprehension by examining the evidence collected and the explanation of findings. In 2016, ERAU launched its Virtual Aerial Robotics Lab which gives students the opportunity to build their own Unmanned Aircraft Systems (UAS). This Lab enhances the online learning environment for students enrolled in engineering, aeronautics, or UAS courses. The Robotics Lab introduces students to various modules, such as a bench test to verify the correct design of the UAS. By simulating a flight, students can test and analyze how well their systems performed (Embry-Riddle Aeronautical University, 2017b).

ERAU has become widely recognized as one of the leaders in online education and has received multiple number one rankings from *U.S. News and World Report*, the *Online Schools Center*, and *College Choice* (Embry-Riddle Aeronautical University, 2017c).

Western Governors University

Western Governors University (WGU) was conceived in 1995 when 19 members at a meeting of the Western Governors Association decided to establish a university that would be competency-based and would offer programs that would be fully online. Utah Governor Mike Leavitt is generally credited with having the foresight to realize that distance learning technologies had the power to tackle one of the western states' most pressing problems: rapid population growth confronted by limited public funds for educational services (Western Governors University, 2017b).

WGU was chartered in 1996, incorporated as a private, nonprofit university in 1997, and began accepting students in 1999. WGU is a totally online university. It operates from an office complex in Salt Lake City, Utah. In addition to its fully online nature, WGU is unique in that its programs are all competency-based rather than seat time based. Students only need to demonstrate competency in a subject to receive credit. It has a full-time teaching faculty who follow scripted course materials developed by master teachers and administrators. WGU also makes extensive use of faculty advisers for course, career, and personal student services. State funding was used for the creation of WGU but it has evolved into a self-supporting institution dependent upon tuition, gifts, and grants. Using mostly an asynchronous learning model, WGU has flourished, serving 84,000 online students from all 50 states (Western Governors University, 2017a). In addition, a number of other states including Indiana, Texas, Missouri, Tennessee, and Washington have created state-affiliated WGUs that offer programs and curricula similar to WGU.

WGU has not been without its critics and has come under scrutiny for a number of issues. For instance, in a CBS Money Watch ranking of best and worst college completion rates, WGU was ranked as having the lowest graduation rate at 6.5% (O'Shaughnessy, 2012). WGU also has a very high student to faculty ratio of 47:1 (Career Index, 2015). Johann Neem in an op-ed piece for the *Seattle Times* criticized WGU's basic premise:

> WGU does not offer a college education. A college education is about going through a process that leaves students transformed. That's why it takes time. Learning is hard—brain research demonstrates that real learning requires students to struggle with difficult material under the consistent guidance of good teachers. WGU denies students these opportunities. In fact, its advertisements pander to prospective students by offering them credit for what they already know rather than promising to teach them something new.
>
> (Neem, 2011)

WGU's role may be to provide a non-profit alternative to for-profit higher education. Gravois (2011), in an article titled "The College For-Profits Should Fear," makes the case that many students who might have enrolled in an online program at a for-profit college find WGU a much more viable alternative. It is less expensive; it provides credit for life experience; and it has good advisement services. Gravois commented:

> The school's enrollment was verging on 25,000 students—up from just 500 in 2003—and its yearly revenues had climbed from $32 million to $111 million. And if 2010 was the worst of years for the for-profits, it was among WGU's best.
>
> (Gravois, 2011)

In a 2017 federal audit, the United States Department of Education, Office of the Inspector General recommended that WGU repay $713 million in federal student financial aid claiming faculty did not have "regular and substantive" interaction with students, something WGU officials dispute. Moreover, the audit says that WGU should be ineligible to receive any more federal aid (USDOE, 2017). At the time of this writing, WGU was appealing the USDOE audit.

Regardless of its critics and federal audit concerns, WGU is an interesting model and the fact that it is being emulated in a number of other universities gives credence to its approach. The concept of competency-based online education is receiving a good deal of attention across the country. Southern New Hampshire University was a struggling institution with 2,000 residential students in 2009. A new president initiated a competency-based online program and enrollments grew to almost 40,000 in five years (Kahn, 2014). It may be that WGU's approach is more appropriate for a niche population of older students who are interested in earning a degree as quickly as possible. Regardless, WGU was made possible by the online education technology movement of the 1990s and has made its mark.

Babson College

Babson College traces its history to the establishment of Babson Institute in 1919 when Roger Babson set out to distinguish the Babson Institute from colleges offering instruction in business. The Institute provided intensive training in the fundamentals of production, finance, and distribution in just one academic year, rather than four. The curriculum was divided into four subject areas: practical economics, financial management, business psychology, and personal efficiency (which covered topics such as ethics, personal hygiene, and interpersonal relationships). The program's pace assumed that students would learn arts and sciences content elsewhere. A major focus of the Babson Institute from its beginnings was on entrepreneurship.

In 1969, Babson Institute became Babson College and formalized its mission to educate entrepreneurial leaders who will create great economic and social value—everywhere. Its vision is:

> . . . to be the preeminent institution in the world for Entrepreneurial Thought & Action—and known for it. We want to expand the notion of entrepreneurship to embrace and celebrate entrepreneurs of all kinds. We want to put the power of entrepreneurship as a force for economic and social value creation in as many hands in the world as we can.
>
> (Babson College Vision Statement, 2017b)

Babson's enrollment is just over 3,000, two-thirds of who are undergraduates and the remainder graduate students. It offers both on-ground and online programs, admission to which is highly selective.

Babson College's contribution to online education is its blended learning MBA programs in entrepreneurship that combine online classes and face-to-face sessions at its San Francisco, Wellesley, or Miami campuses, and provide virtual collaboration activities "to make the most of your time, your learning, your network, and your investment" (Babson College Babson College Blended Learning MBA Program, 2017a). This approach allows a student to finish an MBA in 21 months. It was one of the first colleges to integrate intensive all-day, face-to-face sessions into its blended programs. As described on the College's website:

> Face-to-face sessions occur approximately every seven weeks, Friday-Saturday. Online learning averages 20 hours per week, and reflects readings, case preparation, contributing to asynchronous and real-time discussions, and active participation in team-based exercises and projects. The Web-based elements are delivered via state-of-the-art distance learning tools.
>
> (Babson College Blended Learning MBA Program, 2017a)

Babson College's MBA program is consistently ranked by *U.S. News and World Report* as the number one graduate program in the country in entrepreneurship, ahead of universities such as Stanford, Harvard, and Yale (*U.S. News and World Report*, 2015).

References

American Public University. (2017a). *History*. Retrieved September 9, 2017 from www.apus.edu/about/history

American Public University. (2017b). *Our university at a glance*. Retrieved September 9, 2017 from www.apu.apus.edu/aboutus/index.html

Anderson, T. (2011). *The theory and practice of online learning* (2nd ed.). Edmonton: AU Press.

Apex Learning Virtual School. (2017). *About us*. Retrieved September 14, 2017 from www.apexlearningvs.com/about-us/

Athabasca University. (2016a). *History*. Retrieved September 2, 2017 from www.athabascau.ca/aboutau/history/

Athabasca University. (2016b). *What to expect at AU*. Retrieved September 5, 2017 from www.athabascau.ca/discover/how-au-works/what-to-expect.php

Babson College. (2017a). *Blended learning MBA program*. Retrieved October 17, 2017 from www.babson.edu/admission/graduate/Pages/blended-learning-program.aspx

Babson College. (2017b). *Mission statement*. Retrieved October 15, 2017 from www.babson.edu/about-babson/at-a-glance/Pages/mission-statement.aspx

Boston, W., Diaz, S. R., Gibson, A. M., Ice, P., Richardson, J., & Swan, K. S. (2008). An exploration of the relationship between indicators of the community of inquiry framework and retention in online courses. *Journal of Asynchronous Learning Networks, 12*(1). Retrieved September 13, 2017 from https://onlinelearningconsortium.org/read/journal-issues/

California Community College Online Education Initiative. (2014). *Goals*. California Community Colleges Online Education Initiative Website. Retrieved June 20, 2015 from http://ccconlineed.org/goals

Career Index. (2015). Western Governors University. *Career Index Website*. Retrieved September 23, 2017 from www.educationnews.org/career-index/western-governors-university/

Cavanagh, T. (2017, August 2). Digital learning. *Presentation to UCF*.

Crush, M. (2011, December 14). Monitoring the PACE of student learning: Analytics at Rio Salado Community College. *Campus Technology*. Retrieved June 10, 2015 from http://campustechnology.com/Articles/2011/12/14/Monitoring-the-PACE-of-Student-Learning-Analytics-at-Rio-Salado-College.aspx?Page=1

Embry-Riddle Aeronautical University. (2017a). *A brief history of Embrey-Riddle*. Retrieved September 27, 2017 from https://erau.edu/about/brief-history

Embry-Riddle Aeronautical University. (2017b). *Online technology for the modern student*. Retrieved September 27, 2017 from https://worldwide.erau.edu/online-learning/online-technology-for-the-modern-student

Embry-Riddle Aeronautical University. (2017c). *Online learning*. Retrieved September 27, 2017 from https://worldwide.erau.edu/online-learning/

Fain, P., & Seltzer, R. (2017, April 28). Purdue's bold move. *Inside Education*. Retrieved September 12, 2017 from www.insidehighered.com/news/2017/04/28/purdue-acquires-kaplan-university-create-new-public-online-university-under-purdue

Florida Virtual School. (2016). *Florida Virtual School district enrollment summary*. Retrieved September 13, 2017 from www.flvs.net/docs/default-source/district/flvs-district-enrollment-summary.pdf?sfvrsn=6

Garnham, C., & Kaleta, R. (2002, March). Introduction to hybrid courses. *Teaching with Technology Today, 8*(10). Retrieved September 21, 2017 from www.uwsa.edu/ttt/ articles/garnham.htm

Garrison, D. R., Anderson, T., & Archer, W. (2000). Critical inquiry in a text-based environment: Computer conferencing in higher education model. *The Internet and Higher Education, 2*(2–3), 87–105.

Gootman, E., & Coutts, S. (2008, April 11). Lacking credits, some students learn a shortcut. *New York Times*. Retrieved June 26, 2010 from www.nytimes.com/2008/04/11/education/11graduation.html

Gravois, J. (2011, September/October), The college for-profits should fear. *Washington Monthly*. Retrieved September 24, 2017 from www.washingtonmonthly.com/magazine/septemberoctober_2011/features/the_college_forprofits_should031640.php?page=all

Hanford, E. (2012). The case against for-profit colleges and universities. *American Public Media, RadioWorks*. Retrieved September 10, 2016 from http://americanradioworks.publicradio.org/features/tomorrows-college/phoenix/case-against-for-profit-schools.html

Hartman, J. (2017, September 19). *Quick question*. Email sent to Anthony G. Picciano.

Ice, P., Diaz, S., Swan, K., Burgess, M., Sharkey, M., Sherrill, J., . . . Okimoto, H. (2012). The PAR Framework proof of concept: Initial findings from a multi-institutional analysis of federated postsecondary data. *Journal of Asynchronous Learning Networks, 16*(3), 63–86.

Ice, P., Gibson, A., Boston, W., & Becher, D. (2011). An exploration of differences between community of indicators in low and high disenrollment online courses. *Journal of Asynchronous Learning Networks, 15*(2). Retrieved September 13, 2017 from https://onlinelearningconsortium.org/read/journal-issues/

Kahn, G. (2014, January 2). The Amazon of higher education. *Slate*. Retrieved September 24, 2017 from www.slate.com/articles/life/education/2014/01/southern_new_hampshire_university_how_paul_leblanc_s_tiny_school_has_become.html

Kaleta, R., Skibba, K., & Joosten, T. (2007). Discovering, designing, and delivering hybrid courses. In A. G. Picciano & C. D. Dziuban (Eds.), *Blended learning: Research perspectives* (Volume I). Needham, MA: The Sloan Consortium.

Kaplan University. (2017). *Who we are*. Retrieved September 12, 2017 from www.kaplanuniversity.edu/why-kaplan/about-kaplan-university/

Kinser, K. (2006). *From Main Street to Wall Street: The transformation of for-profit higher education.* San Francisco, CA: Jossey-Bass.

Moskal, P. (2015). Longitudinal evaluation in online and blended learning. In C. Dziuban, A. Picciano, C. Graham, & P. Moskal (Eds.), *Conducting research in online and blended learning environments: New pedagogical frontiers.* New York, NY: Routledge/Taylor & Francis.

Moskal, P., & Cavanagh, T. (2014). Scaling blended learning beyond the university. In A. G. Picciano, C. D. Dziuban, & C. R. Graham (Eds.), *Blended learning research perspectives* (Volume II). New York, NY: Routledge/Taylor & Francis.

Moskal, P., Dziuban, C., & Hartman, J. (2013). Blended learning: A dangerous idea? *Internet and Higher Education, 18*, 15–23.

Neem, J. (2011, April 1). Online university doesn't offer 'real college education'. *Seattle Times.* Retrieved September 23, 2017 from www.seattletimes.com/opinion/online-university-doesnt-offer-real-college-education/

NOVA Northern Virginia Community College. (2017). *About the Extended Learning Institute.* Retrieved September 19, 2017 from http://eli.nvcc.edu/abouteli.htm

Online Schools Center. (2017). *30 most technologically savvy online schools.* Retrieved September 28, 2017 from www.onlineschoolscenter.com/posts/the-30-most-technologically-savvy-online-schools/

O'Shaughnessy, L. (2012). Fifty colleges with the best and worst graduation rates. *CBS Money Watch Website.* Retrieved September 23, 2017 from www.cbsnews.com/news/50-private-colleges-with-best-worst-grad-rates/

Pape, L. (2009). Virtual High School Global Consortium: The past, present and future. *SEEN Magazine: Southeast Regional Network*, November 20, 2009. Retrieved September 15, 2017 from www.seenmagazine.us/Articles/Article-Detail/articleid/212/virtual-high-school-global-consortium

Penn State World Campus. (2017). *Serving our military and veteran students.* Retrieved September 9, 2017 from www.worldcampus.psu.edu/military

Picciano, A. G. (2011). Introduction to the special issue on transitioning to blended learning. *Journal of Asynchronous Learning Networks, 13*(1), 1–5.

Picciano, A. G., & Dziuban, C. D. (2007). *Blended learning: Research perspectives* (Volume I). Needham, MA: The Sloan Consortium.

Rio Salado Community College. (2016). *Who we are.* Retrieved September 17, 2017 from www.riosalado.edu/about/news-resources/Documents/2015-16-RSC-Fact-Sheet.pdf

The RP Group. (2017). *Projects: The California Community College Online Education Initiative.* Retrieved September 18, 2017 from http://rpgroup.org/All-Projects/ctl/ArticleView/mid/1686/articleld/149/California-Community-Colleges-Online-Education-Initiative-OEI-Evaluation

UIC Today. (2016). UIC enrollment hits record high. Retrieved September 23, 2017 from https://today.uic.edu/uic-enrollment-hits-record-high

United States Department of Education (USDOE). (2017). *Western Governors University was not eligible to participate in the Title IV Programs: Final audit report.* U.S.D.O.E. Office of Inspector General Document ED-OIG/A05M0009. Retrieved September 23, 2017 from www2.ed.gov/about/offices/list/oig/auditreports/fy2017/a05m0009.pdf

University of Central Florida. (2017). *UCF facts 2016–2017.* Retrieved September 19, 2017 from www.ucf.edu/about-ucf/facts/

University of Illinois–Chicago. (2017). *History.* Retrieved September 23, 2017 from www.uic.edu/about/history

University of Maryland University College. (2016). *Mission and history.* Retrieved September 6, 2017 from www.umuc.edu/about/mission-and-history.cfm

University of Maryland University College. (2017). *Our students and alumni.* Retrieved September 6, 2017 from www.umuc.edu/about/about-our-students-and-alumni/index.cfm

University of Phoenix. (2015). *About the University of Phoenix Website.* Retrieved April 17, 2015 from www.phoenix.edu/about_us/about_university_of_phoenix/history.html

University of Wisconsin—Milwaukee. (2017). *Facts and figures.* Retrieved September 21, 2017 from http://uwm.edu/facts/

U.S. News and World Report. (2015). *Best graduate schools: Entrepreneurship.* Retrieved June 5, 2015 from http://grad-schools.usnews.rankingsandreviews.com/best-graduate-schools/top-business-schools/entrepreneurship-rankings

Western Governors University. (2017a). *A diverse and successful student body.* Retrieved September 23, 2017 from www.wgu.edu/about_WGU/students_alumni

Western Governors University. (2017b). *The unique history of Western Governors University.* Retrieved September 23, 2017 from www.wgu.edu/about_WGU/WGU_story

Appendix B

Evaluation Criteria for the Administration of Online Education Programs

The criteria for Appendices B, C, and D are derived from the OLC Quality Framework. (OLC Quality Framework, 2017, https://onlinelearningconsortium.org/about/quality-framework-five-pillars/).

Institutional Support

1. The institution has a governance structure to enable clear, effective, and comprehensive decision making related to online education.
2. The institution has policy and guidelines that confirm a student who registers in an online course or program is the same student who participates in and completes the course or program and receives academic credit. This is done by verifying the identity of a student by using methods such as (a) a secure login and passcode, (b) proctored examinations, or (c) other technologies and practices that are effective in verifying student identity.
3. The institution has a policy for intellectual property of course materials; it specifically addresses online course materials and is publicly visible online.
4. The institution has defined the strategic value of online learning to its enterprise and stakeholders.
5. The organizational structure of the online program supports the institution's mission, values, and strategic plan.
6. The online program's strategic plan is reviewed for its continuing relevance, and periodically improved and updated.
7. The institution has a process for planning and allocating resources for the online program, including financial resources, in accordance with strategic planning.
8. The institution demonstrates sufficient resource allocation, including financial resources, in order to effectively support the mission of online education.
9. The institution has a governance structure to enable systematic and continuous improvement related to the administration of online education.

Technology Support

1. A documented technology plan that includes electronic security measures (e.g., password protection, encryption, secure online or proctored exams, etc.) is in place and operational to ensure quality, in accordance with established standards and regulatory requirements.
2. The technology delivery systems are highly reliable and operable with measurable standards being utilized such as system downtime tracking or task benchmarking.

3. A centralized system provides support for building and maintaining the online education infrastructure.
4. The course delivery technology is considered a mission-critical enterprise system and supported as such.
5. The institution has established a contingency plan for the continuance of data centers and support services in the event of prolonged service disruption.
6. Faculty, staff, and students are supported in the development and use of new technologies and skills.
7. Whether the institution maintains local data centers (servers), and/or contracts for outsourced, hosted services or cloud services, those systems are administered in compliance with established data management practices such as the Information Technology Service Management (ITSM) standards which include appropriate power protection, backup solutions, disaster recovery plans, etc.

Course Development/Instructional Design

1. Guidelines regarding minimum requirements for course development, design, and delivery of online instruction (such as course syllabus elements, course materials, assessment strategies, faculty feedback) are followed.
2. Course embedded technology actively supports the achievement of learning outcomes and delivery of course content, and superfluous use of technology is minimized.
3. Instructional materials and course syllabi are reviewed periodically to ensure they meet online course and program learning outcomes.
4. A course development process is followed that ensures courses are designed so that students develop the necessary knowledge and skills to meet measurable learning outcomes at the course and program level.
5. A process is followed that ensures that permissions (Creative Commons, Copyright, Fair Use, Public Domain, etc.) are in place for appropriate use of online course materials.
6. Course assignments and activities are reviewed periodically to ensure they meet online course and program learning outcomes.
7. Student-centered instruction is considered during the course development process.
8. There is consistency in course development for student retention and quality.
9. Course design promotes both faculty and student engagement.
10. A process is followed for evaluating the effectiveness of current and emerging technologies to support the achievement of learning outcomes and delivery of course content.
11. Usability tests are conducted and applied, and recommendations based upon Web Content Accessibility Guidelines (WCAGs) are incorporated.
12. Curriculum development is a core responsibility for faculty (i.e., faculty should be involved in either the development or the decision-making for the online curriculum choices).

Course Structure

1. The online course includes a syllabus outlining course objectives, learning outcomes, evaluation methods, books and supplies, technical and proctoring requirements, and other related course information, making course requirements transparent.
2. The course structure ensures that all online students, regardless of location, have access to library/learning resources that adequately support online courses.
3. Expectations for student assignment completion, grade policy, and faculty response are clearly provided in the course syllabus.

4. Links or explanations of technical support are available in the course (i.e., each course provides suggested solutions to potential technical issues and/or links for technical assistance).
5. Instructional materials are accessible to the student, easy to use, and may be accessed by multiple operating systems and applications.
6. Instructional materials are easily accessed by students with disabilities via alternative instructional strategies and/or referral to special institutional resources.
7. Opportunities/tools are provided to encourage student-to-student collaboration (i.e., web conferencing, instant messaging, etc.) if appropriate.
8. Rules or standards for appropriate online student behavior are provided within the course.

Teaching and Learning

1. Student-to-student and faculty-to-student interaction are essential characteristics and are encouraged and facilitated.
2. Feedback on student assignments and questions is constructive and provided in a timely manner.
3. Students learn appropriate methods for effective research, including assessment of the validity of resources and the ability to master resources in an online environment.
4. Students are provided access to library professionals and resources to help locate, analyze, evaluate, synthesize, and ethically use a variety of information resources.
5. Instructors use specific strategies to create a presence in the course.

Social and Student Engagement

1. Students should be provided a way to interact with other students in an online community (outside the course).
2. Technical assistance is provided for faculty during online course development and online teaching.
3. The institution ensures faculty receive training, assistance, and support to prepare for course development and teaching online.
4. Faculty receive training and materials related to Fair Use, plagiarism, and other relevant legal and ethical concepts.
5. Faculty are provided ongoing professional development related to online teaching and learning.
6. Clear standards are established for faculty engagement and expectations concerning online teaching (e.g., response time, contact information, etc.).
7. Faculty are informed about emerging technologies and the selection and use of new tools.

Faculty Support/Student Support

1. Before starting an online program, students are advised about the program to determine if they possess the self-motivation and commitment to learn online.
2. Before starting an online program, students are advised about the program to determine if they have access to the minimum technology skills and equipment required by the course design.
3. Before starting an online program, students receive (or have access to) information about the program, including admission requirements, tuition and fees, books and supplies, technical and proctoring requirements, and student support services.

4. Throughout the duration of the course/program, students have access to training and information they will need to secure required materials through electronic databases, interlibrary loans, government archives, news services, and other sources.
5. Throughout the duration of the course/program, students have access to appropriate technical assistance and technical support staff.
6. Support personnel are available to address student questions, problems, bug reporting, and complaints.
7. Students have access to effective academic, personal, and career counseling.
8. Frequently Asked Questions (FAQs) are provided in order to respond to students' most common questions regarding online education.
9. Students are provided non-instructional support services such as admission, financial assistance, registration/enrollment, etc.
10. Policy, processes, and resources are in place to support students with disabilities.
11. Students have access to required course materials in print and/or digital format, such as ISBN numbers for textbooks, book suppliers, and delivery modes prior to course enrollment.
12. Program demonstrates a student-centered focus rather than trying to fit existing on-campus services to the online student.
13. Efforts are made to engage students with the program and institution in order to minimize feelings of isolation and alienation.
14. The institution provides guidance/tutorials for students in the use of all forms of technologies used for course delivery.
15. Tutoring is available as a learning resource.
16. Students are provided clear information for enlisting help from the institution.

Evaluation and Assessment

1. The program is assessed through an evaluation process that applies specific established standards.
2. A variety of data (academic and administrative information) are used to regularly and frequently evaluate program effectiveness and to guide changes toward continual improvement.
3. Intended learning outcomes at the course and program level are reviewed regularly to ensure alignment, clarity, utility, appropriateness, and effectiveness.
4. A process is in place and followed for the assessment of support services for faculty and students.
5. A process is in place and followed for the assessment of student retention in online courses and programs.
6. A process is in place and followed for the assessment of recruitment practices.
7. Program demonstrates compliance and review of accessibility standards (Section 508, etc.).
8. Course evaluations collect feedback on the effectiveness of instruction in relation to faculty performance evaluations.
9. A process is in place and followed for the institutional assessment of faculty online teaching performance.
10. A process is in place and followed for the assessment of stakeholder (e.g., learners, faculty, staff) satisfaction with the online program.
11. Course evaluations collect student feedback on quality of online course materials.

Appendix C

Evaluation Criteria for Blended Learning Programs

Institutional Support

1. The institution has a governance structure to enable systematic and continuous improvement related to the administration of blended education.
2. The institution has a governance structure to enable clear, timely, effective, and comprehensive decision making related to blended learning courses/programs.
3. The blended learning program's strategic plan is reviewed for its continuing relevance, compliance with accreditation objectives, and is periodically improved and updated.
4. The institution has defined the strategic value of blended learning to its enterprise and stakeholders (students, faculty, parents, etc.).
5. The organizational structure of the blended learning program supports the institution's mission, values, and strategic plan.
6. The institution has a process for planning and resource allocation for the blended learning program, including financial resources, in accordance with strategic planning.
7. The institution demonstrates sufficient resource allocation, including technology and financial resources, in order to effectively support the mission of blended education.
8. The institution has policy and guidelines that confirm a student who registers in a blended course or blended learning program is the same student who participates in and completes the course or program and receives academic credit. This is done by verifying the identity of a student by using methods such as (a) a secure login and pass code, (b) proctored examinations, or (c) other technologies and practices that are effective in verifying student identification.
9. A process is followed that ensures that permissions (Creative Commons, Copyright, Fair Use, Public Domain, etc.) are in place for appropriate use of all course materials.

Technology Support

1. The course delivery technology is considered a mission critical enterprise system and supported as such.
2. Whether the institution maintains local data centers (servers), and/or contracts for outsourced, hosted services or cloud services, those systems are administered in compliance with established data management practices such as the Information Technology Service Management (ITSM) standards, which include appropriate power protection, backup solutions, disaster recovery plans, etc.
3. The technology systems related to the delivery of blended learning programs are highly reliable and operable with measurable standards being utilized such as system downtime tracking and task benchmarking.

4. A documented technology plan that includes electronic security measures (e.g., password protection, encryption, secure online or proctored exams if applicable, etc.) is in place and operational to ensure quality, in accordance with established standards and regulatory requirements.
5. The institution has an established (updated and continuously reviewed) contingency plan for the continuance of data centers and support services in the event of prolonged service disruption.
6. A centralized system provides support for building and maintaining the blended education infrastructure.
7. Faculty, staff, and students are supported in the development and use of new technologies and skills applicable to blended learning.

Course Development and Instructional Design

1. A course development process is followed that ensures courses are designed with alignment between course materials, assessments and learning objectives so that students develop the necessary knowledge and skills to meet measurable learning outcomes at the course and program level.
2. Guidelines regarding minimum requirements for course development, design, and delivery of blended instruction (such as course syllabus elements, course materials, assessment strategies, faculty feedback) are followed.
3. There is consistency in course development for student retention (enrollment and course completion) and quality (i.e., courses in a program have a consistent navigational structure).
4. A blended course should be designed as one cohesive whole, incorporating both face-to-face and online experiences in complementary ways.
5. Instructional materials (both online and in-class) and course syllabi are reviewed periodically to ensure they meet the blended course's and program's learning outcomes.
6. Course assignments and activities are reviewed periodically to ensure they meet the blended courses' and program's learning outcomes.
7. Student-centered instruction is considered during the course development process (i.e., student engagement, immersion, and personal responsibility).
8. Course design promotes both faculty and student engagement.
9. Course workloads are reviewed to ensure it is appropriate for designated credit allocation.
10. A process is established and followed for evaluating the effectiveness of current and emerging technologies to support the achievement of learning outcomes and delivering course content.
11. Course embedded technology actively supports the achievement of learning outcomes and delivering course content and unnecessary use of technology is minimized.
12. Usability tests are conducted and applied and recommendations based upon Web Content Accessibility Guidelines (WCAGs) are incorporated in the course design process.
13. Curriculum development is a core responsibility for faculty (i.e., faculty should be involved in either the development or the decision making for the blended curriculum choices).
14. Faculty support and resources are provided to promote the best use of blended delivery method in course development and instructional design to facilitate teaching and learning.

Course Structure

1. The blended course includes a syllabus outlining course objectives, learning outcomes, evaluation methods, books and supplies, technical and proctoring requirements, and other related course information, making course requirements and course schedule transparent.*
2. The course structure ensures that all students, regardless of location, have access to library/learning resources that adequately support the blended course.
3. Expectations for student assignment completion, grade policy, and faculty response are clearly provided in the course syllabus.
4. Links or explanations of technical support are available in the course (i.e., each course provides suggested solutions to potential technical issues and/or links for technical assistance).
5. Rules or standards for appropriate student behavior, both online and face-to-face, are provided within the course.
6. Instructional materials are easily accessible to the student, easy to use, with an ability to be accessed by multiple operating systems and applications.
7. Instructional materials are easily accessed by students with disabilities via alternative instructional strategies and/or referral to special institutional resources.
8. The blended course is visually appealing to the student and the course is navigationally sound.

Teaching and Learning

1. Student-to-Student and Faculty-to-Student interaction are essential characteristics and are encouraged and facilitated.
2. Instructor feedback on student assignments and questions is constructive and provided in a timely manner.
3. Instructors use specific strategies to create an engaged, learning-focused presence in both modalities of the course.
4. Faculty teach the course as one cohesive whole, with "presence" in both the face-to-face and the online portions of the course.
5. Resources are provided to assist students in conducting research online and assessing the validity of online resources.

Faculty Support

1. Technical assistance is provided for faculty before and during blended course development and teaching.
2. The institution ensures faculty receive training, assistance, and support to prepare faculty for course development and effective teaching with technology in a variety of modalities.
3. Faculty receive training and materials related to Fair Use, plagiarism, and other relevant legal and ethical concepts.
4. Faculty are provided on-going professional development related to blended teaching and learning.
5. Clear standards are established for faculty engagement and expectations around blended teaching (e.g., response time, contact information, etc.).
6. Faculty are provided training in blended teaching.

Student Support

1. Before starting a blended learning program, students complete an orientation or self-assessment to determine if they possess the self-motivation and commitment to learn.*
2. Before starting a blended learning program, students are advised about the program to determine if they have access to the minimum technology skills and equipment required by the course design.
3. Before starting a blended learning program, students receive (or have access to) information about programs, including admission requirements, tuition and fees, books and supplies, technical and proctoring requirements, and student support services.
4. Throughout the duration of the course/program, students have access to training and information they will need to secure required materials through electronic databases, interlibrary loans, government archives, news services, and other sources.
5. Throughout the duration of the course/program, students have access to appropriate technical assistance and technical support staff.
6. Support personnel are available (24/7) to address student questions and problems of a technical nature.
7. Policy, processes, and resources are in place to support students with disabilities.
8. Students have access to information regarding required course materials in print and/or digital format, such as ISBN numbers for textbooks, book suppliers, and delivery modes prior to course enrollment.
9. Program demonstrates a student-centered focus and intentionality in the integration of online and face-to-face resources.
10. The institution provides guidance/tutorials for students in the use of all forms of technologies used for course delivery.
11. Students are provided clear information for enlisting help from the institution.

Evaluation and Assessment

1. The program is assessed through an evaluation process that applies specific established standards (i.e., accreditor guidelines and/or other recognized agency such as the OLC Scorecard).
2. A variety of data (academic and administrative information) are used to regularly and frequently evaluate program effectiveness in order to guide changes toward continual improvement.
3. Intended learning outcomes at the course and program level are reviewed regularly to ensure alignment, clarity, utility, appropriateness, and effectiveness.
4. A process is in place and followed for the comprehensive assessment of support services for faculty and students.
5. A process is in place and followed for the assessment of student retention in blended courses and programs.
6. Program demonstrates compliance and review of accessibility standards (Section 508, etc.).
7. Course evaluations collect student feedback on the effectiveness of instruction in relation to faculty performance evaluations.
8. Course evaluations collect student feedback on quality of blended course materials.
9. A process is in place and followed for the institutional assessment of faculty blended teaching performance.
10. A process is in place and followed for the assessment of stakeholder (e.g., learners, faculty, staff) satisfaction with the blended learning programs.

Appendix D

Evaluation Criteria for Quality Course Teaching and Instructional Practice

Course Design

1. Consistent course design is used.
2. Clear structure and course organization is provided with opportunities for students to share in the responsibility for their learning.
3. Course design is cohesive and aligns the course objectives, assessments, and activities.
4. Course is designed so that student workload is reasonable and evenly distributed.
5. Content has logical progression and facilitates student interaction/understanding.
6. The course is designed to facilitate easy navigation of course content.
7. Course syllabus is learner-centered and sets the tone for learning and engaging the student.
8. Course module or unit outcomes are stated.
9. Course resources are clearly identified and easy to access.
10. Terms and labels are consistent throughout the course shell.
11. Course offers multiple opportunities for students to gain information (for example—due dates are found in Course Content, Course Calendar, Assignment Listing).
12. Textbooks/Ebooks/Online Tools work seamlessly with LMS.
13. Course is fully prepared and available to students by the first day of the term.

Accessibility, ADA Compliance and Universal Design

1. Course Accessibility is addressed (i.e., videos are captioned, use of color is ADA appropriate, other visual elements meet ADA standards, etc.).
2. Course design adheres to universal design standards.

Course Learning Outcomes

1. Instructor facilitates critical thinking.
2. Learning outcomes build upon existing knowledge.
3. Instructor recognizes and acknowledges excellence in student work.
4. Course learning outcomes are aligned with program and/or institutional learning outcomes.
5. Course learning outcomes are reviewed and updated on a regular basis.
6. Course learning outcomes are stated in syllabus (or in the beginning of modules).
7. Course learning outcomes and content are continuously evaluated for alignment.
8. Course learning outcomes are clearly defined and measurable.
9. There are clear links between learning objectives and outcomes with activities and assessment.

10. Course learning outcomes are related to the appropriate level of learning.
11. All learning outcomes for the course are assessed.

Course Content

1. Course content provided covers all course objectives/competencies.
2. Online activities and assignments are written with explicit instructions for how to participate, when responses or submissions are expected, and how the activities are assessed.
3. Interactive group discussions are written with explicit instructions for how to participate, when responses or submissions are expected, and how the activities are assessed.
4. Course offers opportunities for learners to engage in relevant activities that draw from authentic experiences whenever possible.
5. Course activities are appropriately paced for the intended learners and are evenly distributed across modules.
6. A course orientation is provided that familiarizes students with the learning management system, course navigation, and student support services.
7. Instructor provides information for students regarding computer, hardware, and software requirements, as well as where to receive technical assistance.
8. Instructor includes netiquette behavior guidelines to enhance inclusion.
9. Instructor is aware of and obeys copyright law in using and posting materials.

Assignments

1. Assignments are directly related to the course/lecture learning objectives.
2. Assignments are meaningful, purposeful and relevant to learning outcomes.
3. Assignments include grading rubrics with clear expectations.
4. Instructor provides a variety of assignment types to enable different learners opportunities to demonstrate skills.
5. Instructor structures learning activities to promote student to student interactions.
6. Assignments promote critical thinking and problem solving.
7. A schedule of assignments is provided that includes due dates and time frames.

Instructor Role

1. Instructor provides a personalized bio and statement that welcomes students to the course in text or video format.
2. At a minimum, the instructor checks the course five days out of seven.
3. Instructor utilizes accessible online grade book and posts grades promptly.
4. Instructor demonstrates concern for student issues/outcomes.
5. Instructor sets clear expectations for students regarding course learning outcomes.
6. Instructor provides clear information as to expectations of academic integrity and plagiarism.
7. Instructor is flexible and responsive to student needs, revising course directives as needed.
8. Instructor resolves course-related issues in a timely manner.
9. Instructor proactively addresses problems as they emerge and is responsive to student concerns.
10. Instructor consistently demonstrates enthusiasm for the course subject matter.
11. Instructor provides encouraging feedback.

12. Instructor uses strategies that encourage students to be self-directed and take responsibility for their learning.
13. Instructor demonstrates respect for students.
14. Instructor finds opportunities for student affirmation.
15. Instructor uses tools within the LMS to facilitate the learning experience in an effective manner.

Class Discussion and Engagement

1. Discussions are meaningful, aligned with course learning outcomes, and provide opportunities for critical thinking.
2. Instructor provides clear explanation of how the class discussion will be used.
3. Instructor clearly states expectations for participation in discussion forums and other class communication.
4. Instructor promotes students' awareness of other perceptions or perspectives.
5. Instructor demonstrates presence by engaging actively and frequently throughout the course.
6. Instructor posts critical, reflective questions for discussion forums.
7. Students are expected to post discussion responses as well as interact with classmates and the instructor.
8. Class discussion boards are designed to facilitate student-to-student interactions.

Building Community

1. Instructor provides a space for students to post an introduction and share appropriate parts of their personal life to develop the online learning community.
2. Instructor develops an appropriate personal conversation style for the audience.
3. Instructor creates a safe climate for collaboration.
4. Instructor creates an inclusive, supportive, and engaging climate, with a variety of methods such as using learners' names often.
5. Instructor creates a positive, motivating and encouraging environment.
6. Instructor encourages students to be candid, yet respectful of others.
7. Instructor uses inclusive language, such as we, you, and our.
8. Instructor provides activities/assignments that foster student interaction.
9. Instructor provides clear and specific course expectations for community in assignments/ discussion forums.
10. Instructor facilitates positive communication with students.
11. Instructor creates and promotes respectful interaction.
12. Expectations are communicated for participation or engagement with peers.

Communication

1. Instructor provides ongoing and meaningful communication.
2. Instructor models effective communication techniques and netiquette.
3. Instructor uses a positive, supportive tone in all communications to describe course content and for interpersonal communication.
4. Instructor provides clear, useful, and constructive feedback to students.
5. Instructor provides prompt feedback.
6. Instructor specifies times when students can expect instructor feedback.

7. Instructor messages are clear and appropriate.
8. Instructor sends introductory welcome email message.
9. Instructor uses announcements effectively and appropriately.
10. Instructor communicates to students what they should know in order to focus on learning.
11. Instructor promptly returns all phone calls and emails in compliance with the course communication policy.
12. Instructor shows strong desire to assist students in performing successfully in the course.
13. Instructor informs students when he/she will be out of contact and provides an alternative for students to receive assistance.
14. Instructor encourages students to contact instructor when questions arise.
15. Instructor requires college level writing and communication in all written work and course participation, including email and class discussions.

Continuous Course Improvement

1. Instructor continuously evaluates the effectiveness and content of their online course.
2. Instructor frequently reviews course design.
3. Student feedback (for course improvement) is encouraged and requested.
4. An anonymous course survey is available to encourage student feedback.
5. Instructor provides opportunities for reflection at the end of course (for course improvement).

Appendix E

General Data Protection Regulation (GDPR) Overview

Source: European Union General Data Protection Regulation Website
Retrieved from: www.eugdpr.org/the-regulation.html
Accessed: February 3, 2018

The aim of the GDPR is to protect all EU citizens from privacy and data breaches in an increasingly data-driven world that is vastly different from the time in which the 1995 directive was established. Although the key principles of data privacy still hold true to the previous directive, many changes have been proposed to the regulatory policies; the key points of the GDPR as well as information on the impacts it will have on business can be found below.

Increased Territorial Scope (Extra-Territorial Applicability)

Arguably the biggest change to the regulatory landscape of data privacy comes with the extended jurisdiction of the GDPR, as it applies to all companies processing the personal data of data subjects residing in the Union, regardless of the company's location. Previously, territorial applicability of the directive was ambiguous and referred to data process 'in context of an establishment'. This topic has arisen in a number of high profile court cases. GPDR makes its applicability very clear—it will apply to the processing of personal data by controllers and processors in the EU, regardless of whether the processing takes place in the EU or not. The GDPR will also apply to the processing of personal data of data subjects in the EU by a controller or processor not established in the EU, where the activities relate to: offering goods or services to EU citizens (irrespective of whether payment is required) and the monitoring of behaviour that takes place within the EU. Non-EU businesses processing the data of EU citizens will also have to appoint a representative in the EU.

Penalties

Under GDPR organizations in breach of GDPR can be fined up to 4% of annual global turnover or €20 million (whichever is greater). This is the maximum fine that can be imposed for the most serious infringements, e.g., not having sufficient customer consent to process data or violating the core of Privacy by Design concepts. There is a tiered approach to fines, e.g., a company can be fined 2% for not having their records in order (article 28), not notifying the supervising authority and data subject about a breach or not conducting impact assessment. It is important to note that these rules apply to both controllers and processors—meaning 'clouds' will not be exempt from GDPR enforcement.

Consent

The conditions for consent have been strengthened, and companies will no longer be able to use long illegible terms and conditions full of legalese, as the request for consent must be given in an intelligible and easily accessible form, with the purpose for data processing attached to that consent. Consent must be clear and distinguishable from other matters and provided in an intelligible and easily accessible form, using clear and plain language. It must be as easy to withdraw consent as it is to give it.

Data Subject Rights

Breach Notification

Under the GDPR, breach notification will become mandatory in all member states where a data breach is likely to "result in a risk for the rights and freedoms of individuals". This must be done within 72 hours of first having become aware of the breach. Data processors will also be required to notify their customers, the controllers, "without undue delay" after first becoming aware of a data breach.

Right to Access

Part of the expanded rights of data subjects outlined by the GDPR is the right for data subjects to obtain from the data controller confirmation as to whether or not personal data concerning them is being processed, where and for what purpose. Further, the controller shall provide a copy of the personal data, free of charge, in an electronic format. This change is a dramatic shift to data transparency and empowerment of data subjects.

Right to Be Forgotten

Also known as Data Erasure, the right to be forgotten entitles the data subject to have the data controller erase his/her personal data, cease further dissemination of the data, and potentially have third parties halt processing of the data. The conditions for erasure, as outlined in article 17, include the data no longer being relevant to original purposes for processing, or a data subjects withdrawing consent. It should also be noted that this right requires controllers to compare the subjects' rights to "the public interest in the availability of the data" when considering such requests.

Data Portability

GDPR introduces data portability—the right for a data subject to receive the personal data concerning them, which they have previously provided in a 'commonly use and machine readable format' and have the right to transmit that data to another controller.

Privacy by Design

Privacy by design as a concept has existed for years now, but it is only just becoming part of a legal requirement with the GDPR. At it's core, privacy by design calls for the inclusion of data protection from the onset of the designing of systems, rather than an addition. More specifically—'The controller shall . . . implement appropriate technical and organisational measures . . . in an effective way . . . in order to meet the requirements of this Regulation and protect the rights of data subjects'. Article 23 calls for controllers to hold and process only the data absolutely necessary for the completion of its duties (data minimisation), as well as limiting the access to personal data to those needing to act out the processing.

Data Protection Officers

Currently, controllers are required to notify their data processing activities with local DPAs, which, for multinationals, can be a bureaucratic nightmare with most Member States having different notification requirements. Under GDPR it will not be necessary to submit notifications/registrations to each local DPA of data processing activities, nor will it be a requirement to notify/obtain approval for transfers based on the Model Contract Clauses (MCCs). Instead, there will be internal record keeping requirements, as further explained below, and DPO appointment will be mandatory only for those controllers and processors whose core activities consist of processing operations which require regular and systematic monitoring of data subjects on a large scale or of special categories of data or data relating to criminal convictions and offences. Importantly, the DPO:

- Must be appointed on the basis of professional qualities and, in particular, expert knowledge on data protection law and practices
- May be a staff member or an external service provider
- Contact details must be provided to the relevant DPA
- Must be provided with appropriate resources to carry out their tasks and maintain their expert knowledge
- Must report directly to the highest level of management
- Must not carry out any other tasks that could results in a conflict of interest.

Index

Note: Page numbers in italic indicate a figure on the corresponding page. *Pl'* indicates figures in plate section.